The Fall
of
Imperial China

The Transformation of Modern China Series
James E. Sheridan, General Editor

The Fall of Imperial China
Frederic Wakeman, Jr.

China in Disintegration
The Republican Era in Chinese History, 1912–1949
James E. Sheridan

* The People's Republic of China
An Interpretive History of the First Twenty-five Years
Maurice Meisner

* Chinese Foreign Policy
A Conceptual History
Mark Mancall

* In preparation.

The Fall
of
Imperial China

EARLY CH'ING CHINA

The Fall
of
Imperial China

Frederic Wakeman, Jr.

THE FREE PRESS
A Division of Macmillan Publishing Co., Inc.
NEW YORK

Collier Macmillan Publishers
LONDON

The Free Press
A Division of Macmillan Publishing Co., Inc.
866 Third Avenue, New York, N.Y.   10022

Collier Macmillan Canada, Ltd.

Library of Congress Catalog Card Number: 74–27854

Printed in the United States of America

printing number

    3   4   5   6   7   8   9   10

Library of Congress Cataloging in Publication Data

Wakeman, Frederic Jr.
    The fall of imperial China.

    (The Transformation of modern China series)
    Bibliography: p.
    Includes index.
    1. China--History--Ch'ing dynasty, 1644-1912.
Title.
    DS754.W13   951'.03   74-27854
    ISBN 0-02-933690-2

The poetic extract appearing on page 53 is from Arthur Waley,
Yuan Mei, Eighteenth Century Chinese Poet (New York: Grove Press,
1956), page 108. Reprinted by permission of George Allen & Unwin
Ltd., book publishers, London, England.

To Carolyn and Freddy
Who Helped Keep Koula Away

Contents

Acknowledgments

I COULD NOT have written this book without the benefit of my students' researches. Many of the problems raised here were discussed in seminars, or thrashed out in debates with teaching assistants like Edward Hammond and Karl Slinkard. The dissertation work of other students has been especially helpful in defining my views. James Polachek's study of Soochow in the nineteenth century has profoundly affected my presentation of the T'ung-chih period gentry. Jeffrey Barlow's thesis on Sun Yat-sen would deserve numerous references if this book were copiously footnoted. Joseph Esherick's interpretation of the Revolution of 1911 has, as he will see when he reads this study, thoroughly informed my own understanding. And Angus McDonald's careful analysis of the Hunanese elite gave me confidence in arguing for the class transformation of the gentry in the early twentieth century. Some of these works are in press. All will eventually, I hope, be published so that others can benefit from them as well.

During a portion of the time spent writing this book, I held a Humanities Research Professorship from the University of California, Berkeley; and was awarded a fellowship by the John Simon Guggenheim Memorial Foundation. The good offices of Dr. Christopher Howe and the Contemporary China Institute also provided access to materials in the library of the School of Oriental and African Studies, the University of London. I am especially grateful to Frederic Wakeman, Sr., James Sheridan, and Carolyn Grant for giving me so much critical help with each stage of the manuscript.

Frederic Wakeman, Jr.
Berkeley, February 1975

Introduction

HISTORIANS OF MODERN CHINA are used to contrasting the dizzying changes in post-renaissance Europe with the glacial creep of Confucian civilization. The West's global expansion to new vistas of discovery thus distorts our perspective of those older worlds that resisted European conquest. The most tenacious of these ancient civilizations was the Chinese empire—a nation so proud of its culture that its inheritors were seemingly incapable of recognizing the need for rapid adaptation to the European challenge. According to this familiar historical view, so splendid, so weighty a civilization could not afford to disturb any of its underpinnings lest the entire edifice crumble. And because piecemeal reform was impossible, sweeping revolution became inevitable. The millennial endurance of China's traditional culture is thus used to explain the totality of its demise.

Such a China, incapable of basic internal change, would have had to be pushed into revolution by external force. But if this interpretation is accurate, then one must assume that an undisturbed China would have endlessly repeated the patterns of its native past, statically clinging to tradition, never changing on its own. Were there then no endogenous transformations in China before the mid-nineteenth century? Was China essentially inert before the Opium War began in 1839?

Chinese Marxists have been particularly sensitive to internal change because their periodization of modern history begins with the Opium War.

> If we employ a foreign war of aggression against China to mark
> a division point in the periodization of our history, do we not then

become proponents of external causation? My answer is to deny
this.... Foreign capitalist aggression against China has influenced
China to undergo internal changes. This means that Chinese
society internally already possessed the prerequisite for the appearance of change; and this prerequisite was the high degree of
development that China had attained during the long period of
feudal society.[1]

My own study does not seek prerequisites to modernization, but it
does try to isolate the inner sources of social change in China before
the heyday of European imperialism.

Pre-modern Chinese dynastic history can be schematically divided into six major periods. The first, from the sixteenth to the
third century B.C., began as a bronze age and ended with an advanced iron technology. During this time Chinese civilization in
the Yellow River valley developed writing, a sophisticated bureaucracy, and the great classics of Confucian thought. The second or
early imperial period from approximately 200 B.C. to 200 A.D. coincided with Ch'in centralization and the rule of the Han Dynasty,
which subjugated parts of Central Asia, created a legal code, opened
a state university, expanded and rationalized the bureaucracy, and
turned Confucianism into a state creed. When the Han fell, the
central government disintegrated and a third period from the third
to the sixth centuries saw many different kingdoms, some of them
barbarian, rule portions of the empire. Military feudalism spread,
philosophers abandoned Confucianism for metaphysical Taoism, and
Buddhist monasteries appeared across the land.

Political unity returned to China during the middle imperial
period from about 600 to 1100 A.D. Under the glorious T'ang and
Sung dynasties classical Chinese poetry and paintings flourished as
never before, and Confucianism enjoyed a powerful revival. The
military aristocracy was curbed, while civil bureaucrats administered the most advanced civilization in the world. When the Sung
was driven into the South, a fifth period began which lasted until
the fourteenth century. A series of barbarian regimes took over
north China, and the last of these—the Mongol Yuan Dynasty—
destroyed the Sung and ruled the entire empire. Then, in the fourteenth century, the Ming Dynasty drove the Mongols out of China
and initiated the last great period of pre-modern history. During
this late imperial era, the Ming and Ch'ing dynasties revived Confucian thought, conquered all of Central Asia, and became the symbol of high culture and civilization to most countries of East Asia.

By then Chinese society was dominated by the gentry—a scholarly elite of officials who staffed the formal bureaucracy and of local notables who informally administered rural affairs. Beneath them was the peasantry, the largest segment of the population and the economic foundation of the empire. Their agricultural efforts, coupled with the introduction of new crops, increased the supply of food, causing the Chinese population to more than triple between 1400 and 1800. Such dramatic demographic growth helped trigger most of the other basic social changes of the late imperial period: changes in the peasants' social and economic status, proliferation of the gentry, and commercialization of the economy.

These processes together constituted an extended and dynamic internal development which had a very important influence upon the outcome of China's nineteenth-century struggle with the West and Japan. China did adapt to the European challenge, but its response to this outer stimulus drastically altered those internal social forces that were already evolving on their own. As old elites gave way to new classes and shared accommodations changed into mutual conflict, the political center of the empire began to dissolve. In 1912 the last dynasty fell, and along with the monarchy, traditional civilization crumbled. The nation survived this cultural disintegration, but its political unity was shattered. And although a much more vigorous China eventually emerged, its revolutionary struggles to define a new polity continue to this very day.

CHINESE DYNASTIES

Shang	*ca.* 1523–1028 B.C.
Chou	*ca.* 1027– 222 B.C.
Ch'in	221– 207 B.C.
Han	206 B.C.– 220 A.D.
Three Kingdoms	221– 264 A.D.
Chin	265– 419
North-South Period	420– 588
Sui	589– 617
T'ang	618– 906
Five Dynasties	907– 959
Sung	960–1279
Yuan	1280–1367
Ming	1368–1644
Ch'ing	1644–1912

Note

1. Li Shu, cited in Albert Feuerwerker, ed., *History in Communist China* (Cambridge: M.I.T. University Press, 1968), p. 26.

Peasants

Peasant Stereotypes

THE CHINESE COMMUNIST REVOLUTION has elevated the role of the masses in history. In Mao Tse-tung's formulation, "the people, and the people alone, are the motive forces in the making of world history."[1] Yet however sincere the desire to pay tribute to the peasantry of traditional China, historians find it extremely difficult to go beyond a merely emotional appreciation of the collective importance of the "hundred surnames" (*lao pai-hsing*). Although they occupy the historical chronicles, these "black-haired masses" (*li chung*) who actually tilled the empire's land and supported its rulers seemed even to contemporaries an abstract stereotype. Illiterate and faceless, they could be defined only by their superiors until modern times gave them their own political reality, and they learned to speak for themselves.

Before the twentieth-century revolution the generic mass of Chinese peasants was portrayed in two paradoxically different stereotypes. The first presented the peasant as a diligent yeoman, fondly regarded by Confucian[2] physiocrats as the social mainstay of agrarian society. Because he pursued the "fundamental vocation" (*pen-yeh*) of agriculture, the peasant theoretically stood high in the social order, well above the artisan and merchant and just below the literati who administered the empire. Frugal and hard-working, this idealized peasant toiled productively, paying his taxes gratefully in return for the paternalistic care and devotion which his rulers were supposed to lavish upon him.

But peasants were also viewed as rebellious. In the second,

equally familiar Confucian portrayal, the black-haired masses were seen as sullen beasts of burden, easily transformed into red-turbaned bandits or fanatic sectarians who arose sporadically to attack their masters. When times worsened and famine spread across the land, peasant armies swelled in despair and rage, smashing city walls and attacking local officials. Chinese political theorists attached great significance to these popular movements, believing them to represent heaven's disapproval of the emperor's mode of rule. Even though few rebel leaders ever seized power, the movements they led were regarded as omens of a new dynasty.

Two such simultaneous yet different formulations of the peasants' role are not difficult to reconcile when seen as opposite sides of the same coin.[3] Peasants did constitute the economic foundation of traditional Chinese society, as they still do today. They usually did spend their lives in routine but laborious work, rooted in the land and regulated by the seasons. Yet when political corruption and economic scarcity coincided, they also stepped out of this role and momentarily attached themselves just as firmly to militant Buddhist prophets or ambitious bandit generals at the head of rebel armies. It is easy to see how the 1898 reformer Liang Ch'i-ch'ao could view the centuries of Ch'ing rule as one long and bloody history of convulsive peasant rebellions. In the nineteenth century alone, Chinese official sources mention thousands of incidents of protest, leaving a chaotic impression of fundamental and lasting social disorder. But this is a one-sided view, distorted by the extraordinary class tensions of the late Ch'ing. By 1800 the empire was already experiencing economic difficulties that had gradually accumulated over earlier centuries of nonviolent changes by the Chinese peasantry.

Agriculture and Land Tenure

Another way of understanding the dual nature of the peasantry is by examining the system of agriculture and land tenure that had evolved in different ways in the North and the South since the dawn of Chinese history. Agriculture began in the North along the Yellow River valley, where sedentary farming was well developed by 700 B.C. This region, which was the heartland of early Chinese civilization, was relatively arid. Only about twenty inches of rain fell each year on the north China plain, so that the growing season was short (four to six months) and best suited for dry cereals like millet and wheat. West of what is now Peking, the soil was a loamy yellow wind-deposit called loess. Minerals needed for cultivation lay deep beneath this spongy, capillary surface, and had to be drawn up through the earth with abundant amounts of water in order for plants to grow. Because rainfall was variable, the peasants depended for irrigation on the Yellow River, which had to be channeled and contained by public works projects. Water conservancy was thus a major responsibility of the early Shang (ca. 1523–1028 B.C.) and Chou (1027–222 B.C.) dynasties, and continued to be a fundamental concern of the state under the first great imperial regime of the Han (206 B.C.–220 A.D.). When the Han Dynasty began to lose control of China in the second century A.D., one of the first casualties was public waterworks. The Yellow River flooded repeatedly, driving peasants off the land and into rebel armies. As the Han government grew weaker, Central Asian tribesmen raided north China, forcing the cultivators to seek the protection of local military magnates. By the time the former Han capital of Lo-yang was sacked by barbarians in 311 A.D., China had developed a quasi-feudal class of military aristocrats whose fortifications housed private armies of liegemen to watch over the slaves and tenants tilling their manors.

Central bureaucratic control was reasserted over the peasantry in the sixth century. The Sui (589–617) and T'ang (618–906) dynasties formed divisional militia to reduce the central government's dependence upon the provincial military magnates. Lands were declared the property of the state, which distributed plots to peasants who were now enrolled in household registers by the government. Officeholders were given service-tenure fiefs as a reward for bureaucratic duties, and were forbidden to accumulate manors of their own. But this "equitable fields" land system was difficult to administer and did not survive the weakening of state control in the mid-700s. By the ninth century local magnates had once again acquired vast private holdings.

Such limited seigneurialism was not the same as European feudalism. The imperial government retained formal command of the military structure and did not recognize the aristocratic prerogatives of magnates to fiefs in exchange for military service. Even after the An Lu-shan rebellion (755–763) enabled governors to rule provinces on their own, powerful regional commanders remained bureaucratic satraps and did not become feudal barons. During the early tenth century China did break up into a host of smaller kingdoms, but the empire was reconstituted by the Sung in 960. And thereafter, when the Sung lost north China to Ju-chen and Mongol invaders, the conceptual unity of the empire still persisted. In geopolitical terms China may have potentially been several different countries whose rural inhabitants spoke distinct dialects, but bureaucratic practice and common cultural identity held *t'ien-hsia* (the Chinese under-heaven) together. By late imperial times kingship as such was inextricably identified with an ideally unified realm that embraced the whole of Chinese territory.

Ideally, too, landed manors—which in Ming times (1368–1644) encompassed tens of thousands of acres in north China—either were reserved as imperial benefices for court favorites or were used to support the imperial family. The Ch'ing Dynasty (1644–1912) extended this to include the maintenance of a conquering Manchu–Mongol military elite. After capturing Peking in 1644, the Manchus not only seized the former Ming imperial manors for the Ch'ing royal family; they also settled their 169,000 bannermen (the soldiers who had conquered China for the Ch'ing) on the more than two million acres of land confiscated for that purpose in a 175-mile radius around the capital. The Ch'ing government provided these homesteads in the hope of strategically preserving its own foreign military elite apart from the conquered Chinese. That expectation was disappointed, and the bannermen soon found that they had to treat their Chinese serfs like favored tenants because so much land had fallen fallow during the conquest period that the peasants could flee the manors and easily reclaim plots of their own elsewhere. And, since Manchu bannermen preferred expensive townhouses in Peking to mud castles in the countryside, they were quick to lease parcels of their manors to Chinese tenants who tilled the land for themselves. When the bannermen fell into debt, individual plots of land were mortgaged to local moneylenders and landlords, who foreclosed to collect their investment. The Ch'ien-lung Emperor (reigned 1736–1795) did try in 1740 to restore the Manchu homesteads by reconfiscating some of the land, but the same process was simply repeated. By the early 1800s most of the land in north China had been broken up into small family farms and, over the course of the nineteenth century, the size of these holdings gradually diminished because Chinese custom forbade primogeniture.

Land and Labor in North China

Manchu extravagance and the practice of dividing property among all male heirs were sufficient reasons for the fragmentation of these manors, but the level of northern Chinese agricultural technology was certainly another contributing cause. The food and fodder staple of the plain had originally been a cereal grass called millet. By the time the Manchus marched across these provinces, wheat and cotton had also become major crops. Under the Ch'ing other commercial plants were cultivated: tobacco, soybeans, peanuts, and eventually opium. Some of these crops would have been more efficiently grown on large landholdings if there had existed techniques and machines for extensive farming. But instead of making capital improvements to raise productivity, agriculturalists increased their investment of labor by intensifying the efforts of every available member of a farming family.[4] The propulsion for greater productivity was the individual peasant's physical energy, and since labor determined productivity, the size of any single family's cultivation was economically limited. A family of five needed four acres of land to subsist. In order to raise its standard of living above the subsistence level, the family had to intensify its labor on the land already held, then use the surplus profits to acquire more land up to the optimum size its small labor force could handle. (At times like the early Ch'ing period when untilled land was plentiful, many households did precisely that.) For a family of five, this would be about twenty-five acres.

As each family farm reached its optimum size, aggregate productivity increased proportionally, providing the food to feed a larger population and hence enlarging the labor supply to the maximum level which the available land could support. But this continuing increase in population ultimately reduced the pool of land available for each peasant family to cultivate. Over the later eighteenth and nineteenth centuries single farms steadily declined in acreage, until many actually dropped below the level of human subsistence.

Simply to survive, then, the northern Chinese peasant had to find new outlets for his unused labor. Cottage industry like cotton weaving afforded one such form of subsidiary income. Seasonal migration to work in the cities provided another. Some economic historians even argue that this additional income enabled tenants[5] to purchase small plots of land, thereby acquiring property which they could mortgage in the event of crop failures. In their opinion, land transfers of this sort cushioned the effects of drought or flood and evened out the problem of labor distribution.

> Those households which rented and leased land were merely attempting to use available land more efficiently to maximize household income. Where land was transferred to another party as a by-product of the credit system, it did not lead to undesirable consequences for the rural economy, because land as a form of near money played an important role in the transfer of credit from lender to debtor.[6]

In this view, the peasant was not a helpless tenant or day laborer, bullied by landlords. Rather, he judiciously invested his supplementary income in land, which then became collateral used to borrow money from city-dwelling creditors. When north China's agricultural economy reached a point of crisis in 1940—so the argument goes—it was because of technical backwardness, not because of the unequal distribution of wealth.

The rural credit system may not have appeared quite so advantageous to farmers who did turn to the usurer and pawnbroker, gambling that future harvests would be good enough to keep them from falling hopelessly into debt. Interest rates were cruelly high, and—as Chinese peasants today bitterly describe their pre-revolutionary experiences—put the poorer farmers completely at the mercy of loan sharks. Of course, moneylenders were resented and hated long before revolutionary times, but their presence was usually taken for granted in the late imperial period. Peasants turned to pawnbrokers because they had no choice; external elements beyond their control dictated that necessity for them. Men could only pray, burn incense, and sacrifice pigs in the hope of making the heavens rain. But ultimately the forces of nature were decisive where so narrow a margin of subsistence was concerned.

The most feared disaster in north China was drought. Between 1876 and 1879, for instance, it rained not at all in the province of Shansi. During the terrible famine that followed, the people first ate their seed-grain, then the wild grass, and finally each other. Corpses were heaped in "ten thousand men holes" or dropped into dry wells. When the government sent relief grain by muleback, the desperate peasants slaughtered the pack animals for food, preventing further supplies from reaching them. In the bitter year of 1877–1878, ten million people perished in north China.

An abundance of water could, however, be just as fatal. The Shansi mountains, which had been cultivated for thousands of years, were denuded of forests and ground cover. Erosive runoff filled the Yellow River with silt up to 11 percent of its entire volume, and this earth slowly settled to the bottom, gradually forcing the water level to rise. The river was normally kept within its meandering course by man-made dikes which stood thirty feet above the northern plain. But the dikes were expensive to maintain and the silt hard to dredge. If an emperor preferred to rebuild a burned palace rather than keep the river in check, or if the officials he appointed to the vast Yellow River Waterworks Administration pocketed the labor costs themselves, then the brown waters rose higher and higher. When the rains came, the swollen river would push up and out, spilling over its banks to flood the plain below in search of other outlets to the sea. At times like this, the Yellow River might shift its course hundreds of miles and devastate entire provinces.[7]

When such natural calamities struck, the peasants of north China reacted like a force of nature themselves, pouring across the same plains that were so quickly engulfed by floods. The core of these rebel movements was often an army of professional bandits, but their ranks were swollen with refugees from drought or flood, from other bandits or from the regime's tax collectors. If it is permissible to speak of social movements in topographical terms, then the rebellions in the North were extended and broad, like the plains and river valleys which they covered. Mounted rebels swept easily across entire provinces, difficult to contain and crush. Yet, in the end, when the flood waters had receded or a new dynasty promised peace, the peasants returned to their villages to reclaim the once abandoned land.

The Human Geography of South China

South China presented a much different human geography. Below the Yangtze River the physical landscape of high mountains and wet river valleys was fragmented and differentiated, its population density unevenly scattered. While the fertile deltas and highly irrigated flatlands hummed with farming activity around marketing centers, the hilly borderlands were spare of people, sheltering brigands and aboriginal tribesmen. Lineages competed among themselves for local wealth and power; rival ethnic groups disturbed the evenness of the human horizon.

The peasants themselves were Han Chinese,[8] originally from the North. The periodic disasters of climate and the continuous human pressure upon natural resources above the Yangtze had gradually propelled the Han out of the Yellow River basin and into the South. Sometimes, as in the Southern Sung period, there were immense waves of migration, but the flow of population was not always so perceptible. By tabulating the construction of waterworks mentioned in local gazetteers, historians can now tell that significant numbers of Chinese settlers first began drifting across the Yangtze into the monsoon climate and tropical jungles of the South by the third century A.D. Migration increased sharply during the T'ang period (618–906), rising to a peak in the late thirteenth century, then declining to a point of stability about 1700, when slightly more than half of China's population dwelt below the Yangtze River. During this long time span, ethnic differences came to distinguish the populations of the two zones. Northerners spoke varieties of Mandarin Chinese, while the physically smaller southerners developed mutually unintelligible dialects like Cantonese, Hakka, or Hokkienese. Religious differences also existed, and the corporate lineage was far more extensive in the South than elsewhere.

The immigrants discovered a lush new landscape beyond the Yangtze River. Water was plentiful; thirty to sixty inches of rain fell each year. Polders (diked fields) were built, new types of dams constructed, and treadle water pumps devised to flood the paddies for high-caloric rice crops. Since the gentler climate lengthened the growing season by three months, a new species of early ripening rice was imported from Southeast Asia by the imperial government in the eleventh century. Using these new seeds and organic manure, the southern peasants were able to harvest two or three crops each year. By 1300 south China possessed the most advanced agricultural technology in the world, permitting a demographic leap forward to a national population figure of over one hundred million.

Wet-field irrigation projects were on a smaller scale than the water conservancy works of the North, but they demanded a higher investment of labor and continuous management. While the state assumed responsibility for controlling the Yellow River, private enterprise accounted for most of the canals, dikes, and dams of the lower Yangtze. In the eighteenth and nineteenth centuries, such projects were vested in the hands of official gentry who were not always large landlords. Before 1700, however, the expense of irrigation works in the Yangtze delta seems to have largely been assumed by wealthy landowners who lived off the rents from large estates.[9]

These estates may once have been integrated demesnes, but by the Ming period, at least, they consisted of the landowner's household and directly supervised labor force, plus outlying and scattered plots tilled by tenants. The development of such a landlord system in south China was intimately related to the rise of the bureaucratic gentry, which will be described in the following chapter. One of the privileges of being a member of the official gentry was virtual exemption from *corvée* or labor service. That, plus the gentry's political influence, often meant that gentry-held land was kept off the property tax rolls. As more and more estate land thus became tax exempt, the burden on remaining freeholders increased. Unable to pay their taxes, these freeholding peasants had little choice but to turn their lands over to the more influential landlords and gentry, and become *their* serfs or tenants. The line between serfdom and tenantry was not clearly drawn. Serfs were bought and sold like slaves after binding their bodies to a life of personal service—a status which was often inherited by their offspring. Tenants, on the other hand, were bound to the soil, and might be sold with the land when it changed hands. Legally, only bureaucratic families were permitted to own serfs, but nongentry households did so as well under the fiction of adopting indigent children, thus acquiring a bound labor force to cultivate their estates.

In the late fourteenth century, the first Ming emperor confiscated the Yangtze valley estates and returned the land to its peasant tenants. However, there were still so many loopholes for the southern gentry in the Ming tax collection system that peasants were once again forced to commend their holdings to the ownership of the great households. By the sixteenth century tenancy rates were as high as ever, even though the commercialization of the economy was starting to weaken the status system that kept tenants and serfs in their place. As more and more intermediate market towns increased opportunities for communication among lower peasants, the personal resentments of the subservient were magnified into a collective class animus against the great landlords of the lower Yangtze. In 1644 when the Ming Dynasty fell in the North, serfs and tenants broke into riot in the South, demanding that their service contracts be torn up or their lands returned.

The new Ch'ing Dynasty abolished serfdom in the 1730s. And although tenantry persisted, about half of the land in south China would eventually be held by the peasants themselves. This was also a result of the declining profitability of investment in farming land. The wealthy found that they could obtain better profits by putting their money into urban real estate, or by turning to moneylending. Nevertheless, landlordism was much more predominant in the South than it was in the North (see Figure 1–1). The spread of property among middle and rich peasants was almost equal above and below the Yangtze: about 30 percent of the population held 40 percent of the land. But in the South there was a great discrepancy at the extremes of wealth and poverty. Three percent of the population controlled about half of the cultivated land, which was occupied by a poor peasant class that was almost three times larger than its counterpart in the North.

One reason for this unequal distribution was the amount of corporately owned property in south China. Wealthy lineages invested huge amounts of money in family trusts and estates, which were managed by clan officers. These estates purchased land and pawnshops in order to earn income for clan rituals, welfare, and education. Other organizations—gentry-run charity bureaus, village leagues (*yueh*), irrigation corporations, even secret societies—made south China appear much more socially complex than the rural society of the North. This complexity was also a reflection of the higher degree of commercialization along and below the Yangtze River. Interregional and international trade increased during the late imperial period, making independent farmers of peasants who had before then been basically unaffected by market relationships. In the commercialized districts of Hunan and Fukien, for instance, farmers carefully planned to take the best advantage of commercial crop prices, which they tried to manipulate to their own benefit when paying rents to absentee landlords. In this respect, the individual cultivator was enmeshed in a web of impersonal economic forces: fluctuating rice prices in a distant provincial capital, a changing demand for tea in London, or an altered style of silk clothing in Osaka.

Figure 1–1. *Landholding in North and South China in the Twentieth Century*

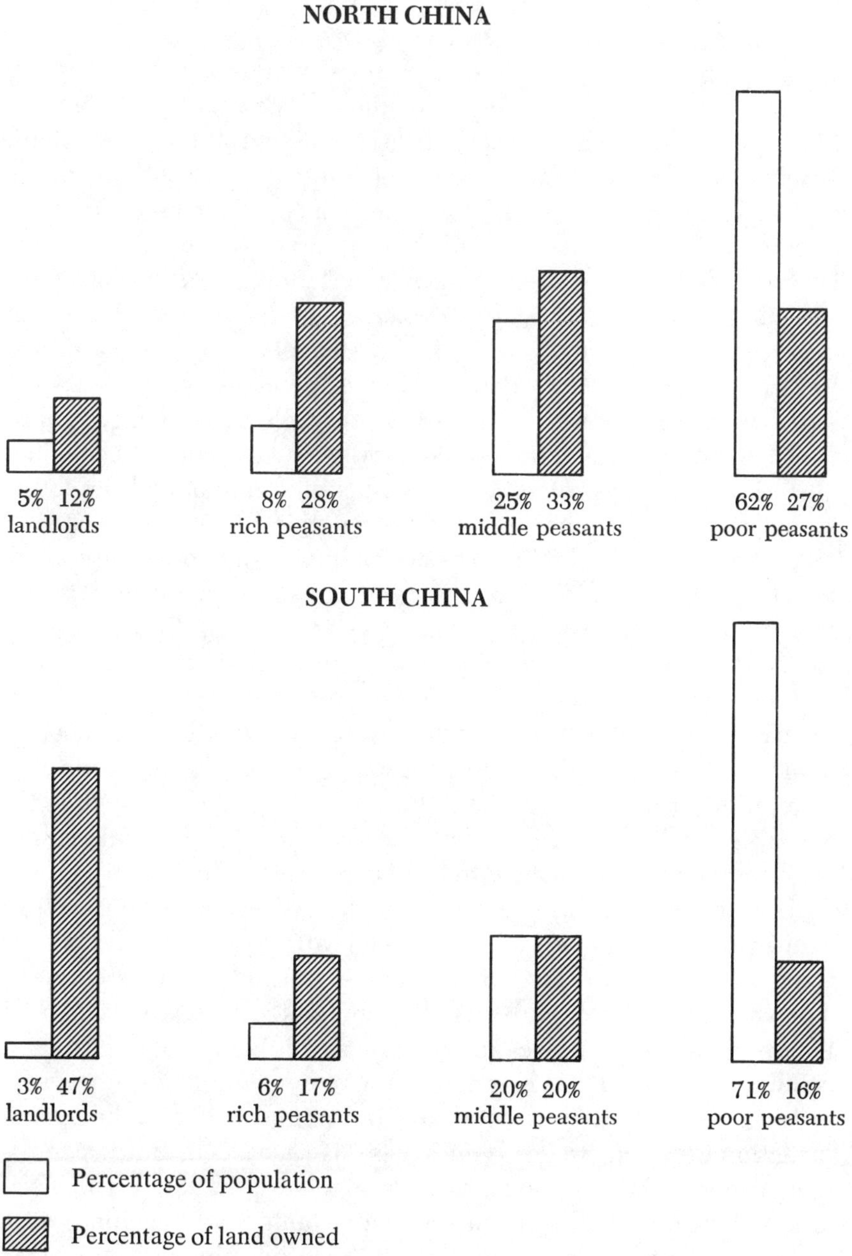

NORTH CHINA

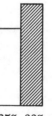

5% 12%
landlords

8% 28%
rich peasants

25% 33%
middle peasants

62% 27%
poor peasants

SOUTH CHINA

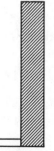

3% 47%
landlords

6% 17%
rich peasants

20% 20%
middle peasants

71% 16%
poor peasants

☐ Percentage of population

▨ Percentage of land owned

Source: Data derived from Chen Han-seng, *The Chinese Peasant* (Oxford: Oxford Pamphlets on Indian Affairs, 1945), p. 22. Professor Chen has been criticized by some scholars for overestimating landlordism. He based these figures on twentieth-century field studies.

Personal Relationships and Class Conflict

The direct impact of these impersonal market relationships was sometimes softened by the cultivation of personal ties between higher and lower, buyer and seller. Although there were many absentee landlords during the seventeenth and eighteenth centuries, the conscious paternalism of the elite helped alleviate some of the uncertainty of rural life and reduced putative class conflict. Tenant contracts from the late Ming show how familial relationships were extended to cover rental agreements. In exchange for special services at family weddings and funerals, tenants expected their landlords to feast them on particular religious holidays. In the far South many peasants were actually tenants of their own lineage and so could expect welfare, famine relief, and even education if the elders abided by the clan's rules. When there existed no familial ties, other kinds of personal connections were strengthened through a code of mutual rapport (*kan-ch'ing*) between upper and lower classes, so that if a harvest failed or crop prices dropped, a tenant might hope to persuade his landlord to reduce the rent. Naturally his chances of success were influenced by economic considerations. At times, certain regions (central Hunan in the late 1600s, for example) were relatively depopulated and tenants were in high demand. There a landowner would take special care to retain his subordinate's loyalty. At other times, when the supply of labor exceeded the available land (Kiangsu in the 1820s), a landowner could afford to be much less concerned with his tenant's interests.

The inevitable consequence of paternalism is ambivalence. Just as the upper classes viewed the peasant with mixed feelings, so did the tenant farmer or day laborer mingle gratitude with resentment. The very contract he had signed to guarantee his own security of tenure might well prove an instrument of bondage if economic conditions changed.[10] When the supply of land and labor was evenly apportioned, both parties stood to gain by good will, and the accommodation between landlords and peasants succeeded. But if population burdened the land too heavily, social relations suffered. There was only a short distance between economic comfort and genuine want, and when the balance tilted too far against him, the peasant discovered that the devices he had learned to manipulate in his own favor (rapport with the landlord, dependence upon the moneylender for quick and easy credit, reliance upon shifting market prices for his cash crops) trammeled his ability to survive. Then animus flared into hostility, hoes became weapons, and the villas of the rich were burned to the ground. Yet once the balance was restored, and productivity moved ahead of population growth, the peasant slipped back into the personal relations most familiar to him and regular rural life resumed.

Throughout the late imperial period, then, peasants in both north and south China alternated between order and disorder, agriculture and rebellion. The balance inclined toward rural stability as long as natural resources were sufficient for human subsistence. But continuous population growth eventually disturbed this balance, especially after the sixteenth century, when Portuguese and Spanish mariners introduced the Chinese to food plants which they had discovered in America: maize, sweet potatoes, Irish potatoes, and peanuts. These new sources of nutrition flourished in sandy soils and on dry hillsides that had never before been farmed. As cultivated acreage doubled between 1600 and 1850, the population almost tripled, increasing from 150,000,000 to 430,000,000 Chinese in the same period. Sparsely inhabited parts of China like the Yangtze highlands were settled. Millions of southern Chinese emigrated overseas. Millions more from the North were to filter into Manchuria. But despite such outlets, the pressure of population continued to grow. By the 1770s, the Chinese had multiplied more rapidly than their land allowed. In 1796, the White Lotus revolt erupted. Although this rebellion was defeated, it was only the first in a series of major revolts that were to shake the foundations of the empire and destroy the ancient accommodation between the peasants and the gentry.

Notes

1. Mao Tse-tung, *Hung-ch'i,* cited in the *New York Times,* November 6, 1971.
2. "Confucian" is used throughout this study to denote the political and moral orthodoxy that prevailed after the T'ang period (618–906 A.D.).
3. Or if placed within the historical context of the theory of the Mandate of Heaven (see Chapter IV).
4. Landowning was not a profitable enterprise. By the 1930s, Hopei farms returned only about 3 percent a year on capital investments,

whereas urban real estate or pawnshops brought a return on the original capital of 30 to 45 percent.

5. The separation between tenantry and freeholding was not always clear. A peasant household might rent one plot from a landlord while at the same time owning other plots and having its own tenants.

6. Ramon H. Myers, *The Chinese Peasant Economy: Agricultural Development in Hopei and Shantung* (Cambridge: Harvard University Press, 1970), p. 234.

7. In 1938 the Chinese Nationalists deliberately broke the Yellow River's dikes to stop Japanese soldiers from advancing to the south. The river changed its course from above Shantung to the Huai River valley, where it remained until redirected in 1947. Conservative estimates of the flood damage showed that 44 counties were flooded, 900,000 people killed, and 3,900,000 driven from their homes as refugees.

8. "Han" was the self-styled racial appellation of the Chinese as opposed to the other minority ethnic and religious groups (Miao, Yao, and Lolo aborigines; Manchus, Mongols, Muslims, and so forth) living in China during the later imperial period.

9. The Chinese word for the northern manor and the southern estate is identical (*chuang*), and the two are not absolutely different. One broad distinction was the formal recognition of the manor as an imperial gift, while the estate was an informal (and in the case of Kiangnan's "public lands" in the Ming period, illegal) acquisition. The division which I have made between northern manors and southern estates is not an absolute one. Some of the complexities of nomenclature and historiography about this topic are discussed in Ramon H. Myers, "Transformation and Continuity in Chinese Economic and Social History," *Journal of Asian Studies* (February, 1974), 265–277.

10. Then, and now, so much depends upon point of view. The contracts binding the tenant to the soil and enabling the landlord to sell him like a serf were also designed to protect the tenant against arbitrary expulsion from his plot. The customary practice of *sui-t'ien tien-hu* (tenants accompany the plot) meant that a new landlord did not have the right to throw tenants off recently purchased land and guaranteed the peasant's tenure as long as he continued to pay the rents due. The recognition of ground and surface rights (*i-t'ien liang-chu*) provided protection of a similar sort.

II

Gentry

The Dual Nature of the Gentry

THE POLITICAL SYSTEM of late imperial China is easy to schematize at its higher and more formal levels. At the top ruled the emperor, surrounded by relatives and trusted councillors who were sometimes granted hereditary titles of nobility. Below the emperor, carrying out his orders, were the bureaucrats, whom Westerners used to call "mandarins." The bureaucracy was staffed with scholar-officials who had achieved a higher degree in the state civil service examination. Their ranks extended down to the level of district magistrate and a few of his subordinates. But between the formal magistracy and the peasant population at large there existed another informal level of government and social service performed by a group usually defined in English as the "gentry." This word does not adequately translate *shen-shih*, which was the Chinese phrase most often used to describe the local elite. "Gentry" does aptly evoke the gentlemanly status and rural residence of the *shen-shih*,[1] but fails to suggest the bureaucratic derivation of that status. Other terms—"mandarin," "degree-holder"—describe the official rank of the *shen-shih*, but overlook the non-bureaucratic status that was independently derived by members of the gentry from wealth, education, and even birth alone. We shall use the word "gentry" to describe this group as a whole, but only after showing that the *shen-shih* was neither a purely bureaucratic status group, nor an aristocratic local notability. Unlike its English counterpart, the binomial Chinese term—*shen* and *shih*—captures both components,

19

attesting to the gentry's bureaucratic and aristocratic tendencies alike.

Bureaucratic Rank: The Gentry as a Status Group

The single word *shen,* for instance, denotes the meritocratic quality of gentry status. *Shen* originally referred to the embroidered sash which imperial officials once wore as a badge of rank. This corresponded in the late imperial period to the official degree won by passing the state civil service examinations.[2] Individuals who earned these degrees were consequently entitled to wear gold and silver buttons along with lynx and sable furs, to participate in official Confucian ceremonies, to receive municipal and imperial subsidies, to be exempted from the labor service tax, and to be immune from punishment by the local magistrate. Such formal status could not be passed on to one's heirs. Descendants of a gentryman had to earn their own degrees in order to acquire the same official privileges.

These sumptuary rewards and legal perquisites were all gifts of the state. As *shen,* therefore, the gentry was a creation of the imperial government. In fact, the gentry had originally risen in the world because of the T'ang emperors' need for a bureaucratic counterweight to the influential aristocracy which had monopolized land and military power after the fall of the Han. Between the third and seventh centuries authority in China had been divided between the monarch and the lineages of noble birth. The great families provided ministers for the bureaucracy and consorts for the emperor, possessing as much social prestige as the royal family itself. Successive T'ang rulers fought for their independence by fostering a new bureaucracy open to men of talent. Because these civil servants borrowed their prestige from the throne, they would presumably be the monarchy's servants and not its masters. Indeed, once established, this bureaucratic corps did implement the institutions and procedures that were needed to strip the aristocracy of seigneurial prerogatives, restoring population, land, and military strength to an imperial state as strong as the Han had been. Thus, by pitting its bureaucracy against the aristocracy, the monarchy eventually won the long inconclusive struggle between nobles and emperor. But once having defeated the aristocracy, the throne discovered that its own weapon—the new bureaucracy—had become a new competitor. Eager to be more independent of the state, the civil service corps sought a manorial base outside the government by developing into a landed gentry during the twelfth and thirteenth centuries. Within the bureaucracy, it managed to secure the hereditary privilege of *yin*, which gave the sons of high-ranking officials automatic gentry status as *chien-sheng* (students of the imperial academy). The monarchy, on the other hand, tried to uproot the newly entrenched gentry, first by making tax exemption and serf ownership the exclusive privileges of men actually in office; and second by channeling all access to official rank or *shen* status through an open examination system.

The early Ming emperors were crucial in this regard. During the late fourteenth century, Ming T'ai-tsu (reigned 1368–1398) confiscated the estates of the Yangtze gentry, and abolished the prime ministership, thereby depriving the civil service of a powerful spokesman at court. Successive fifteenth-century Ming emperors withdrew the *yin* privilege and debased the prestige of imperial students.[3] At the same time the monarchy encouraged mobility in and out of the bureaucratic gentry by vastly expanding a civil service examination system which was available to men of all but the meanest social background. Through its control of the content, frequency and difficulty of the examinations, the central government could manipulate the ideology, size, and calibre of the influential elite that governed the empire on its behalf.

The Ming examination system, which grew increasingly complex over the sixteenth century, was perpetuated without major modifications by the Ch'ing Dynasty. There were basically three levels of proficiency, tested every two or three years. At the lowest prefectural level was the *sheng-yuan*[4] degree, popularly called *hsiu-ts'ai*, or "cultivated talent." A successful *sheng-yuan*[5] was allowed to compete at the provincial level for a *chü-jen* (recommended man) degree. If he passed that examination and became a provincial graduate, then he was eligible to sit for the metropolitan and palace degree in the capital. Success at these national examinations was rewarded with the title of *chin-shih* (presented scholar). In brief:

chin-shih	national exams
chü-jen	provincial exams
sheng-yuan	prefectural exams

Westerners in China during the nineteenth century frequently thought of the *sheng-yuan* as a bachelor's degree, the *chü-jen* as a

master's degree, and the *chin-shih* as a doctoral degree. This designation is mnemonically helpful, but not entirely apt.

Originally, a degree-holder at any level was eligible for office,
but by 1850 only *chin-shih* degree-holders could be sure of getting
posts.[6] Entry into all ranks was strictly controlled by government
quotas, which were widely opened at the *sheng-yuan* level but
narrowed drastically the closer one got to the top. Each time the
examinations were given, approximately two million aspirants
(*t'ung-sheng*) sat for the district degree. Of these only thirty
thousand were made *sheng-yuan*. Among their ranks another fifteen
hundred would make it past the *chü-jen* provincial examinations
and, out of the *chü-jen*, only three hundred would manage to
acquire the highest *chin-shih* rank. An aspirant looking up the ladder
realized that he had only about one chance in sixty of getting the
lowest degree. Once a *sheng-yuan*, his possibility of passing the
provincial level was a depressingly low one in twenty; but if he could
satisfy the *chü-jen* requirements, the odds against his becoming a
chin-shih were only five to one. To put it another way, each of the
two million students waiting outside the prefectural examination
halls of the empire in any given year knew that he had only one
chance in six thousand of ever reaching the top rank where a bureaucratic post would be guaranteed him. For the total 1.4 million
degree-holders, high and low, in the realm, there were only twenty
thousand available civil appointments.

Competition was keen and social mobility in and out of gentry
ranks was high. At any single time, one-third of the examination
gentry was fresh blood—people whose immediate ancestors had
never held a degree. And of every ten who were admitted into the
ranks, only two had immediate heirs who perpetuated the family's
official position by gaining a degree of their own in the second
generation. If degree-holding is considered the sole sign of status,
then elite membership fluctuated constantly, making the Chinese
gentry much more labile than the squires of Hanoverian England.
Nor was the proportion of examination gentry nearly as large, say,
as that of the nobility in eighteenth-century France. Only 1.7
percent of the population in the late 1800s belonged to gentry
families in all of China.[7]

Because it was so difficult to reach the higher echelons, provincial and metropolitan degrees conferred immense social prestige.
The upper gentry (*chü-jen* and *chin-shih*) were noticeably distinguished from lower degree holders (*sheng-yuan*) who were often

referred to as "gentry commoners" (*shih-min*). Only a handful of men ever became metropolitan gentry (between 1723 and 1795 there were only 6,884 *chin-shih* degrees presented), and their names were famous throughout the empire. So honored was the title that the remotest chance of acquiring it spurred millions of scholars, year after year, to study for the examinations. A dramatic jump from rags to riches, from starving student to fêted metropolitan scholar, was uncommon. But the possibility of success, however unlikely, alleviated social discontent and gave the civilization tenacious staying-power.

The examination system also perpetuated a high culture common to all the gentry. During certain periods, like the early Ch'ing, subjects like law and administrative practices were tested. But the most prevalent examination questions concerned literary and philosophical subjects, which had to be answered in a prescribed and formulaic *pa-ku* (eight-legged) essay style which was exceedingly difficult to master. The questions themselves were based upon Confucian classics which the candidates were all expected to memorize in advance. Thus, however different their regional or social backgrounds, all scholar-officials wrote a universally understood classical Chinese and had educated themselves with an identical set of Confucian texts. This shared high culture distinguished the gentry from commoners who could not read classical Chinese, write elegant calligraphy, or understand the basic content of the Confucian canon. Unfortunately, the examination system also placed a premium upon the rote learning of works which the government had decided were orthodox. Critics of the system argued that it stultified creative thought and rewarded drones rather than original intellects. A better-than-average apprenticeship for the examinations meant beginning to learn to write characters at the age of 5, memorizing the Four Books and the Five Classics by the age of 11, mastering poetry composition at age 12, and studying *pa-ku* essay style thereafter. If a student could maintain this rigorous schedule without flagging, he would make a first experimental try at passing the prefectural exams when he reached 15. These he almost invariably failed at the first sitting, but by dint of repetition, he might be able to bring honor to himself and his family by acquiring the *sheng-yuan* degree at the relatively tender age of 21. Most people actually did not pass the prefectural level until the age of 24, while the average *chü-jen* was 31 and the average *chin-shih* 36. Truly, the life of an aspirant must have seemed to be one of constant examinations. The prefectural exams, for instance, were actually three different sets of tests; and if one actually made it past *sheng-yuan*, the degree-holder had to take examinations every three years until old age just to retain his gentry status. An average gentryman who had reached the metropolitan level could easily have spent over 160 days of examination-writing getting there.

Yet for all the toll it took, few really questioned the rationale behind this system. Those who did pass the examinations acquired a commitment along the way because of the time they had invested. They had a stake, so to speak, in seeing that others followed the same difficult route and devoted a lifetime to the mastery of classical culture. But what of those who failed? The aspirants at the bottom who tried unsuccessfully to scale this sharply rising pyramid must have experienced a sharp sense of disappointment and frustration. And the ones who did manage to become lower *sheng-yuan* well knew that all those years of study would still not get them office unless they scrambled higher up the ranks. The central government did try to alleviate resentment by periodically rewarding senior *sheng-yuan* with titles like *kung-sheng* (senior licentiate or imperial student) that made one eligible to purchase sub-magistral posts. Nonetheless, the frustration continued to produce its share of malcontents. The trouble was that each man knew just what his chances of success were: exactly one in six thousand. Although late imperial Chinese society was more upwardly mobile than any traditional civilization and most modern ones, advancement within the elite was maddeningly restricted and unsuccessful *sheng-yuan* often found an outlet in social protest. Many revolts, and even large-scale rebellions, were led by dissident lower degree-holders or aspirants who had tried for years to pass the higher examinations. But local prestige (as distinct from national office) kept this discontent from getting entirely out of hand. Evinced by the visible decorations mentioned earlier, social recognition satisfied the vanity of even the lowliest degree-holder and set him apart from simple commoners.

Local Prestige: The Gentry as a Class

The degree was not all: the sash (*shen*) was not the only determiner of status. The figure of the seedy *sheng-yuan* became something of a stock comedy character (like the English rural parson) in Ming and Ch'ing fiction. Living from hand to mouth, the lower degree-holder was often depicted as a down-and-out opportunist living on his uppers, "plowing with the pen" by tutoring the scions of the county's great families (*ta-hu*). Thus, looking behind such caricatures, the historian immediately grows aware that a degree-holder stood lower in the social hierarchy than certain other kinds of local notables whose families were regarded as *shih-chia* or *wang-tsu*—eminent lineages of a high social pedigree. Indeed those households, even if devoid of degree-holders, apparently also belonged to what would be regarded by contemporaries as the local gentry of a county. Consequently, one sees only half the picture when viewing the gentry from their *shen* side; that is, by defining gentry membership solely in terms of degrees conferred by the imperial government.[8] What then of *shih*—the second word in the compound term for "gentry?"

In the classical texts of the Chou period, the word *shih* described the nobles who served the king, the most acceptable definition being: one who assumed an administrative position. Before the sixth or seventh century B.C. these officials were invariably of aristocratic birth. Because Confucius himself was a *shih,* the word's meaning was gradually extended to include literati—a nobility of education rather than birth. By the Ch'ing period, *shih* was loosely used to describe leading members of the local elite who were not necessarily *shen* (degree-holders). Magistrates' handbooks defined them as "heads of the masses," and singled them out as being "exactly the ones to rely upon in persuading the people to follow the instructions of the officials."[9] As *shih,* the gentry was not just the ascribed creation of the state; it held an independent status of its own because of local prestige which was based upon wealth, education, power, and influence.

In its most extreme forms such a definition contrasts sharply with the degree-holding criteria given earlier. Instead of being a status group, the gentry in this guise appeared to be a class, identified with the landlords who owned the estates of Ming times and who in the Ch'ing period were so deeply involved in urban real estate and usury. After all—it is argued—where else would degree-holders come from than from the ranks of the wealthy? It took money to pass the examinations—tutors were expensive, and the average peasant family could hardly afford to spare the labor of one of its members in the futile hope that studying would bring immediate rewards. Wealth and informal social status had to precede the formal acquisition of a degree which—if office were gained—perpetuated a family's holdings by providing bureaucratic connections and political influence.

The *shih* interpretation thus transfers the definition of the gentry from the individual degree-holder to the socially prominent family or clan. Indeed, the rise of the Chinese gentry after 1000 A.D. coincided with an emphasis by scholar-officials like Fan Chung-yen (989–1052) upon the social responsibilities of the clan to instill Confucian moral values and look after the social welfare of its poorer members. By investing in corporate property, the clan ideally acquired the means to subsidize examination preparation, support indigent widows, nourish orphaned children, and in general palliate economic discontent by distributing individual wealth to poorer kinsmen. All this the government naturally favored, provided the clan neither became an instrument of elite domination, competing with the magistrate for control over the peasantry, nor fought so excessively with other lineages over property and water rights as to throw the countryside into clan warfare.

Success bred success. Lineages grew by acquiring corporate wealth, which in turn provided both a *raison d'être* and the resources for securing even more property. From the point of view of its members, the clan maximized their potential for garnering formal gentry status by sharing the financial burden of preparing the scholarly in their midst for civil service competition. The most successful lineages were those which functionally assigned careers to members according to aptitude.[10] Some kinsmen remained farmers, others engaged in commerce, and the bookish were encouraged to try for academic degrees that would reflect luster on them all.

And the luster was not just the glow of social success. It represented the real sheen of government salaries in silver. Although terms of office were short during the Ch'ing period,[11] a bureaucrat stood to make a fortune for himself and his kinsmen while in the civil service. Regular salaries were high (an eighteenth-century governor-general earned 18,000 taels, or about 23,400 silver dollars per year), and added to that were numerous customary fees such as *ts'ao-kuei* (grain tribute fees, which were a percentage of the taxes collected), and gifts. For a district magistrate these amounted to 30,000–40,000 taels per annum. The combined formal and informal income of his superiors were even greater, and a Ch'ing governor-general in a single year easily earned the equivalent of over a quarter million silver dollars. A portion of these riches was bound to find its way back into the coffers of the family that had nurtured such an official during those long years of study. Many lineages automatically assessed their officeholders a tithing of their salary and fully expected further contributions to enhance the clan's prosperity. These usually involved the purchase of *i-t'ien* (welfare fields), whose rents became income for the clan trust. In Soochow prefecture, for instance, there were almost two million *mou* (approximately 300,000 acres) of welfare fields owned by important lineages in the late nineteenth century. Nor was land the only outlet for investment. Beginning about 1700, wealthy families began to put more and more of their money into pawnbroking, so that control of rural credit was by the nineteenth century a major source of gentry wealth.

Officeholding was by no means the sole prop of such fortunes, but it certainly paid enough of a share to explain why lineages were eager to cultivate a future official among their own kin. If a wealthy clan lacked promising candidates for the exams, then it might adopt a bright neighborhood boy for that purpose, or contract a marriage alliance with other lineages by betrothing its daughters to their heirs. One study[12] of 91 notable clans of the lower Yangtze region during the late imperial period shows that most influential lineages were able to preserve their social position in this way for eight generations, or well over two centuries. And the truly eminent *wang-tsu* (notable lineages) managed to retain prestige for as long as 21 generations, or 550 years. An exceptional example of this longevity was Fan Chung-yen's clan in Soochow. The estate which he established in the eleventh century survived well into the 1900s, becoming a major landlord bursary after the Taiping Rebellion. This does not mean that members of these families necessarily held high bureaucratic posts during all that time. Only one lineage in all of China—the famous Lin clan of P'u-t'ien (Fukien)—consistently produced high officials throughout the Ming Dynasty. But many other notable lineages, while lacking metropolitan prominence, were likely to remain *shih* (gentry) until major political upheavals brought prominence to other families.

The dual dimensions of gentryhood (*shen* and *shih*) indicate the multilayered complexity of Chinese society under the later dynasties. Before the thirteenth-century gentry and commoners had been discretely distinguished, and the social distance separating them was often vast. By the Ming and Ch'ing periods the social landscape was much harder to sketch in stark outline. Early Confucianists did not find it difficult to order social ranks hierarchically by *shih* (scholar), *nung* (peasant), *kung* (artisan), and *shang* (merchant). But a sixteenth-century observer, even while noting the visible status symbols of the official elite, would quickly discover how impossible it was to compartmentalize society in such an absolute form. A rural county contained at least its share of metropolitan bureaucrats connected to the highest political levels of the empire, gentry-commoners working as tutors or local clerks, great families lacking formal rank yet accorded high status, moneylenders and market brokers, rich peasants, freeholders, successful tenants, and poor farm laborers. And if the district boundaries enclosed a major city, the urban setting made matters even more complex. Such a composite defied any absolute separation between elite and mass; and intermarriage, bureaucratic mobility, commercial success, and social disorder all combined to keep this cluster of different social types in visible flux. It may have been impossible for a poor peasant to leap suddenly and dramatically to the pinnacle of this society; but by fits and starts, with small increments of wealth an ambitious and talented family of farmers could eventually wend its way first into larger landholding, then into commerce and pawn-broking, lower gentry status, and perhaps in some future generation even into that small group of cultivated gentlemen who ran the affairs of the realm.

Public Service and Private Interest

Just as historians emphasize one side or the other of the *shen-shih* dichotomy, so do they also divide over the moral character of the gentry's social role. To nineteenth-century Western observers the gentry often appeared to be the mainstay of orderly society, paternalistically guiding the peasants toward higher moral principles, altruistically dispersing charity and administering public works, and through a kind of *noblesse oblige* assuming a major responsibility for the safety and security of their peasant charges. To many contemporary historians who have witnessed the Chinese revolution, on the other hand, all those homiletic attributes seem a thin disguise for the rapaciousness and exploitation of a class which consistently sought its own profit at the expense of the commonweal.

Perhaps the difference here lies between the Confucian ideal of public service and the reality of the gentry's self-interest. Every gentryman was, after all, deeply schooled in ethical Confucianism which insisted that the duty of a gentleman (*chün-tzu*) was the moral improvement of society. The *Analects* which he knew by heart likened the *chün-tzu* to the wind and the masses of the people to the grass which swayed at his moral touch. By late imperial times, this implied more than acting as a moral example. A gentleman lived up to his station in very concrete ways by mediating local legal disputes, caring for the underprivileged, and contributing conspicuously to charity—all of which earned him an honorable citation in the local gazetteer or in his own clan genealogy.

The Role of the Gentry in Local Government

These activities were honored, in part, because the imperial government realized that it could not govern the fifteen hundred districts of the empire without the informal help of the gentry. By 1800 the average district magistrate was responsible for the legal control, taxation, and care of approximately two hundred thousand people. Sometimes, owing to dialect differences, he could not even communicate with this enormous population because of the Ch'ing law of avoidance, which prohibited bureaucrats from serving in their native provinces for fear they would entrench themselves in office or enrich their relatives. Each magistrate did have a regularly appointed registrar or warden serving under him and also employed a clerical staff, policemen, and tax collectors. In earlier periods these might have been sufficient to govern the average district, but the population had outgrown such a modest bureaucracy by the late imperial period. The government could have hired more sub-bureaucrats to help out the harried magistrate, but the decision had been taken early in the Ming period to reduce the cost of local government by not formally appropriating salary funds for the magistrate's staff members, leaving it up to him to fill those positions through labor service taxes. The succeeding Ch'ing Dynasty did not fundamentally alter this policy,[13] which had two important consequences. First, the magistrate's clerks and underlings were forced to rely on informal fees for their livelihood, which often led to extortion and bribery. Second, since the magistrate was mainly concerned with keeping his personnel record clean by clearing the legal docket and meeting tax quotas on time, his responsibility for serving as a "parent to the people" devolved more and more upon the gentry.

This latter practice well suited Confucian ideals of social self-regulation which accompanied the orthodox abhorrence of Legalism.[14] Since at least Sung times most Confucian political writers preferred social *laissez faire* to bureaucratic regulation, fearing that price controls and other social welfare measures would be the opening wedge of a dangerous form of statism which could eventually stifle the individual, strengthen imperial despotism, and dehumanize civil government. Legalist models did play an important part in actual administrative practice. The *pao-chia* control system, for example, was supposed to enroll the populace in hundred-family units which maintained household registers and made neighbors mutually responsible for each other's good behavior. But Confucianists could easily point out that *pao-chia* was a form of self-policing that encouraged community solidarity rather than a ubiquitous public security system and that it was preferable to have people control each other than to create a repressive secret police authority. Many regular functions of local government were thus kept out of the hands of bureaucrats and assigned to the citizenry. Earlier, under the Sung, peasants were chosen to be local service officers for routine police duties, tax collection, and land registration. In the fourteenth century the Ming government appointed wealthy commoners to the post of *liang-chang* (tax chief) and rewarded them with court audiences for transporting grain taxes to the capital in Nanking. Although this system did reduce the government's budget and helped keep tax collection from being monopolized by "rapacious and ravenous" yamen[15] clerks, the position of *liang-chang* soon became an onerous burden for hapless collectors left stranded when others evaded their taxes. By the seventeenth century the Ming tax system was hopelessly snarled, and the succeeding Ch'ing Dynasty adopted more direct methods of revenue collection. But it continued to allow non-officials to assume other administrative duties, partly because a much larger reservoir of gentry managerial talent was available in each rural district. As lower degree examination quotas were enlarged after 1400, the numbers of *sheng-yuan* swelled from forty thousand to six hundred thousand in three centuries. Blocked from higher rank and office by the slim quotas above them, these gentry-commoners increasingly took on informal roles in district government.

By the early nineteenth century the local gentry had assumed a preponderant role in five different categories of local government, each of which provided an important source of income:

1. The mediation of legal disputes between peasants, who in turn paid retainer fees to their gentry spokesmen.
2. The supervision of local schools and academies, of which the endowment provided for principals' and teachers' salaries.
3. The supervision of irrigation works, which sometimes grew into ambitiously organized rural contract associations (*hsiang-yueh*) that paid their managers handsome wages.
4. The recruiting and training of local militia, which depended upon public subscriptions to pay the rank-and-file, as well as the annual salaries of their gentry officers.
5. The proxy remittance (*pao-lan*) of the peasants' taxes to the yamen clerks, for which the gentry collected customary fees amounting to tens of thousands of taels per district.

After 1700, then, all of these new sources of managerial income began to replace landed wealth as the essential economic ingredient of gentry status. When the Ch'ing was founded, the class character of the majority of the gentry was primarily defined by landlordism. By the time the dynasty fell, it was determined by managerial expertise.

Gentry Fees and Corruption

Yet the late imperial Chinese gentry was never an integral whole; there were significant differences between the metropolitan gentry who gained much income from regular office and lower degree-holders dependent upon informal fees.[16] The upper bureaucratic gentry earned salaries generous enough to afford vast clan properties and private land of its own. Farming investments were less prone than urban real estate or pawnshops to social disorder and monetary inflation, but they paid very low dividends. However, the upper gentry's office income was so great that it was willing to sacrifice liquidity and profit for stability and security. Landholding also suited the upper gentry's image of itself in retirement— benevolent gentlemen farmers composing poetry at their villa windows while loyal tenants toiled patiently in the distant fields.

Bureaucratic income therefore subsidized their identity as a landed notability, permitting them to perpetuate an ideal of landlordism that would otherwise have been economically impossible.

The lower gentry was usually unable to support such a way of life. Commerce was ostensibly beneath them,[17] and the physical labor of farming was demeaning to their intellectual dignity. Ostensibly unqualified for regular bureaucratic posts, they had to contrive a management income which was far from munificent by upper gentry standards, and which was much more directly extracted from the peasantry. A governor-general's fortune was built with informal bureaucratic fees, too, but these were raked off the higher levels of tax revenue. A *sheng-yuan,* on the other hand, appeared to be more exploitative because his source of income was not so far removed from the populace, based as it was upon influence peddling and rural peculation. As the lower gentry grew in numbers and competition for legitimate management fees intensified, the *sheng-yuan* had to abuse their informal offices just to survive. Legal mediation turned into pettifoggery. Educational endowments, irrigation funds, and militia subscriptions were embezzled. Above all, proxy remittance fees were raised higher and higher until the peasant was paying the gentry middlemen two or three times as much money as his actual tax quota.

These irregularities, which often amounted to outright extortion, convinced many contemporary observers that the *sheng-yuan* were betraying the Confucian ideal of gentry paternalism. The late Ming and Ch'ing periods witnessed a spate of private and official appeals to the gentry's sense of moral integrity. These hortatory pleas did help curb *sheng-yuan* venality, although the fact remained that a class of unemployables was in many parts of China the scourge of the countryside. The government could, of course, reduce the size of the lower gentry by regulating examination quotas. But that would have dangerously denied the expectations of millions of aspirants, losing their support of the regime. Instead, political commentators either continued to deplore the degeneration of political standards, while calling for a moral regeneration of the literati; or else drew a sharp distinction between the more ideal behavior of the upper gentry and the very real venality of the *sheng-yuan.*

The latter point of view was especially developed by Ku Yen-wu (1613–1682), the widely read statecraft (*ching-shih*) writer who had a profound influence upon nineteenth-century reformers. Writing just after the Ming Dynasty had collapsed, Ku appeared to be calling for contradictory solutions to the manifest problems of local government in China. On the one hand, he was convinced that the empire would be better administered if the local gentry's management of local government was formally recognized. But on the other he angrily condemned the *sheng-yuan* for meddling in yamen affairs and abusing their social position to cheat the peasant out of his earnings. If the *sheng-yuan* were only restrained by the imperial government, then in his view many problems of local administration would promptly be solved.

The contradiction was really just an apparent one. Ku Yen-wu's prescription for gentry home rule actually meant government by the upper gentry. The lower *sheng-yuan* were condemned because they lacked the moral self-control of metropolitan scholar-officials who presumably were more ethical because they had climbed higher up the examination degree ladder. That is, the level of status within the official gentry's ranks was supposed to reflect education. And since Confucian education was believed to be a process of moral self-cultivation, the higher one's degree the more elevated were one's virtues. Behind this assumption, which was open to question, was Ku's own special perception of the changing class character of the gentry. He wrote at a time when large landowning was fast on its way to becoming the reward of high office and the economic foundations of estate management were slipping. Indeed, Ku Yen-wu's own family property in the lower Yangtze had been lost because of a disloyal serf. He was thus almost nostalgic for a disappearing rural society in which a landed gentry paternalistically handled its own local affairs and infused district government with "the spirit of feudalism." To restore that presumed benevolence, he proceeded to idealize the responsibility and morality of members of the upper gentry who by then could lend themselves to this glorification because they were more disinterested landlords than their predecessors. The *sheng-yuan* rural managers, on the other hand, had no land to fall back on and therefore "treated the peasants as their fish and meat."

The Ch'ing government certainly shared Ku Yen-wu's animus against the *sheng-yuan*. Strong rulers like the Yung-cheng Emperor (reigned 1723–1735) curtailed the lower gentry's petitionary privileges and forbade them to engage in proxy remittance. Though checked by such setbacks in the short term, the rural gentry continued to occupy a crucial (though not yet paramount) position in district affairs. Perhaps the one thing that kept a balance of power between central control and gentry home rule was the reluctance of the upper gentry to condone, justify, and promote *sheng-yuan* interests. Politically influential metropolitan gentrymen were often embarrassed by the lower gentry's excesses, which could so easily jeopardize their own privileges vis-à-vis the throne. Moreover, with less of a stake in property, the lower gentry did not have so much to lose if its tax evasion[18] drove the peasantry into rebellion by increasing the financial burden upon small free-holders. The higher gentry evaded taxes too; but it was more sensitive to the dangers of social disorder, and so more likely to condemn wholesale corruption and welcome official efforts to correct economic abuses. Then, too, the upper gentry's commitment to office was genuine—it held a true stake in the integrity of the empire.

The Changing Balance between the Central Government and the Local Gentry

The result, until the 1800s, was a fairly consistent balance between the central government and the local gentry. If the gentry appropriated too much, then some in its midst, or the government itself, curtailed the *shen-shih* privileges. If the throne, on the other hand, ordered its magistrates to ignore gentry interests altogether, then censors were certain to complain of overly zealous bureaucratic intervention and urge a more relaxed policy upon the regime. Ch'ing monarchs did claim, and receive, greater despotic powers at the administrative center of the empire. Yet this was matched by the gradual entrenchment during the eighteenth century of the rural gentry on the periphery of regular government. The reason the center continued to hold and the balance was maintained was simple enough—the key group, the upper gentry, never acquired fiscal independence and military power. The gentry certainly flourished as a social estate, but this was at the expense of political independence.

Naturally, there were occasions when the gentry did possess independent military and economic means. These occurred during times of disorder like the White Lotus rebellion at the end of the eighteenth century when the monarchy was forced in self-defense to order the mobilization of gentry militia. But then, as before, the central government was able to disband those armies soon enough to avoid the creation of regional military machines. This capacity was lost in the nineteenth century. When the monarchy confronted both internal rebellion and external aggression after 1839, it found it much more difficult to rescind the military and police powers which had been temporarily ceded to the gentry. During the previous century, partly because of increased population pressure upon the limited resources of the regular bureaucracy, the lower gentry had become skilled in and habituated to irregular local government. Now, too, the upper gentry discovered that both the external and internal enemies were unfamiliar and novel threats to its own position, necessitating the formation of an entirely new local infrastructure of militia bureaus and tax offices. At such a moment the most committed of metropolitan literati found even the worst of venal *sheng-yuan* a welcome ally.

Faced with unbeatable foreign and rebel armies, the Ch'ing Dynasty had no choice but begrudgingly to allow the upper and lower gentry to cooperate in creating and commanding the kinds of private armies which contemporaries likened to those of the late T'ang magnates. But military feudalism was not to be the issue. The progeny of this new alliance was plural: a modern form of warlordism and a Western concept of gentry political sovereignty which together upset the old balance between capital and district, center and periphery, and ended by destroying the dynasty altogether.

Notes

1. Even during the late nineteenth century, when there was a marked trend toward the development of an urban rentier class, 40 percent of the gentry still lived in rural areas. Y. C. Wang, *Chinese Intellectuals and the West, 1872–1949* (Chapel Hill: University of North Carolina Press, 1966), p. 13.
2. Or to the lower degrees or ranks which could sometimes be purchased from the imperial government.
3. This was also an effect of the government's desire to raise military revenue in the 1400s to combat the Mongols. Sorely in need of funds, the monarchy adopted the practice of selling studentships in the imperial academy for 1,000 ounces of silver (taels) apiece. The *chiensheng* degree entitled the bearer to lower gentry status. As more and more were sold, the degree's prestige declined. Despite the great in-

flation of currency between 1450 and 1850, *chien-sheng* only sold for 108 ounces of silver in the mid-nineteenth century.

4. Hereafter in the text I shall use *sheng-yuan* (government student) as a convenient term for all lower-degree holders, including regular *ling-sheng, tseng-sheng, fu-sheng, wu-sheng,* and *kung-sheng;* and irregular *chien-sheng.*

5. That is, one who had passed the triennial *k'o* examinations.

6. Even after the Taiping Rebellion, when office-holding was more widely shared, only 3 percent of all *sheng-yuan* held official posts, while 40 percent of the *chü-jen,* and 75 to 100 percent of the *chin-shih* were appointed to office. Only the top third went on to the very peak of the pyramid, which was the Hanlin Academy.

7. There were 1,443,900 regular and irregular gentry in late nineteenth-century China. Figuring a family average of five persons, this meant that 7,219,500 people shared gentry status by virtue of degree-holding. At a conservative population estimate of 377,500,000, only 1.9 percent were gentry. At a more amplified estimate of 450,000,000 only 1.6 percent were gentry.

8. Limited definitions of the gentry as degree-holders fit well with theories of oriental despotism. If it is impossible for an elite to exist apart from the state, then historians who think of China as an example of such oriental despotism can substantiate their claims of total state control, even over the local elites which commanded so much power and authority in their own districts.

9. Cited in Chang Chung-li, *The Chinese Gentry* (Seattle: University of Washington Press, 1955), p. 32.

10. Hence the importance of fortune telling at the time of birth, and of phrenology or physiognomy.

11. A magistrate served about 2.3 years in any single locale.

12. P'an Kuang-tan, *Ming-Ch'ing liang-tai Chia-hsing ti wang-tsu* [The Notable Lineages of Chia-hsing during the Ming and Ch'ing Periods] (Shanghai: Commercial Press, 1947), pp. 94–96.

13. During the 1720s the Yung-cheng Emperor did order that more districts be created in China so as to reduce the scale of the average magistrate's duties, but this was insufficient to lessen the burden as population continued to increase.

14. The theory of state which flourished under the Ch'in Dynasty (221–207 B.C.) and which called for a harsh system of laws to regulate society.

15. The yamen was the official residence of a civil servant.

16. Both strata were of course prepared to follow civil service careers, though the training created classicists instead of legal or fiscal ex-

perts. Ironically, those who did go on to join the regular civil service remained classical generalists, whereas the ones who failed to pass the provincial examinations actually learned the administrative skills to serve their superiors as clerical experts or to act as unofficial administrators below the county magistrate.

17. In fact, many merchants purchased degrees. Moreover, even high-ranking gentrymen were often involved in business. See Maurice Freedman, *Chinese Lineage and Society: Fukien and Kwangtung* (New York: Humanities Press, 1971), p. 70.

18. Members of the lower gentry frequently connived with non-gentry landowners to bribe yamen clerks and falsely register property under *sheng-yuan* names, thus becoming exempt from labor service tax.

Merchants

The Social Position of Merchants

MERCHANTS WERE RANKED lowest in the social order by Confucian physiocrats. Peasants and artisans produced food and artifacts, but merchants profited from the non-productive exchange of others' goods. Peasants merited praise because they formed the economic foundation of society, contributing the fruits of their labor to feed the populace. Merchants deserved an inferior status because their commerce encouraged frivolous luxury and distracted the peasant from his appointed task. Money as such seemed to interfere with the kind of economic self-sufficiency that agrarian idealists tried to perpetuate in China.

This deprecation of merchants contradicted social reality. In fact, classical Confucianists scorned businessmen precisely because commerce had played such an important part in Chinese history. Confucius (551–479 B.C.) himself wrote during a period when powerful merchants had begun to challenge the established aristocratic order, so that his disesteem of commerce was normative, not descriptive. The implication that merchants should be lowly ranked, in other words, did not mean they really were held in contempt by peasants and artisans, who were only their nominal superiors. By the late imperial period when merchants occupied a crucial role in state monopolies, even ordinary businessmen were recognized as valuable members of society. Nevertheless, lingering agrarian prejudices sometimes adversely influenced the government's policy toward commerce, and literati certainly continued to pay lip service to the old scholar-peasant-artisan-merchant rank order.

The category of merchants was a broad one, ranging from street peddlers to merchant princes. The Chinese themselves often distinguished three subcategories: simple traders (*tso-ku*), brokers (*ya-seng*), and wealthy consignment merchants (*k'o-shang*). Such functional differentiations accompanied the growth of trade after the tenth century A.D. when canal building helped create a national market, foreign commerce expanded, paper money and bills of exchange were brought into use, and large cities began to sprawl beyond the confining walls of old administrative capitals.

The Development of Commerce and the "Sprouts of Capitalism"

Commerce continued to develop during the Ming period. After the Ming founder, Chu Yuan-chang, reunified the empire in the late fourteenth century, China once again possessed a coherent internal market. High transportation costs continued to hinder the inter-regional exchange of staples, but the private sector opened new trade routes for luxury items while public conveyances like the north-south Grand Canal carried private goods as well as the grain taxes for which they were intended. And if there was enough demand for, say, Shansi raw cotton in the Yangtze delta, private initiative often supplied the appropriate means of transport. For example, Cantonese merchants wished to exchange their salt and iron for bullion and cloth from the North. Consequently, there grew up around the Mei-ling pass whole new communities of navvies, porters, teamsters, and convoy guards to build, man, and protect the elaborate system of way stations and roads that hauled goods over the Fukienese mountains.[1]

The easing of transportation difficulties was only one factor that accounted for increasing commercialization under the Ming regime. Another was the growing relaxation of hereditary attachments to land and craft. By creating royal manors in the North, the Ming emperors inadvertently drove many peasants into the cities, creating a modest labor force. The government also encouraged the development of a skilled artisanate by trying to maintain hereditary occupational groups of workers who were forced to contribute a portion of their labor for constructing palaces, weaving imperial silks, and firing the world-famous porcelains of the period.

In the later Ming period, government controls loosened and these carpenters, masons, weavers, and potters were able to buy their way out of hereditary state service to become private craftsmen.

The relaxation of service attachments and the liberation of many from subordinate status by market forces, synergistically affected the commutation of tax payments from kind to money. Chinese Marxist historians have argued that the single-whip tax reform, which combined service and land taxes into monetary payments, watered the "sprouts of capitalism" (*tzu-pen meng-ya*) in the late sixteenth century: once taxes were paid in money, farmers cultivated more cash crops, landowners moved to the cities, handicrafts were more widely consumed, and merchants accumulated commercial capital. But from another point of view, the monetization of tax payments was less the cause of commercialization than its effect. Thus, several other social and economic changes that occurred between 1550 and 1650 deserve greater emphasis.

For instance, the late sixteenth century saw an appreciable growth in the number of intermediate-level marketing centers. Great cities like Yangchow and Hangchow dated from the Sung period, when 10 percent of the population lived in urban areas. During the Ming, China experienced another surge of urbanization. Intermediate cities proliferated between the major cities and the countryside. Periodic marketing towns (*hsu*) expanded into permanent commercial centers (*chen*), and whole networks of rural, semi-urban, and urban markets spread around the lower Yangtze, K'ai-feng, and Szechwan. These marketing complexes encouraged new habits of consumption, introducing clothing fashions and theatrical entertainment to millions of people who had never before experienced the high life of the major cities.

Landlords, too, found the new intermediate cities a more congenial place to dwell than the countryside.[2] If we are to believe contemporary subjective impressions, land ownership grew more concentrated between 1550 and 1650, especially in the lower Yangtze where it was said that "one man holds a hundred people's dwellings, and one household occupies a hundred household's fields." Gentry families used their tax privileges to acquire thousands of scattered acres of land, whose tenants' money rents permitted the wealthy to move to the city. Soochow's magnificent garden villas and flourishing theatrical companies were expensive to maintain, increasing the upper classes' need for rents in money rather than kind. The Chinese did not mine sufficient silver to meet this ex-

panding demand for currency, but overseas trade with Japan and
the Philippines brought in millions of silver dollars[3] over the last
century of Ming rule. Such vast amounts of currency helped pay for
the many cash crops which were now grown, and encouraged the
diversification of local products for sale: Soochow's iron goods and
fancy embroideries, or Chekiang's brushes, linens, and rush mats.
Traders carried Anhwei's metal tools to the southeastern coast,
where the profits from their sale were plowed back into Fukienese
wigs that were in turn sold in Kiangnan. Cottage industry became
more sophisticated in response. During the thirteenth century, for
instance, only urban artisans were skilled enough to weave delicate
damasks. Yet by the sixteenth century, dextrous peasant children
were performing the same art. Cotton weaving also became a
routine handicraft, and in the late Ming, three out of every four
districts in China manufactured cotton cloth. Peasants who lacked
the land to grow cotton purchased the raw material from urban
brokers and managed to live almost entirely off a manufacturing
income. Many such weavers—so a study of clan genealogies shows[4]
—went on to purchase several looms and hire other workers until
they could afford to construct a manufactory. Silk weaving, too,
made it possible for peasant families, over generations, to become
manufacturers, then traders, and finally major dealers owning chains
of silk shops in major cities like Nanking.

Yet the "sprouts of capitalism" never grew into an industrial
revolution. In spite of being so widespread, cotton spinning and
weaving were never technologically improved. China failed to develop anything like the Saxony spinning wheel or the flying shuttle,
perhaps because an ample supply of workers, coupled with a limited
amount of raw material, meant that there was little incentive for
labor-saving inventions to process greater quantities of cloth. Besides, household industry was the most prevalent form of cotton
manufacture, with each family producing most of the cloth for its
own needs. Even in the lower Yangtze, where textile weaving
manufactories were the largest and most advanced, spinning continued to be dominated by the individual peasant household. The
entire industry was therefore based upon an enormous reserve of
subsidiary labor—labor which "was coordinated through a market
mechanism by merchants with no direct involvement whatever in
the process of production itself."[5] The multiple tasks of preparing
cloth (ginning, spinning, dyeing, weaving) were not joined in a
unitary manufacturing enterprise. Instead, technologically primitive

and scattered individual industries were commercially unified by a sophisticated and complex series of functionally specialized putting-out merchants, wholesale buyers, brokers, and retailers. Under these circumstances command of a market was far more important than manufacturing improvements, so that habile commerce became a substitute for efficient management. Besides, wholesale purchasers of cotton cloth were so far removed from manufacturing that they scarcely knew how the cloth was made. Even merchant manufacturers were separated from actual cotton production by intermediaries. The 70-odd major dealers of Soochow in the 1600s paid labor contractors a fixed price per piece of cloth without hiring artisans themselves. Under these circumstances entrepreneurs were hardly in a position to recognize more efficient techniques and satisfied themselves with the ample profits to be made by adapting to the market mechanism of changing prices. Chinese merchants thus ranked among the world's best businessmen, but they hardly qualified as large capitalists.

Mercantile Insecurity

Commercial success in the Ming and Ch'ing periods did not automatically confer social security upon the Chinese merchant. Wealth did purchase political influence, but it never commanded bureaucratic obedience. Merchants lacked even a bailiwick of their own, a refuge where they could rule as municipal syndics or town councillors. The cities that did spread during the sixteenth century were not at all autonomous boroughs. Most large commercial entrepôts were primarily identified as administrative centers which housed the empire's governors, prefects, and magistrates. Regardless of the Chinese word for city (*ch'eng*, which means wall), there was not the fixed boundary between urban and rural societies that is often found in other civilizations. Most important urban centers were not vividly set apart from the surrounding countryside. Marketplaces melted into suburbs and then dwindled on into densely populated farmlands. The administrative buildings of the district, prefectural, or provincial capital were surrounded by walls, but these were boundaries of an earlier era and could not contain the sprawling urban landscape of the 1600s and 1700s.

The centers of such cities were regarded by officials as the

spawning ground of a *lumpenproletariat* inimical to social order. By
the Ch'ing period, secret society hoodlums, bordello owners, gam-
blers, and even marketplace rioters all seemed to flourish in this
urban environment, which rowdily symbolized the new commercialization that so conflicted with the physiocratic notion of economic stability. The authorities therefore took great care to retain
control over the city, which remained a seat of centrally appointed
bureaucratic administration and never evolved its own municipal
form of government. Until the early 1900s, merchants were effectively prevented from acquiring any form of political autonomy in
their own natural urban setting.

They were also denied organizational autonomy. Merchant guilds
(*hang*) began in T'ang times as craft and trade associations organized by the government. *Hang* originally meant row or street,[6]
and so referred to the bureaucratic assignment of occupational
groups to a single city block in the highly planned T'ang metropolis.
All jewelers, for example, had to open their shops on the "goldsmith
street" and were supervised by a government-appointed *hang-t'ou*
(guild head) who controlled quality, membership, and prices, while
ensuring the government's collection of a *hang* tax. Trade, in short,
was a privilege which had to be purchased from the emperor. The
Sung guild was a more voluntary association, but it never entirely
shed its original function of keeping artisans and merchants under
government control. The same was true for late imperial *hang*,
though by the Ch'ing period other kinds of guilds existed as well:
kung-so (public associations), which were especially prevalent in
central and south China, and *hui-kuan* (provincial lodges).

Hui-kuan were especially prominent during the eighteenth century because of the continuing growth of interregional commerce.
Anhwei merchants residing in Peking, for instance, joined together
to found a provincial lodge in the capital. Such a *hui-kuan* served
as an inn or social club as well as a cooperative business association
to provide letters of introduction and limited commercial credit.
Several of these provincial lodges in Peking were originally built by
merchants to house literati visiting the capital to take the metropolitan examinations. The *hui-kuan* thus provided businessmen with
an opportunity to solidify their ties with future gentrymen and
symbolized the merchants' ultimate reliance upon bureaucrats for
official protection. The higher one moved in the business world, the
more important were bureaucratic connections. A simple trader
(*ku*) tried to avoid contact with the government, but a broker (*ya*)

or merchant (*shang*) found it impossible to operate without official sponsorship. Under the pretext of controlling trade and regulating prices, bureaucrats frequently conferred monopoly trading rights upon individuals or guilds in exchange for a fee from the merchants. A typical case of this arrangement was the grain broker, who applied to his prefect for permission to regulate the prices of the local rice market. After paying the prefect, the broker was empowered to control the commerce between wholesale buyers and the farmers who brought their grain to market. His reward, besides the opportunity to finagle prices to his own advantage, was the collection of a percentage fee on all sales. Sometimes the broker's cut became larger than the farmers would accept; but if they tried to break away from the controlled grain exchange in order to establish their own free rice market, the broker had recourse to the prefect's police, who closed down the farmer's market and supported the broker's personal monopoly.

Private Monopolies

Monopolies of the above sort are not unknown in other societies. In fact, they amount to a form of licensing comparable to a liquor sales permit. But the Chinese instance was often characterized by a personal relationship between the licensing authority and the licensee. The broker did not purchase a formal license guaranteed by law; he paid a personal fee to an individual bureaucrat, and when that official was replaced by someone else, the contract had to be renegotiated. The advantage clearly rested with the bureaucracy. Since licenses were always temporary, their sale and resale benefited the officials, whereas a permanent license that might have been sold at an inflated price by one broker to another would have kept the profits in the private sector. Then, too, the monopoly arrangement was extremely responsive to market conditions and ideally prevented the broker from abusing his position. If the broker extorted too much money from the farmers, their displeasure would alert the prefect who had only limited tolerance for any single monopsonist. Because the official could always recall the license and appoint someone else, the broker was theoretically checked from being overly exploitative. However, this system was prone to break down in practice simply because the broker could increase his

payoff to the prefect, who in turn would be tempted to collaborate
at the expense of the farmers. The line between licensing and corruption, payment and bribery, was never clear enough to prevent
such collusion, and—true to the general precepts of Confucian political thought—depended more upon the moral integrity of the
scholar-official than upon institutional checks and balances.

Hereditary licensing did exist, however, at the highest financial
levels of the empire. During the eighteenth and nineteenth centuries, national banking was virtually monopolized by the three families who owned the famous Shansi banks. These banks were independently founded in the early 1700s to transport currency across
the empire, and most of their early clients were officials who wanted
to remit their bureaucratic salaries home without risking highway
robbery. For a fee, the Shansi banks convoyed the officials' silver
under the protection of their own *pao-piao* (guards). As their
reputation for reliability grew, the Shansi banks opened local offices
and issued bills of exchange which could be cashed at one of their
branches. So responsible were the bankers that by the 1850s the
imperial government was depositing funds in these branches to be
loaned out at high interest. In return, the three Shansi families made
favorable loans to promising civil service candidates, who gratefully repaid the gifts by depositing or investing money in the banks
when they came to occupy bureaucratic posts later in their careers.
Eventually the Shansi banks became semi-official intermediaries
between the imperial treasury and provincial fiscs, certain of their
government sponsors' determination to keep other bankers from in-
truding upon this valuable business without the three families'
permission.

In contrast to the more private sector, the public forms of commerce and finance moved away from multiple merchants toward
concentration. Instead of proliferating in function and numbers, the
businessmen who became involved in bureaucratic forms of capitalism steadily diminished in number, with a corresponding increase
in each individual's wealth. Yet favored as they were, the Shansi
bankers did not acquire the financial strength of, say, the Rothschild
banking house in Europe. Unlike European bankers, they had no
place to start small, no principality or duchy where they could
become the entire mainstay of a regime. They remained a convenience, and never became a real necessity, to the imperial government. The closest the Shansi bankers came to the Rothschilds or to
Lombardy financiers was during the mid-nineteenth century when

they helped bankroll regional viceroys like Tso Tsung-t'ang. They would not, however, be able to compete successfully with the much larger and more established Western banking interests that accompanied imperialism in China in the 1890s.

The Salt Industry

While bureaucratic control tinctured every aspect of high level finance, it most vividly colored the state monopolies, especially in salt. The imperial government had tried since Han times to monopolize salt production. Salt was universally consumed; if taxed, it provided a population-wide levy. But the bureaucracy was spread too thin to tax salt at the retail outlet. Consequently, the government controlled its production, which by the Ch'ing period was an enormous enterprise, comprising 11 huge salt yards throughout the country. The largest was the Liang-huai salt-producing zone near Yangchow, where the Grand Canal joined the Yangtze River. That single yard contained 30 factories, employed 672,000 workers, and annually supplied 4,000,000 taels to the government, or 6 percent of its total revenue.

A thousand years earlier, salt-producing zones like the Liang-huai yard had been entirely administered by bureaucrats. The T'ang Dynasty's salt commissioners had been regular civil servants specially trained to supervise the production, storage, transportation and financial accounting of salt manufacture. From the standpoint of the throne, there appeared to be two disadvantages to such bureaucratic management. First, it created a technocratic corps of commissioners whose professionalism made them and their staffs somewhat impervious to central control, especially when it was exercised by classically trained generalists. Second, it provided an opportunity for regional officials to develop sources of income independent of the capital, thus laying the foundation for provincial military autonomy. The military governors who carved up the T'ang empire relied heavily upon the loyalties (and revenue-producing skills) of their local salt commissioners.

By the Ch'ing period, however, the salt industry was organized along different lines, mixing top-level bureaucratic supervision with merchant management of production and distribution. The salt commissioners themselves had to share policy-making responsibili-

ties with the emperor and the Board of Revenue. They were also
chosen from among the emperor's most trusted personal officials:
the staff of the Imperial Household (*Nei-wu fu*), which was composed of bannermen or the ruler's bondservants whose loyalty to
the throne was unquestionable. Part of their duty, in fact, was to
funnel salt revenue directly to the emperor's privy purse, even if
that meant failing to meet the regular Board of Revenue quota.

The role of the salt commissioner was fairly constant over time,
but the complex pattern of merchant management beneath him
varied greatly in the course of the late imperial period. Production
was put in the hands of salt households (*tsao-hu*) who turned the
salt over to saltern merchants (*nei-shang* or *ch'ang-shang*) within
the yard. The saltern merchants were then supposed to convey the
salt to Yangchow at the bidding of the salt commissioner's office,
which taxed the shipments when they were sold to the transport
merchants (*shui-shang*) who actually distributed the salt to retailers. When this system was first elaborated in the fourteenth
century, the transport merchants could not ship the salt unless they
presented a special certificate, proving that they had helped provision the government's frontier military garrisons. This complicated
arrangement, which was supposed to make salt merchants contribute to the military logistics of the Ming empire, soon broke down.
By 1500 the Shansi and Anhwei transport merchants were able to
move right into the yards and buy salt certificates directly from the
commissioners.

During the next century the transport merchants gradually became more and more indispensable to the salt trade, and their
purchases of certificates were a major source of imperial revenue.
When the Ming Dynasty's military expenses increased because of
Manchu attacks on the frontier, the government tried to raise additional revenue by forcing the merchants to buy certificates for
future shipments—two or three years in advance of the actual date.
The merchants quietly rebelled by refusing to purchase these advance certificates unless the salt commissioners enlarged the quota
and let them ship out salt on the old ones already in their possession. Some of the more confident in their midst were even buying
up others' old certificates on speculation. The salt commissioners
could, of course, break the transport merchants' grip on the salt
monopoly by ruling that the old certificates were invalid. The commissioners realized, however, that the salt trade had grown so vast
that the existing merchants were the only people with sufficient

capital to finance future shipments. At the salt commissioners' pleading, therefore, the central government agreed in 1617 to a crucial compromise. Whoever bought new certificates would also earn permanent options on all shipments in the foreseeable future. The 1617 compromise was a great victory for the small group of 24 transport merchants who soon transformed their options into family licenses— "rooted nests" (*ken-wo*) of privilege which would enable their eighteenth-century heirs to amass enormous fortunes.

The number of saltern merchants (*ch'ang-shang*) within the yards also grew fewer as their individual wealth increased. By 1700 the Liang-huai salt households were completely dominated by a handful of 30 *ch'ang-shang*. This concentration also reflected the government's recognition that only the wealthiest merchants could afford the capital risk of aging the salt in storage for a year. There was always the possibility of spoilage, and the salt commissioners had to be sure that the saltern merchants had enough cash reserves to survive warehouse damage that would easily bankrupt smaller businessmen. Concentration was thus a matter of economic scale. In so vast a commerce, one of the few which was truly empire-wide, management came to rest in the hands of a few—in sharp contrast to the profusion of many smaller merchants involved in marketing at the local level.[7]

Commercial concentration was also a desideratum of bureaucrats hoping to regulate the trade more effectively. The government even encouraged the domination of the monopoly by a few top merchants in the hope of curbing illegal salt sales and smuggling. The senior merchants thus stood surety for smaller businessmen who could not trade without their permission. In theory at least, this sort of monopsony also stabilized salt prices because it was less responsive to labile market fluctuations. For all of these reasons, then, the number of leading merchants steadily declined. By 1730 the transport and saltern merchants were brought together under the single aegis of five chief salt merchants (*tsung-shang*) who agreed to accept the major risks of the trade in return for a lion's share of the profits.

The chief merchants were expected to demonstrate their gratitude for these highly visible profits. Gross receipts were all subject to an automatic charge which paid for the gifts, banquets, and bribes that were routinely offered to successive salt commissioners supervising the yards. The throne was also directly given holiday and birthday contributions. In a sense, of course, these payments

were customary recompense for the hereditary licenses that allowed
the chief merchants to enjoy their monopoly. But the capriciousness
and informality of the fees encouraged particularly greedy officials
to find pretexts (increases in smuggling, the sale of private salt)
for extorting even greater sums from those who stood bond for the
trade. Bureaucratic capitalism thus carried high risks along with
enormous rewards, which totaled 250 million taels of profits over
the course of the eighteenth century and provided the salt merchants with as much as 80 million taels of available capital.

Because that capital was necessary for the steady maintenance
of salt production and distribution, merchants were usually spared
outright economic ruin. The typical salt commissioner was an Imperial Household official who had spent considerable money of his
own to acquire the coveted appointment from palace superiors. The
throne, too, expected remuneration from the salt commissioner, and
if this was not forthcoming in the form of expensive presents, the
emperor could easily stock his privy purse by fining his commissioner for malfeasance. Given these financial hazards, the average
salt commissioner was highly motivated to squeeze as much from
his brief tenure as possible. At the same time, he also realized that
if he drove the merchants into bankruptcy and even momentarily
curtailed the trade, the Imperial Household quota of salt revenue
could not be met. Ch'ing emperors regularly overlooked a commissioner's failure to meet the regular Board of Revenue quota, but
when their privy income suffered they were most unforgiving. To
save his own head, a commissioner was understandably wary of
provoking too much merchant opposition. Consequently, the heart
of bureaucratic capitalism was a strong nexus between official and
commercial interests. What might have appeared to outsiders as an
utterly corrupt system of arbitrary levies and haphazard bribes was
in fact a well oiled and subtly regulated mechanism of informal
payments limited by custom and circumscribed by economic reality.[8]

The Bourgeois Adoption of Gentry Culture

Even though the salt merchants did (however infrequently) use
their considerable economic resources to defy bureaucratic supervisors, they remained steadily in thrall to their superiors' social
values. One reason for their acceptance of the official gentry's right

to rule was the accessibility of elite status. Given the opportunity to purchase lower degrees, the openness of the examination system, and the absence of an aristocratic order impenetrable to the low-born, chief merchants like the Ch'eng family were able to acquire official gentry status for half of their male members. Such lineages could afford to hire the finest teachers of the realm to staff their household academies and prepare their scions to sit for the quota of examination degrees set aside by the government especially for them.[9] Since they could so readily enter the elite themselves, individual merchants did not have an incentive to overturn the Confucian ranking system. They did not share with other potential members of the bourgeoisie the aspiration to raise their caste status collectively. In fact, they were not consciously aware of themselves as a bourgeoisie at all. Lacking the motive to justify themselves ideologically, these merchants were not inspired to conceive of a Chinese analogue to the Calvinist ethic because they could easily ascend as individuals into the gentry world they coveted so dearly.

Nor did they adopt a distinct class manner, or style of life, of their own. Emulating the gentry's status manner on a colossal scale, they consumed their capital conspicuously, dissipating the possibility of more productive investments and reaffirming the hegemony of the literati's high culture. There was a uniquely mad and millionairish quality to the "salt fools" (*yen tai-tzu*) who lavished fortunes on mechanized toys, Lake T'ai rock decorations, and exotic pets, but this was still just a magnified perversion of gentry fashion. And for all the squander, families like the Ma clan of salt merchants not only presided over one of the most famous literary salons of the eighteenth century and patronized many of the noted artists of the day, they also amassed private libraries of rare editions which were the envy of the Ch'ien-lung Emperor. Their enlargement of traditional gentry style was a definite contrast to the Osaka rice merchants of Japan, who at just about the same time were enjoying their own particular brand of urban culture. Kabuki plays, puppet drama, the "floating world" of Saikaku's novels, and Hiroshige's genre prints, were a soft-hearted and sensual counterpoint to the sterner values of orthodox samurai culture in Japan. But in eighteenth-century Yangchow, the old elite cultural forms changed very little. This was the age of China's greatest vernacular novel, to be sure; but *The Dream of the Red Chamber* concerned the family of an Imperial Household salt commissioner and not the merchants ostensibly in that commissioner's thrall.

Some of the eccentric paintings which the Yangchow salt merchants commissioned did reflect fresh tastes, but Kao Ch'i-p'ei's
fingernail paintings or Chin Nung's twisted landscapes did not represent what might be thought of as bourgeois concerns. They expressed the deliberate amateurism of literati artists revolting against
the professionally polished style of the old imperial academy. One
had to be deeply schooled in the brush techniques and calligraphic
conventions of Sung, Yuan, and Ming painting just to be able to
appreciate the witty and iconoclastic distortions of these scholarly
painters, who were far more concerned with effortless awkward-
ness than with glossily pleasing the tastes of aesthetic parvenus. In
fact, these literati directed their paintings almost entirely to an
audience like themselves, capable of appreciating the multiple allu-
sions to T'ang and Sung motifs. Such extremely mannered connoisseurship depended, in the words of one art historian,

> upon an elaborate dialogue between present and past, between
> an individual of the highest sensibility and a cultural heritage of
> which he was perhaps excessively aware.[10]

The past weighed heavily upon the present. The eighteenth-
century eccentrics were determined to flaunt their individualism,
but they expressed their originality by inverting past conventions.
They could not, in others words, find a new graphic language of
their own. Perhaps the very crassness of their patrons discouraged
experimentation by keeping the artist within the bounds of high
cultural allusion. After all, it was the bourgeois buyer who had to
educate himself to the painter's taste. But the price of the Yangchow
artists' cultural superiority was the continual repetition, however
inventive, of Sung, Yuan, and Ming motifs.

The same limitations characterized poetry. Yuan Mei, the great
lyricist of the eighteenth century, was also patronized by the "salt
fools." Like many of his contemporaries, he felt the burden of past
conventions and attacked slavish imitators of middle imperial poetic
styles. His own eclectic verse was designed to move the reader and
stir the listener, but it was still impossible for him to do this without using T'ang and Sung scansion. However individualistic and
bold his impulses, Yuan Mei's artistic medium remained the classical
language of his audience.

The overwhelming antiquity of Chinese civilization and the
sheer volume of its cultural artifacts[11] were unwittingly parodied in
the Ch'ien-lung Emperor's thirty-six thousand-volume *Ssu-k'u ch'üan-*

shu (The Complete Writings of the Four Treasuries)—a collectanea which was designed to bring together all of the great editions of the past. It was for such a purpose that the rarest volumes of the salt merchants' libraries were packed off to Peking, where scores of prestigious scholars labored over the vast compendium, deleting unorthodox works and copying acceptable ones. Yuan Mei—despite his romantic individualism and rejection of past convention—longed to become a part of that same bibliographic project. When a friend of his was appointed an editor for the *Ssu-k'u,* Yuan wrote (apparently without irony):

> I still do not seem to avoid being classed as an ignoramus,
> Narrow in what I have heard and seen, careless in my researches.
> I turn and look towards the city and in vain heave my sighs;
> If only I might come and join you and drudge as your secretary!
> As it is, what you might do is send me a list of the titles,
> Then I should have some vague idea of what is going on,
> And should not feel that I gain nothing by living under a sage's
> rule.[12]

From one point of view, then, all cultural ambitions were ultimately political, focussing on the seat of power at the very pinnacle of society. Just as merchants, however wealthy, aspired to gentry connoisseurship, so did literati, however nonconformist, hope one day to serve the emperor in Peking.

Notes

1. However, provincial jealousies and communication difficulties hampered the development of a completely rational exchange system. In the case of the Mei-ling pass, the differential transport rates (the small bulk of bullion and cloth required only a few hundred donkeys whereas thousands of pack animals were needed for iron and salt) were not regulated by the market. Rather, they inflamed prior hostilities between the Fukienese and Cantonese to the point of commercially destructive feuds between *routiers* on either side of the pass.

2. Despite their urban residence, the upper gentry rather self-consciously accentuated rural values during this period. The literati composed their poetry in rustic temple courtyards, sketched their albums in mountain hermitages, and entertained their friends with lute and zither in country villas.

3. The Manila galleons brought silver from Mexico to exchange for Chinese silks and damasks which were taken back to adorn the altars of New Spain. This trade flooded China with a new medium of exchange during the eighteenth century in the form of the Carolus, or Spanish silver dollar.

4. Fu I-ling, *Ming-Ch'ing shih-tai shang-jen chi shang-yeh tzu-pen* [Merchants and commercial capital during the Ming and Ch'ing periods] (Peking: Jen-min ch'u-pan she, 1956).

5. Mark Elvin, *The Pattern of the Chinese Past* (London: Methuen, 1973), pp. 276–277.

6. Or more literally, "a street block consisting of shops engaged in the same trade." Kato Shigeshi, "On the *Hang* of Merchants in China," *Memoirs of the Research Department of the Toyo Bunko*, No. 8 (1936), p. 49.

7. There are certainly obvious analogies with modern corporate giants, especially in the connection between national and multinational corporations and executive government. It might not be too farfetched to compare the political ties of the Yangchow elite of salt merchants with similar relationships of large corporations in the United States, Japan, or Western Europe. However, the salt merchants merely tried to monopolize an existing market which could not be readily expanded. Most modern corporations are as concerned with exploiting new resources and expanding their markets as they are with cornering existing ones.

8. In the 1830s, statecraftsmen like Wei Yuan and his friend, the salt commissioner T'ao Chu, bridled at this collusion between the government and a handful of powerful merchants. However, they found it impossible to change the system.

9. This quota was conferred as a reward by the regime for the merchants' contributions to the imperial treasury. Whether or not this was deliberately intended to keep the merchants within the prevailing system, the policy of special examination quotas did have the effect of disarming a potentially powerful bourgeois opposition to the Confucian gentry.

10. James Cahill, *Chinese Painting* (Lausanne: Skira, 1960), p. 192.

11. At this time China had more published works than all the rest of the world combined.

12. Arthur Waley, *Yuan Mei, Eighteenth Century Chinese Poet* (New York: Grove Press, 1956), p. 108.

The Dynastic Cycle

Dynastic and Secular Change

SECULAR CHANGES among the peasants, gentry, and merchants were outside the perspective of most traditional Chinese historians. Chroniclers were certainly aware of social and economic conditions, but these were only a backdrop for the much more dramatic history of dynastic politics, which played itself out in patterns as seemingly repetitive as the seasons. And those few institutional historians who discerned long-term social changes like the demise of feudalism or the rising economic influence of merchants did not project them into a progressively altered future. History was not linear for the Confucianist; it was a series of whorls moving forward through time without necessarily reaching a higher end. Individual dynasties rose and fell like man himself, obeying a cycle of life and death that governed all animate beings. This notion of a dynastic cycle was the primary political concept of the Chinese. By the late imperial period it incorporated three related elements: moral retribution, ritual magic, and historical voluntarism.

The Moral Factor

Moral retribution was the earliest significance attached to the notion of a dynastic cycle. In 1027 B.C. the Shang empire was conquered by the Chou Dynasty. Until then the Shang had governed in the name of Shang-ti, a deity who ruled over the bureaucratically ranked ancestral spirits of the Shang royal family. Although Shang-ti may originally have been an ancestral spirit, by the twelfth century B.C. it was sufficiently abstracted to be identified with an entirely impersonal force called *t'ien* or heaven. Since heaven could not be the anthropomorphic personal property of the Shang kings, the Chou Dynasty believed it could legitimately claim the right to usurp the throne. After defeating the Shang, the Chou rulers thus proclaimed that they had won because their enemy had lost the Mandate of Heaven (*t'ien-ming*) by ruling immorally.

As elaborated in later canonical texts like the *Book of Documents* (*Shang shu*), the Mandate of Heaven theory was enthusiastically adopted by Confucius and his disciples in the fifth century B.C. According to the *Analects,* and then later the *Mencius,* the sage ruler fulfilled heaven's mandate by cultivating his own moral propriety. If an emperor observed the Confucian rites (*li*) of social intercourse by being filial to his parents, attentive to his ministers, and paternalistic to his subjects, then the empire would prosper and civilization flourish. As the Chinese state took shape after the founding of the Han, these Confucian prophecies proved to be self-fulfilling. The ruler's moral propriety did, in effect, influence the political order. Lacking elaborate institutional checks upon bureaucratic performance, dynasties had to rely upon Confucian norms of behavior, and hence upon their officials' own sense of self-restraint. If the emperor was a paragon of virtue, then officials were likely to emulate him. But when a ruler was amoral, demanding favors and gifts from his minions, officials were likely to lose that modicum of self-control, and—like the emperor—look to their own private interests at the expense of public welfare. If corruption spread too far, so that taxes became inequitable or riverworks collapsed, peasant rebellions were sure to follow, apparently creating the conditions for a new dynasty to arise and take over the heavenly mandate.

Pushed to the extreme, this aspect of the dynastic cycle suggested that a single lax ruler might easily forfeit the mandate of his entire royal house. It also gave carte blanche to usurpers by providing a right to rebel whenever social conditions deteriorated. Fearing political instability and recoiling from the prospect of recurrent revolts, Confucianists therefore added certain safeguards to the mandate theory. A metaphorical parental relationship was established between impersonal *t'ien* and the emperor, who was often called "the Son of Heaven." Rules of legitimate succession were carefully observed. Ambitious ministers were discouraged from regicide by being taught to regard the monarch as their figurative father. And in the later imperial period, subordinate officials were indoctrinated with the ideal of unswerving loyalty (*chung*) to the throne, which led many of them to commit suicide rather than serve a usurper. Because of this concern with proper succession and hierarchy, founders of new dynasties had to behave with ritual caution, moving through a circumspect minuet by seeking public support for each step of the process toward emperorship. Many victorious generals, rebel leaders, and provincial aristocrats were able to take the first steps, but very few indeed ever made it all the way to the throne.

The Ritual Factor

A ritual element was added to the dynastic cycle concept during the Han period, and it too discouraged usurpation and helped prevent political instability. Under the Han emperors, an increasing amount of attention was devoted to imperial ceremony as a means of retaining the Mandate of Heaven. Influenced by Taoist numerology and astrology, Han philosophers such as Tung Chung-shu (c.179–c.104 B.C.) set out a complicated theory of the dynastic cycle which related the reign of a monarch to certain colors and natural elements. By carefully observing an astrological calendar and conducting sacrifices in accordance with those relationships, a ruler could help ensure the success of his reign. Since Han Confucianists had declared the emperor to be semi-divine, the act of keeping heaven and earth in the proper and harmonious balance was seen as his proper duty. This cosmic role both underscored the importance of the monarch's personal virtue and provided him with greater confidence in the routine preservation of his regime through the use of magic. Social reactions to misrule thus seemed a consequence of ritual lapses, as well as signs that heaven and earth had been thrown out of balance by the ruler's religious and political negligence. Consequently, peasant rebellions were viewed as natural calamities of the same magnitude as earthquakes, meteors, volcanic eruptions, and other omens of heaven's displeasure—mere thunderbolts which signified a changing of the mandate without being decisive in themselves.

The Voluntary Factor

Although the emperor regulated the cosmic-historic balance of the universe in person, the Han theory of the dynastic cycle did not give any individual ruler ultimate control over the mechanical and necessary succession of one cycle by the next. When a new calendrical stage had arrived, a reign or dynasty had reached its appointed term, and there was little that human agents could do to forestall its decline and fall. But by the time of the great Sung Dynasty, philosophers like Ch'eng Hao (1032–1085) had begun to restore a measure of voluntarism, arguing that the duration of the heavenly mandate was affected by men's individual efforts.[1] The historian Ssu-ma Kuang (1019–1086) asserted that a wise emperor and his councillors could study the history of the past and apply its lessons to the present, reforming an ailing government so as to postpone its demise. No dynasty would last forever, but sagacious leadership might overcome the worst of times.

Individual Emperors and the Dynastic Cycle

Those three elements—retributive, ritualistic, and voluntaristic— had by the late imperial period merged into a single resonant idea that aptly represented the relationship which was supposed to exist between an emperor and his officials. The monarch was ritually exalted, but he was saved from becoming a religious figurehead, or a puppet of consorts and courtiers like the Japanese emperor, by the Confucian regard for his moral self-cultivation and his day-to-day involvement in government. On the other hand, the same theory served to justify the independence and moral integrity of his ministers. Since heaven evaluated a monarch's reign in terms of his subjects' welfare, an emperor had to know when his policies failed. Slavish courtiers might soothe his vanity, but he needed ministers bold enough to advise him when he had erred. To Confucianists, who highly valued an honest ruler-minister relationship, the truest sign of loyalty was frankness, even if it meant *lèse majesté* and the loss of one's head. By speaking truthfully to one's monarch, a loyal minister helped the emperor reform and enabled him to preserve the mandate.

Dynasties were not immortal, but neither did they have a fixed life span. No one could confidently predict how many years the Ming or Ch'ing was destined to rule. Responsible men could not even be certain that a newly founded regime would last beyond a generation. The historical annals of certain periods, like the tenth and fourteenth centuries, were littered with accounts of princedoms too ephemeral to deserve the dynastic titles their founders had arrogated. Often such claims were too untimely to succeed. The adoption of imperial regalia and ranks by a weak rebel regime only aroused mirth and contempt and—in the eyes of Confucianists— called down destruction by affronting heaven. Even when firmly established by a dynamic founder, however, an imperial regime risked collapse when a second generation of heirs struggled over the throne.

The Ming, fortunately, was strong enough to survive such a battle in 1402 when the Prince of Yen usurped the throne from his nephew, the Chien-wen Emperor (reigned 1399–1402). Once succession was secured, a regime like the Ming was assumed by contemporaries to be following the general pattern of the dynastic cycle: after the political and military vigor of its youth (fourteenth century), a mature middle age of peace and stability (the fifteenth century), to be succeeded by feebleness and eventually fatal decline (the sixteenth century). Temporary restorations, such as the first decade of the Wan-li reign (1573–1619), helped stave off the inevitable demise, but the dynasty was bound to end sometime. And when contemporaries of high and low station began to sense that the Ming was on its way out, the decline accelerated. Officials defected to foreign enemies or internal rebels. Omens were heard across the land. Magicians and shamans found ready audiences for their predictions of a change in the mandate. The time had come— in the words of the *Book of Changes*—for dragons to take flight and a new Son of Heaven to appear.

At such moments, when heaven's mandate had been lifted from a dying regime and seemed poised to redescend to someone sufficiently audacious and promising to accept it, men across the empire stirred expectantly. The prospect of a new mandate feverishly excited rebellions, which seemed in turn to prove that the previous dynastic cycle had reached its term.

POPULAR REBELLIONS

Such rebellions came from many quarters. Taoist religious sects, for example, were often quick to revolt. In peaceful times, tantric Taoists attracted the support of social elements on the margin of settled peasant society. But when the administrative routine of the empire was severely disturbed and the regular political order seemed about to fail, the sects' promises of protection and salvation appealed to much wider audiences. Some of these thaumaturgic movements during the late Han provided physical refuge for peasants who had been driven off their land by natural or human catastrophes. Their leaders enrolled hundreds of thousands of people in religious societies which provided food and security, spreading across entire provinces.

After the T'ang period, chiliastic Buddhism added the promise of eternal salvation to such movements. The White Lotus sect predicted the coming of a messiah, the Buddha Maitreya, who would lead his followers into a third great age, or kalpa, of human history. The passage would not be easy: the second kalpa would end with death and destruction, and the forces of darkness[2] would try to keep the true creed from being propagated. But those who joined the elect band of Maitreya's followers and helped the White Lotus society defeat its enemies would survive the catastrophes to enjoy a paradise on earth during the coming third age. Maitreyan Buddhism was less credible in stable times than when the natural order of life was disturbed. The harsher the peasants' dearth and suffering, the easier it was to believe that mankind had begun to endure the terrible conditions prophesied for the end of the second kalpa, and the greater the need for eventual respite in a new paradisiacal age.

There was nothing particularly Chinese about this willingness to hope for a miraculous salvation, but what made the Chinese peasants' response unique was their identification of cosmic instability with the supposed life cycle of the dynasty. So linked were the natural and political orders in the popular conception of the Mandate of Heaven that dynastic change as such was a symbol of total chaos. And, correspondingly, dynastic stability was a sign of cosmic regularity. When a new dynasty finally did restore unity to the empire, chiliastic movements lost their mass appeal. Peasants returned to the land and sects went underground, their membership dwindling to a marginal peacetime group of true believers for whom prophecies never fail. The best example of this occurred when the Ming was founded by Chu Yuan-chang, a mendicant Buddhist monk who joined White Lotus rebels in overthrowing the Mongol Yuan Dynasty.[3] Chu used these White Lotus elements to build a private army which enabled him to consolidate a regional government in central China. After eliminating his military rivals one by one and carefully wooing influential gentry support, Chu inaugurated the Ming Dynasty in Nanking in 1368. Once secure, he turned against the White Lotus rebels who had helped make him emperor, proscribing the sect and executing many of its adherents. But the cult was never extirpated entirely; it reappeared periodically during periods of political and social turmoil until the twentieth century.

Chiliastic movements ebbed and flowed with the dynastic cycle because Confucian political theories and folk religion held that human acts and natural phenomena were causally linked. They also shared a mutual respect for hierarchical order. A peasant's private worship was devoted to his own ancestral spirits or to Buddhist-Taoist deities, but his public religious obligations centered on the local earth god (*t'u-ti*) who was the patron of his community and a subordinate of the district's city god (*ch'eng-huang*). The relationship between a worshipper and the city god was analogous to the attitude taken by a peasant petitioner toward a district magistrate. In fact, the *ch'eng-huang*, who was originally a protective god for the city walls, was not so much an individual deity as an official in the underworld. Each city god's rank depended, like the civil bureaucrat after which he was modeled, upon the size of the area the god administered. The central government even "appointed" the spirits of deceased officials to the position of given city gods for regular three-year terms and announced that "while it is the magistrates who rule in the world of light, it is the gods who govern in the world of shadows. There is close cooperation between the two authorities."[4]

Religion was also bureaucratized in the concept of the afterlife, which the peasant regarded with the same terror as a magistrate's court with its judicial torture and powers of legal inquisition. Yama, god of the underworld, was usually depicted seated on a judge's throne, dressed like a Confucian magistrate and aided by demonic lictors, while a dead soul's record of good and evil deeds was read aloud by the devil-clerks. Yama then meted out sentences strikingly similar to the rewards and punishments of a human courtroom.

The parallels between secular and sacred orders were not a

clever invention of the imperial authorities to keep the masses in
their place. Since the dawn of history Chinese peasants had assumed
that the world was organized hierarchically and expected to obey
officials who lived up to their own bureaucratic obligations. But
the populace's submission was conditional upon benevolent government, and if officials failed to observe this tacit covenant they deserved to be attacked. When "the officials [thus] forced the people
to rebel" (*kuan pi min fan*), revolts were likely to be directed
against individual magistrates or in opposition to onerous supplementary taxes. Such protest movements were often led by lower
degree-holders, who formulated specific political demands. But
when peasants led their own uprisings, they acted more from desperation than decision. Rather than making negotiable demands,
they revolted to express general social grievances.[5] Yet even such
unfocused popular movements were motivated by the peasants' continual concern for order.

Many peasant uprisings, for example, occurred when bandits
threatened their region or armies fought nearby. The contemporary
chronicles that record such incidents convey an atmosphere of un-
utterable forces of darkness, of rising waves of chaos about to sweep
over the land. Someone in the marketplace might report that black-
turbaned bandits had been seen beating farmers to death several
villages away. Another peasant might insist that across the nearest
hills, out of sight, armed militiamen were massacring the people.
As anxieties multiplied, the peasants would arm themselves and
then convulsively arise en masse, assaulting strangers and attacking
gentry homes. Yet at the same time, one senses in the very midst
of unruly turmoil a longing for the previously predictable routine.
The appeal of movements like the White Lotus sect may even have
derived from their promise of a comforting order which civil society
had momentarily lost.

Peasants were frightened by the threat of disruption precisely
because the prospect of social disorder was so prevalent in late
imperial China. Banditry was endemic in most parts of the country.
Many varieties of outlaws—professional salt smugglers, pirates,
highwaymen, strongarm extortionists, footpads, experts in boxing
and the martial arts, bowmen of the green wood—were glorified in
vernacular literature and drama. Heroes to the young, they ideally
robbed the rich to help the poor or took to the hills to resist barbarian invaders. Living by a military code of honor, these *yu-hsia*
(knights errant) were admired for being rash, quick-tempered, and

bold enough to challenge established authority. They were, in short, the alterego of the settled peasants, and like all steppenwolves were alternatively admired and feared.

Whether hijacking merchant convoys or controlling urban rackets, ganglords enjoyed a marginal degree of official tolerance during the late imperial period. Conscientious officials sometimes tried to extirpate all banditry in their districts, but most magistrates were willing to overlook a modicum of criminal activity, partly because law enforcement agents were spread too thin to both patrol distant border regions and police the populous urban complexes of the late Ming and Ch'ing. There was no official tolerance, however, for any acts that implied political rebellion. If a ganglord attacked a district yamen or proclaimed himself the leader of a rebellious army, then the authorities were almost certain to mobilize troops against his band.

Despite the knowledge that political rebellion endangered their bailiwicks and illegal sources of income, outlaws were among the first to engage in the Great Enterprise—the competition for the mandate—during periods of dynastic instability.

In contrast to social bandits elsewhere, Chinese outlaws were imbued with a political self-consciousness because of the traditional belief that men of resolve could win heaven's mandate. In other traditional civilizations, like pre-colonial India, the official political world was hermetically separated from autonomous social units beneath it. But in China, especially during times of crisis, state and society were not so distant. By the fourteenth century, at least, many different social elements were responsive to signs of political change. Outlaws were merely the most vivid examples of this sensitivity, repeatedly revolting in the name of restoring an old or founding a new dynasty. In the Ming period rebels fought to restore the Sung; during the Ch'ing they struggled to return the Ming to the throne. Historically speaking, then, secular social forces constantly reacted to the political rhythms of seemingly repetitive dynastic cycles. Ganglords frequently used military revolts to widen their own following. By adopting an imperial title, a small-time bandit chieftain with fifty or a hundred henchmen could quickly attract other ancillary bands to serve under his banner. These confederations were inherently unstable, but the leader could sometimes stabilize his control over the new bands by proclaiming imperial pretensions. Chinese history offered enough examples of rebel generals actually founding a dynasty, like the Han or the Ming, to make such success seem possible. But any rebel leader hoping to make the transition from bandit chief to emperor had to enlist gentry support. It was therefore unlikely that these aspirants to the throne would abandon the imperial Confucian model of the state. On those rare occasions when rebellions came close to succeeding, egalitarian slogans were largely forgotten and the old familiar dynastic panoply was once again adopted. Whether religious uprisings or bandit revolts, peasant rebellions did not basically threaten the existing order or fundamentally change the polity.

The Gentry and Dynastic Change

The civil gentry, for instance, radically changed its composition when a new dynasty took the throne. During the Yuan-Ming and Ming-Ch'ing transitions, hundreds of new notable lineages (*wang-tsu*) rose to the fore by supporting the winning side in the dynastic struggle. But increased individual mobility at such times did not fundamentally change the social qualities of the gentry, which was ill equipped to improve its own position by taking advantage of the throne's momentary weakness. Although versed in the civil arts, the local gentry was unable to stand alone against the military skills of peasant rebels or bandit warlords. Consequently, when the empire's administrative structure weakened and the dynasty's hold failed, the gentry grew all the more aware of its dependence on central authority and military protection.

Unable to become a local aristocracy in its own right, the gentry did have one major weapon when a dynasty perished. Since its social support and Confucian skills were indispensable those who planned to form a new government, the literati could influence the formation of a dynasty by favoring one contender for the throne or by tutoring a rude militarist like Chu Yuan-chang, the founder of the Ming, into his imperial role. But the gentry seldom had the opportunity to lend support to a new regime. Because of the Confucian stress on legitimate succession and loyalty, only three dynasties occupied the throne between 1300 and 1900. The 34 emperors who ruled China during those six centuries ultimately relied upon the gentry's acceptance of their regimes, but an individual monarch's favor was more in demand by his subjects than vice-versa. With the immediate balance of power in the monarch's favor, imperial despotism grew discernibly stronger and gentry influence waned beneath the apparently repetitive pattern of dynastic cycles.

Increased Imperial Despotism

Before the thirteenth century the literati had been represented at court by chancellors or prime ministers who had enough stature to oppose absolute autocracy. The gentry's standing slipped sharply under the Yuan Dynasty, however, when Mongol emperors preferred to employ foreigners, like the Uighur Yeh-lü Ch'u-ts'ai or the Venetian Marco Polo, and introduced such demeaning practices as the public flogging of defiant Chinese ministers. Although the early Ming emperors ceased using foreigners, they continued to deny the civil service a strong voice at court, thereby perpetuating the erosion of corporate gentry political power. In 1380 the Ming founder abolished the post of prime minister altogether, and while Chu Yuan-chang's successors gave their personal grand secretaries *de facto* chancellorial powers, the latter basically remained courtiers. Their position—even that of so powerful a grand secretary as Chang Chü-cheng in the 1570s—ultimately depended upon the emperor's personal choice, so that they did not provide an effective check on the power of the throne. Moreover, by the late sixteenth century factional court intrigue had displaced bureaucratic policy divisions. The emperor's eunuchs defied the law by setting up schools within the Forbidden City to teach themselves how to draft edicts for compliant emperors like Hung-chih (reigned 1488–1505) and Wan-li (reigned 1573–1619). They also formed a secret police, the infamous Eastern Depot, which superintended imperial armies and tortured opponents of the regime. Lacking the cultural independence of the literati, the eunuchs seemed more reliable (and pliable) servants than the regular bureaucrats, and were eventually able to decisively influence the emperor's appointment of grand secretaries. The metropolitan gentry bridled at these developments after 1582, demanding the right to memorialize the throne directly and impeaching grand secretaries who collaborated with the eunuchs. But the confrontation between the inner court and the regular bureaucracy broke down into factional squabbling on both sides. The last Ming emperor, Ch'ung-chen (reigned 1628–1644), grew so weary of this strident antagonism as to forbid such discussions entirely. The net result of over a half-century of political debate was the weakening of the metropolitan gentry's influence in Peking (the Ming capital after 1421), while the local gentry tried to entrench itself at the economic expense of the central government.

THE FALL OF THE MING DYNASTY

Years later, after the Ch'ing had conquered China, Confucian historians frequently blamed the Ming Dynasty's defeat upon its eunuchs and sycophantic courtiers. But this change in heaven's mandate had other, much more momentous causes. More than three centuries of official abuses and awkwardly implemented reforms had turned the land tax system into a refuge for the wealthy and a curse for the poor. Unable to increase its revenue without alienating the influential local gentry, the central government could only meet its rising frontier defense costs by imposing commercial taxes which cost the throne public popularity. Public works also suffered from shortsighted economy measures. In the 1620s a series of bad harvests and famines struck the Northwest, which was then the most economically depressed area of China, and revolts broke out in Shansi and Shensi. Military costs increased correspondingly, bankrupting the central government. The regular Ming armies had long been underequipped and undermanned. Now the government had to meet the threat of rebellion by allowing professional soldiers to form their own private armies, which lived off the land and proved more rapacious than the rebels themselves. Meanwhile, small bandit units, army deserters, and peasant rebels were coagulating into major military confederations which at various times occupied entire provinces in central and northern China.

One of these rebel confederations was commanded by a groom named Li Tzu-ch'eng. After losing his job in the government postal service in 1629, Li became a Ming soldier, who mutinied the following year to join one of the many gangs then flourishing in the impoverished Northwest. Over the next decade, and despite numerous defeats by government troops, he steadily increased his influence among the rebels. By 1641 Li was strong enough to establish a provincial base in Honan where he attracted a few gentry supporters and adopted tax reduction slogans to appeal to the peasantry. The ancient city of Kaifeng held out against his repeated sieges, but in

October, 1642, Li finally reduced its defenses after cutting the Yellow River's dikes and killing hundreds of thousands of people. From Honan the rebel leader moved to southern Hukuang and then transferred his base to Shensi, where on the lunar new year's day of 1644 he canonized his ancestors, ennobled his generals, and inaugurated the Shun Dynasty.

Ready now to make a bid for the capital, Li Tzu-ch'eng divided his cavalry and infantry into two armies which poured through the T'ung-kuan pass and swept across Shansi onto the plains of northern Chihli. One group turned south to take the important garrison of Pao-ting, which surrendered without resistance. The other, personally commanded by Li, moved north to capture Ta-t'ung and thus descend on Peking from the west. Although the Ming forces in the capital could not possibly have expected to defeat Li's rebel troops, an army was hastily assembled by the civil minister, Li Chien-t'ai. Loyal but militarily inexperienced, Li Chien-t'ai inspired no confidence in his troops, whose ranks melted away even before reaching the battlefield. Li Tzu-ch'eng's path to the capital was then unobstructed. By April 18, 1644, his soldiers were plundering the Ming tombs west of the city, and within a week they had occupied the suburbs. Watching the smoke of burning buildings from his own inner palace walls, the Ch'ung-chen Emperor finally realized that the mandate was lost. Stupefying himself with wine, he donned his ceremonial robes and wrote a final message to his ministers. Then the emperor walked to a pagoda on Coal Hill just behind the Forbidden City and hanged himself from a rafter. His suicide note read:

> Seventeen years ago I ascended the throne, and now I meet with heaven's punishment above, sinking ignominiously below, while the rebels seize my capital because my ministers have deceived me. I die unable to face my ancestors in the underworld, dejected and ashamed. May the bandits dismember my corpse and slaughter my officials, but let them not despoil the imperial tombs nor harm a single one of our people.[6]

The Ming was dead; long live the Shun.

But the mandate had not yet truly passed on. Despite the defection of many Ming officials, Li Tzu-ch'eng's triumphal entry into Peking did not augur well for his regime. Chroniclers apocryphally recorded that when his horse reached the city gate, Li, an excellent bowman, drew an arrow from his quiver, aimed at the character *chung* (central) inscribed upon the lintel—as if to prove that the

Central Kingdom (*chung-kuo*) was now his alone. To his surprise the shaft missed the target. Li laughed and a courtier tried to explain away the malignant omen, but its meaning was clear enough to the Chinese historians who recorded this act.[7]

A councillor once told the Han founder Liu Pang that the empire could be conquered on horseback but it had to be ruled from the throne. Though soldiers could win the mandate, only Confucian emperors could retain it. Li Tzu-ch'eng was unable to make that transition. While Li harangued the civil servants who tried to appease him, his soldiers raped and looted throughout Peking. Wealthy citizens were seized and then tortured if they could not ransom themselves with precious metal and jewels. The poor suffered as well. According to one citizen's diary:

> The bandit soldiers filled the city from top to bottom. Several hundred rebels rushed forward, flying on their steeds into the Forbidden City. The common people all held up incense to welcome them. Phrases like "Shun" or "the Heavenly King of Shun" or "long live the new emperor in the first year of Yung-ch'ang" were written [on paper] and pasted up on all the gates. Some had the words, "a subject of Shun," pasted on their foreheads. On foot and horseback, [the rebels] wove through every alley to expropriate horses and mules. Throwing off all restraints, some murdered and robbed. Men and women milled about, calling out [each others'] names. Crowds suddenly assembled, and just as quickly scattered—running, stumbling, hacked at with swords, pierced by arrows, knocking each other to the ground in their panic. Some hanged themselves, others threw themselves into wells; women miscarried in their flight, and abandoned their swaddled infants to escape. As the crowds squeezed together, people were crushed or trampled to death by horses' hooves. Hands were amputated, legs severed, stomachs ripped open, ears sliced off, hair cut away. The streets and alleys were as though filled with wolves, the groans [of grief] a dull roar. Some bandit soldiers were in a rage, while others were benign. Some murdered, others used persuasion. If a single [Shun] soldier arrived, hundreds of people would throw themselves down and beg or implore [to be spared]. All [that the soldiers] carried were swords and bows. The children among the bandits sported short knives. Yet the people's spirits were snatched away at the very sight of them. No one dared oppose them. At first, they only stole gold and silver. The ones that came after stole jewelry. And finally the very last to come [stole the people's] clothing.[8]

Within a few weeks the populace's loyalty was totally alienated from the new Shun Dynasty, and Li Tzu-ch'eng found that his soldiers had squandered the short respite they could enjoy before other rivals challenged their hold on Peking. To the northeast forces were gathering against the Shun. The Ming commander at Ningyuan beyond the Great Wall was already moving toward the capital. Behind him yet another army of barbarian Manchus was preparing to enter the Central Kingdom. When the two allied at last, Li's fate was sealed. In spite of all his ministries, his reign titles, his canonized ancestors, and even his Chinese nationality, Li Tzu-ch'eng held less appeal for Ming subjects than did barbarians from beyond the wall. The Manchus had set their sights on Peking long before Li Tzu-ch'eng had thought to establish a Shun Dynasty. For decades they had sought to accommodate their own native institutions to Confucian modes of rule. No one could doubt the seriousness of their intention to found a lasting government when their time came to dismount and ascend the imperial throne. Less than two months after Li Tzu-ch'eng first entered the capital, the Manchus were to proclaim the accession of their own Ch'ing regime from the steps of the Great Audience Hall in Peking, and a new dynasty once more began the ancient cycle of imperial rule.

Notes

1. *T'ien-ming* in this case referred to the bestowal of human nature upon each individual as well.

2. Many historians believe that the White Lotus rebel sect (as distinct from the White Lotus monastic sect) was influenced by Manichaeism, which depicted the universe as engaged in a cosmic battle between the forces of light and darkness. Manichaeism was a syncretic doctrine, preached by the Persian prophet Mani (d. 274 A.D.), with elements borrowed from both Christianity and Zoroasterianism. The Uighurs, who served as mercenaries under the T'ang dynasty, probably introduced the Chinese to Manichaeism. The latter would have been only one of many elements in White Lotus doctrine, which combined vegetarianism, some Islamic practices, and Taoist deities with the idea of the coming Maitreya Buddha.

3. Romeyn Taylor, "Social Origins of the Ming Dynasty, 1351–1360," *Monumenta Serica*, 22.1:13.

4. This statement appears on a sixteenth-century Ming stele, cited in
   C. K. Yang, *Religion in Chinese Society: A Study of Contemporary
   Social Functions of Religion and Some of Their Historical Factors*
   (Berkeley and Los Angeles: University of California Press, 1967),
   p. 157.

5. This was because their covenant with officialdom was only implicit,
   and specific service obligations were not formally recognized. In
   contrast, Japanese peasant risings during the Tokugawa period
   (1600–1868) were often based on the sense of injury felt by villagers
   whose much more explicit covenant with their local *daimyo* or lord
   had been broken by the authorities. Japanese revolts were therefore
   much more likely to be accompanied by petitions, citations of
   customary precedents, and specific political demands. My understanding of Tokugawa revolts is drawn from Irwin Scheiner's work
   on that topic.

6. Hsiao I-shan, *Ch'ing-tai t'ung-shih* [A Complete History of the
   Ch'ing Dynasty] (Taipei, Commercial Press, 1963), Vol. 1, p. 265.

7. The sources vary considerably concerning this famous incident. Some
   say, for instance, that he fired at the character *t'ien* (heaven) and
   succeeded in striking the target. See, for example, Liu Shang-yu,
   Ting-ssu hsiao-chi [A Modest Record to Settle My Thoughts], in
   Chao I-shen and Wang Ta-lung, eds., *Ting-chou ts'ung-pien* [Selec-
   tions Compiled in 1937] (Wu-hsi: N. P., 1937), 2nd *ts'e*, p. 4b.

8. Ch'en Chi-sheng, *Tsai-sheng chi-lüeh* [A General Chronicle of
   Rebirth] in Cheng Chen-to, ed., *Hsuan-lan t'ang ts'ung-shu* [Col-
   lectanea of Hsuan-lan Hall] (Nanking: Nanking Central Library,
   1947), ch. 1:11b–12b. It should be noted, however, that the rebels
   did not begin extensive looting until several weeks after they had
   first entered the capital.

The Rise of the Manchus

The Frontier Zone

NORTH OF PEKING ran the Great Wall, stretching from the sea at Shan-hai-kuan to the Kansu corridor in Central Asia. Begun in the third century B.C., the wall had been strengthened and extended many times. Beyond it lay the world of the nomadic barbarian—the home of tribesmen who had often conquered north China and at times controlled the entire empire. But the wall was more than a defense line. To the Chinese it marked the border between civilization and the barbarian hordes of Huns, Turks, Khitan, Ju-chen, and Mongols that successively threatened native dynasties. To the nomads it was a barrier that challenged and beckoned—a gateway from the bleak steppes and forests to the settled villages and cities of the Central Kingdom. Between the wall and the outer reaches of barbarism was the meeting ground of two different worlds. In this frontier zone between agrarian civilization and the nomadic hinterland, Chinese and barbarians traded, intermarried, and sometimes even created new hybrid forms of social life. Here Chinese political skills and military technology enhanced tribal power, and it was usually this zone that gave birth to the barbarian confederations that actually succeeded in conquering the empire.

The area directly beyond the Great Wall was divided into two distinct regions. One, to the north and northwest, was called Jehol. From its grass steppes the horse-riding Khitan had emerged to found the Liao Dynasty in 907 A.D. And from there too came a wing of the Mongols, sweeping down into China through Shansi to establish the Yuan Dynasty (1280–1367) under Khubilai Khan. Ming armies drove the Mongols out of China in the fourteenth century, but they never managed to oust them from the frontier zone of Jehol. Oirat Mongols settled there, attracted Chinese blacksmiths and artisans to outfit them and continued to harass the Ming throughout its period of rule. To keep out such enemies, the early Ming emperors succeeded in creating an elaborate frontier defense system of *wei-so* (guards and posts units numbering 5,600 men each) which garrisoned self-supporting military colonies along the frontier zone.[1] By the early fifteenth century, however, the Ming government had decided for financial reasons to abandon several of these advance posts and fall back on the Great Wall as its main line of defense. Thus in the 1400s the wall was fortified with masonry and considerably strengthened with watchtowers and artillery. Nevertheless, Oirat Mongols continued to break through and raid sporadically within China. In 1550 their khan, Altan, even led a Mongol army to the walls of Peking, demanding special trading privileges in exchange for withdrawal.

The Manchus

The second region to the northeast comprised what is now known as Manchuria. It was from here that the Manchus[2] would begin their conquest of China. This area, which extended to the Korean border, was dominated by the Liaotung peninsula where several Chinese garrison-towns were located, and where enormous stud farms supplied the Ming army with mounts. The hinterland was characterized by forests and marshes, rich in humous soil but cursed by midges and blackflies. The native inhabitants of this area, Mongols and Tungusic tribesmen, were forest people, not steppe horsemen. Instead of herding cattle or sheep, they hunted, trapped, and fished for a living. Their most valuable products were sable furs and the medicinal plant called ginseng, both of which were exchanged with Chinese traders for salt, cloth, and iron tools.

The economic patterns of tribal life evolved slowly over the centuries. Manchu tribesmen along the distant Aigun River remained hunters and trappers, but those closest to the Korean border and to the Chinese settlements in Liaotung emulated their agrarian neighbors by adopting farming. The Manchu chiefs (*beile*) and commoners (*irgen*) of the frontier zone established estates and farms which were tilled by serfs and slaves captured in battle. From

MANCHURIA IN THE SEVENTEENTH CENTURY

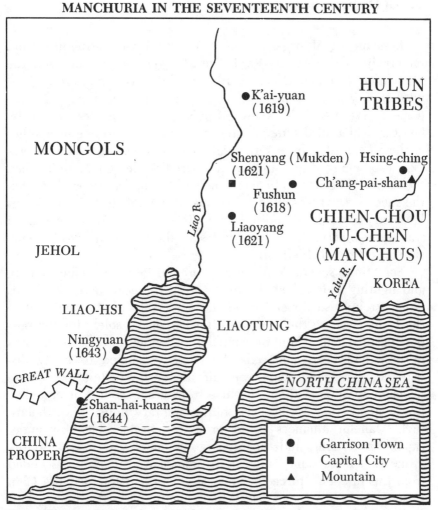

Note: Dates in parentheses indicate the year in which the city was conquered by the Manchus from the Chinese.

their Sino-Korean captives, who served them also as artisans, the
Manchus had learned by the end of the sixteenth century how to
mine and smelt iron for tools and weapons.

Tribal Organization

Manchu tribal organization was both highly structured and
remarkably fluid. At one level, fixed by genealogical descent, the
Manchu and Manchu-Mongol tribes of the Northeast were divided
into twenty-seven clans (*hala*) which were geographically dispersed.[3] Every Manchu knew his own genealogical designation by
heart and identified himself forever as belonging to one or another
of these *hala*. At a lower territorial level, however, that same tribes-
man also belonged to a smaller and more flexible agnatic unit called
the *mokun*. The size and cohesiveness of the *mokun* depended upon
the success of its *mokunda* (a clan head, nominally selected by his
kinsmen) in the hunt and in battle. Since the position of clan head
was often inherited by the eldest son, the *mokunda* was actually
similar to a tribal chieftain.
        Sometimes several Manchu clans united into a common hunting
and fighting unit called the *niru* (arrow). The coherence of this
larger group also depended on the leadership of its chief, called
the *beile*. Because the *niru* was often organized solely for the purpose of a particular hunt or campaign, it tended to dissolve once its
purpose had been achieved—the game consumed or booty distributed. As we shall see, it was difficult for any *beile* to perpetuate
his confederation without recourse to external models of organization, copied from Mongol or Chinese military units. Nevertheless,
such Manchu alliances could grow to considerable size under
capable chieftains, and the Ming government was uncomfortably
aware that these same Tungusic tribesmen were loosely descended
from the Ju-chen (Jurced) barbarians who had founded the Chin
Dynasty in 1115 A.D. and driven the Sung out of north China.
        For this reason the Ming maintained a strong military presence
both in Liaotung and across the North China Sea on the opposite
littoral of Liao-hsi. At first this consisted of 25 *wei-so* garrisons.
Over the course of the fifteenth century, however, the *wei-so* system
declined in quality, and by 1500 many of the commanderies were
phantom units, existing only on paper. During the next century

Peking had to rely more and more on a kind of frontier feudalism to defend its borders. The Chinese soldiers that garrisoned Manchuria became quasi-hereditary retainers of powerful Ming generals like Li Ch'eng-liang in the late sixteenth century and Mao Wen-lung in the seventeenth century. These lords of the marches held regular bureaucratic appointments and were pledged to defend the Ming, but the armies they commanded were literally their own.

The most important concern of Ming frontier officials in Manchuria was to prevent the tribes from confederating under a single khan strong enough to attack China. They therefore followed the time-honored policy of divide-and-rule which had been perfected as far back as the Han period and was widely used in central Asia. Each chieftain was placed in a tributary relationship to the Chinese emperor and was supposed to be his vassal. In exchange for acknowledging Chinese suzerainty, the chieftain was given an official Ming title. If any particular leader appeared to be growing too powerful, the Chinese government took care to favor a rival with higher rank. The Chinese title, which was accompanied by tribute payments from Peking, carried enough prestige to elevate one Manchu chief at the expense of another. By thus inciting jealousy and rivalry Ming frontier commanders usually succeeded in keeping the tribesmen disunited.

Between 1552 and 1582, when the Ming general Li Ch'eng-liang controlled Manchurian affairs, a tribe called the Hada was singled out to receive the highest imperial honors. In 1582, however, the Hada Khan died, leaving a power vacuum which Hulun tribes like the Yehe and Hoifa tried to fill. As feuding broke out, a Suksuhu chieftain named Nikan Wailan[4] became the new Ming candidate for khan. By 1583 Nikan Wailan managed to secure enfeoffment, but only after killing several of his rivals. Two of these were the father and son who commanded a Chien-chou clan called the Aisin Gioro.[5]

The Rise of Nurhaci

Their deaths left the chief's 24-year-old grandson, Nurhaci, in command of the Aisin Gioro. Although indemnified by Li Ch'eng-liang, the young chief was resolved to avenge the murder of his father. With the two leading elders gone, Nurhaci's tribal command was precarious and the loyalty of his kinsmen by no means assured.

By declaring a vendetta—as Genghiz Khan had done with the
Mongols four centuries before—Nurhaci hoped to knit the clan
together into a crusade that would leave the Aisin Gioro stronger
than ever. Promising victory, he impetuously led his kinsmen
against Nikan Wailan in 1584 and two years láter succeeded in
killing the new khan—throwing Manchuria into political turmoil
once again.

Nurhaci now proved to be as judicious as he had earlier been
audacious. First he contracted crucial marriage alliances with some
of the Hulun clans. Then, by bringing several unruly Yalu River
tribes under control, he won both General Li Ch'eng-liang's favor
and the Ming title of brigadier general. Partly to defend his earlier
gains and partly to ensure continued hegemony over his sub-chiefs,
Nurhaci embarked upon further conquests, challenging the Hulun
tribes to the north. His great victory at the Battle of Jaka (1593)
over a confederation led by the Yehe not only elevated his status in
the Ming government's eyes but also strengthened his hold over
peers within the Manchu confederation. This was because each
new victory brought additional prisoners of war to be distributed
as serfs and slaves for the estates of the Manchu *beile*.[6]

As Nurhaci's following widened through diplomacy and conquest, it became necessary to find some new mode of organization to
perpetuate the confederation. In 1601 he divided his troops into
three-hundred-men *niru* (arrows, or companies) which were then
formed into four permanent banners, identified by the color of their
standard. These banners were copied from the Mongol *gūsa* fighting
units.[7] Later on, they were given the Chinese name *ch'i* (banner),
which was taken from the Ming *wei-so* system. In 1615 the four
existing banners were subdivided, forming a permanent total of
eight Manchu banners. Each of the *niru* within the banners constituted a single military-civil unit under an hereditary captain.
The members of that unit included soldiers and dependents who
worked and fought together. The banners themselves were headed
by *hošoi beile* (great princes) chosen from among the sons and
nephews of Nurhaci.

The formation of the banners marked the transformation of a
loosely confederated structure of shifting *niru* into a bureaucratically
organized army under the rule of Aisin Gioro nobles. This evolution
from a clan federation into a military state was not a novel
phenomenon on the frontier, where there had been a long history of
tribal and bureaucratic interaction. The Chinese policy of divide-

and-rule had already confused tribal leadership with bureaucratic rank: khans and clan elders were both chieftains and officers of the empire, using conferred military titles to endow their temporary authority with permanence. The hybrid forms of government that were thus formed in the frontier zone drew their impetus from both sides of the border,[8] with a marked tendency toward military feudalism characterizing each group. Just as Ming border generals tended to form private armies, so were tribal-bureaucratic leaders likely to become an hereditary aristocracy.

This incipient Manchu feudalism was physically symbolized by the castle town which Nurhaci built at Hsing-ching in 1605, using Chinese masons.[9] The design of the city—with Nurhaci's castle at the center, encircled by the Manchu lords' fortifications and the whole surrounded by rural estates—further indicated Nurhaci's transformation of temporary loyalties into a hierarchical system of rewards and benefices in exchange for military services. Because slaves, not land, were the basic form of Manchu aristocratic property, Nurhaci's new order lacked the economic foundation of manorial feudalism prevalent in medieval Europe or Japan. But the military banners were certainly a form of appanage, just as the Aisin Gioro *hošoi beile* comprised a hereditary aristocracy.

Nurhaci's own position was not threatened by the powerful *hošoi beile* because he commanded so much personal authority. As khan (a title assumed in 1616), he had openly declared his supremacy over the other Tungusic chieftains of Manchuria—an assertion enforced three years later when Nurhaci's forty thousand bannermen defeated his last major rival, Prince Gintaisi of Yehe.[10] It was in 1616, too, that Nurhaci adopted an even more awesome source of authority by employing his Ju-chen descent to found the Latter Chin Dynasty under the reign title Heavenly Mandate (*T'ien-ming*). As an emperor on the Chinese model, Nurhaci spontaneously generated a large stock of princely titles and bureaucratic ranks to hand out to his Manchu followers. At the same time he also pitted himself against the Ming Dynasty.

Nurhaci had stopped sending tribute to Peking as early as 1609. Now, by taking the name of a barbarian dynasty that had once humiliated the Sung, he was implicitly announcing his intention to attack the Ming—a plan realized in 1618 when he took the imperial garrison at Fu-shun. Three years later he succeeded in capturing the major Ming headquarters of Liaoyang, and from there he drove most of the Ming forces out of the Liaotung peninsula altogether, controlling all the land east of the Sungari River. In February, 1626, however, his troops were repulsed at Ningyuan, and eight months later Nurhaci died.

The Reign of Abahai

Nurhaci had intended that his heirs, the *beile*, should rule as a council of peers. Before his death he had seen to it that each controlled one of the eight banners and that the four senior *hošoi beile* took turns governing the central administration. One of them would have to be elected khan, but the bearer of that title was supposed to be no more than a *primus inter pares*, a first among equals. Such was not at all the intention of the khan actually selected by the other *beile* when Nurhaci died. The new ruler, Abahai (reigned 1626–1643),[11] was a brilliant military strategist and diplomat who quickly determined to replace feudalism (the domination of many skilled in war) with patrimonialism (the domination of one who uses officials) by curbing the power of his fellow *beile* with the authority he commanded as a Chinese-style emperor. In his capacity as a tribal khan, Abahai was expected to share administrative duties with his brothers. But as an imperial monarch, authority was decreed by him alone. In 1629, therefore, he put an end to the practice of administrative rotation among the *hošoi beile* and began using former Chinese officials to control military appointments within the banner system.[12] By 1633, in fact, he had brought three of the original eight banners under the direct command of the throne.

Abahai also realized how important it was to use Chinese military experts against the Ming forces. The great victories of 1618 and 1621 had placed eastern Manchuria under the Latter Chin's rule. But further expansion down the Liao-hsi coast toward the Great Wall had been blocked by the Ming commander, Yuan Ch'ung-huan, whose Portuguese artillery had repulsed Nurhaci at Ningyuan in 1626. Although the Manchus had excellent cavalry and armored infantry, their line of battle was vulnerable to Chinese firearms.[13] And because they did not understand how to use artillery themselves, they were often forced to retreat from well defended castle walls. Unable to obtain a decisive advantage over Ming forces, Abahai recognized that the stalemate of 1626 would not be broken unless he trusted captured Chinese soldiers to wield firearms and artillery on his behalf.[14]

Chinese elements had joined the Manchu armies as early as 1618 when the Ming commander Li Yung-fang surrendered at Fu-shun. Li was made a banner general, was given gifts of slaves and serfs, and was betrothed to a young woman of the Aisin Gioro clan. Although Li's surrender at the time was exceptional, his integration into the Manchu elite was only the first of many such defections by border generals and their subordinates, who shaved their heads and accepted Manchu customs.[15] It was upon these prisoners, then, that Abahai relied to form new military units to fight their former master, the Ming emperor.

While Abahai proceeded to organize these new units, he also opened diplomatic negotiations with Yuan Ch'ung-huan, thus freeing his own troops for campaigns in Korea and against Mongol enemies. In 1629 Abahai even managed to bypass the Ming defenses facing Manchuria and briefly threatened Peking from the west, disgracing Yuan and causing his downfall. But because this foray was only a raid, it had no lasting military significance. The military stalemate was really only broken two years later, when Abahai sent his new Chinese artillery force against the walls of the Ming garrison at Ta-ling-ho. There he not only won a decisive battle but proved that the Sino-Manchu forces had finally mastered siege warfare.

The victory of Ta-ling-ho inspired the Manchu emperor to take his people one step nearer the conquest of China by establishing six administrative boards on the Ming model in 1631. Further raids on China were followed in 1636 by Abahai's announcement of a new dynastic title, the Ch'ing, which freed the Manchus' claim on the mandate from any connection with their Chin ancestors. At the same time he solidified his military control over the Amur basin and sent another raiding party across the Great Wall in 1639. But in 1643, one year before his plans for the conquest of China were realized, Abahai's health failed and he died.

Dorgon and the Occupation of Peking

When the *beile* convened to name Abahai's successor, one among them was best equipped to fulfill the dead emperor's plans to defeat the Ming. Abahai's younger brother Dorgon, a *hošoi beile* commanding the Plain White Banner, had early decided that the historical mission of the Manchus was to conquer China. He also recognized that success depended on forming a shadow government and attracting Chinese defectors to its cause. In 1631 he had become president of the Board of Civil Appointments in Abahai's facsimile of the Ming administration, and in that crucial capacity had managed to interview all prominent Chinese captives, diverting the better educated into bureaucratic positions. Civilians were wooed with Confucian deference. Whereas Manchu officials necessarily addressed themselves as "slaves" to the throne, Chinese mandarins were entitled to call themselves "ministers." Such measures reflected Dorgon's realization that a loyal civil bureaucracy and not merely military support would be necessary if the Manchus were ever to occupy Peking.

Dorgon's eagerness to sinify the Ch'ing regime seemed to some of the other *beile* a betrayal of Manchu culture. Remembering the earlier days of tribal vendettas, Manchurian manors, and Chinese slaves, these nobles' instincts were to continue raiding from redoubts beyond the Great Wall and leave the Ming empire to itself. Any more permanent involvement in Chinese affairs was going to mean an end to the way of life that had already served the aristocracy so well. Yet Dorgon did enjoy strong support from some of his other brothers and cousins, and when the votes were finally cast he took over the government, along with his cousin Jirgalang, as regent for Abahai's five-year-old son, the new Shun-chih Emperor (reigned 1644–1661).

Dorgon assumed the regency just as the rebel Li Tzu-ch'eng was making final preparations to attack Peking. Li's victory and the suicide of the Ch'ung-chen Emperor gave the Manchus the decisive opportunity they had been awaiting. The only force in north China likely to challenge Li Tzu-ch'eng's armies was the Ming border garrison at Ningyuan which guarded the approaches to the Great Wall. Its Chinese commander, Wu San-kuei, was the son of a former border general. Responding to Peking's pleas for aid, Wu decided to abandon Ningyuan and move his army toward the capital, but his progress was too slow to save the dynasty. Five hundred thousand Chinese civilians were said to have joined Wu San-kuei's army on the trek south to the Great Wall at Shan-hai-kuan, and it took 16 days for all of them to pass through the frontier gates. Of course, the moment the last Chinese contingent marched through Shan-hai-kuan that strategic post was promptly occupied by Manchu bannermen following close behind.

Wu's march toward Peking was halted by the news that Li Tzu-ch'eng had taken the capital and that the Ming Dynasty had fallen.

Envoys from Li Tzu-ch'eng soon met his column with a promise of forty thousand taels if Wu San-kuei surrendered.[16] In the meantime, Li was leading sixty thousand of his own men towards Shan-hai-kuan should Wu refuse the offer. Wu San-kuei could not hope to defeat such a large rebel force alone. Suspecting Li's treachery, he contacted Dorgon who urged him to join the Ch'ing cause in exchange for a princely rank and an hereditary fiefdom. The former Ming general hesitated between the regicidal Li and the barbarian invaders who promised to punish the usurper. Then, as the first elements of Li's army drew near, Wu shaved his head and invited Dorgon over the Great Wall.

On May 27, 1644, while the forces of Wu San-kuei and Li Tzu-ch'eng were engaged in battle, the Manchus rode through Shan-hai-kuan under cover of a dust storm. Their intervention was decisive. Li's men were driven back into Peking, pursued by the combined armies of Dorgon and Wu San-kuei. As the Manchus and Ming frontier forces entered the capital from the east, Li's soldiers fled in the opposite direction as rapidly as they had come, strewing looted antiques and jewelry behind them.[17]

Dorgon entered Peking on June 1, 1644. His first decree to the people read:

> In former days our realm wished to have good and harmonious relations with your Ming, [hoping] for perpetual peace. Since we repeatedly sent letters which were not answered, we invaded deep [into your country] four times, until your dynasty showed regret. How stubborn it was not to comply! Now [the Ming] has been extinguished by roving bandits, and its service [to heaven] is a thing of the past. Let us speak no more [of that]. The empire is not an individual's private property. Whosoever possesses virtue, holds it. The army and the people are not an individual's private property. Whosoever possesses virtue commands them. We now occupy [the empire]. On behalf of your dynasty we took revenge upon the enemies of your ruler-father. We burned our bridges behind us, and we have pledged not to return until every bandit is destroyed. In the counties, districts, and locales that we pass through, all those who are able to shave their heads and surrender, opening their gates to welcome us, will be given rank and reward, retaining their wealth and honor for generations. But if there are those who disobediently resist us when our great armies arrive, then the stones themselves will be set ablaze and all will be massacred. Scholars of resolve will reap the harvest of upright administration, meritorious fame and the

opportunity to pursue a vocation [as our officials]. If there are those who lack faith in us, then how are they to serve the empire? Special edict.[18]

Having announced the accession of the Ch'ing Dynasty to the Chinese throne, Dorgon took immediate measures to gather public support. Ming loyalists were mollified by his attention to the burial rites of their last emperor. Civil servants were reassured by offers of amnesty and employment. And the residents of Peking were convinced of the benevolence of the new regime by Dorgon's harsh punishment of Manchu ravishers and looters. The contrast with Li Tzu-ch'eng's rebel government was strikingly clear. By the time Dorgon had sent to Manchuria for the Shun-chih Emperor, none doubted the Manchus meant to stay. Yet few indeed could have predicted that the Ch'ing Dynasty would occupy Peking for the next 268 years.

Notes

1. These were the garrisons to which the salt merchants were supposed to send grain. (See Chapter III.)

2. The word "Manchu" was formally adopted by the Chien-chou Ju-chen leader Abahai (see below) in 1635 as a name for his people. Its origins are unknown, though some historians have tried to connect it with the name of one of his ancestors, Manjusri. As we shall see, the Manchus were a "people" that grew out of conquests by the Aisin Gioro clan of the Chien-chou Ju-chen. By the time the Ch'ing Dynasty occupied the throne in Peking, the word "Manchu" referred to a combination of different tribes: the original Chien-chou Ju-chen, the Hulun tribes, some Manchu-Mongol tribes, and outlying groups like the Solons, Dahurs, and Hulunbuir. Here, I shall use the word "Manchu" to refer to the Ju-chen tribesmen even before they applied that word to themselves.

3. "The Manchu clan is a group of persons united by the consciousness of their common origin from a male ancestor and through male ancestors, also united by the recognition of their blood relationship, having common clan spirits and recognizing a series of taboos, the principle of which is . . . exogamy." S. M. Shirokogoroff, *Social Organization of the Manchus: A Study of the Manchu Clan Organization* (Shanghai: Royal Asiatic Society, North China Branch, 1924), p. 16.

4. Nikan Wailan may have been a nomadized Chinese. His name in Manchu simply means "Chinese official."

5. The Aisin (gold) branch of Gioro came from Hurka (the Sungari River valley), whence it had migrated to the Ch'ang-pai-shan area.

6. Before 1631 many Chinese who were captured became bondservants (*booi*, or in Chinese *pao-i*) of the Manchus and were attached to the Manchu military banners. Those assigned to the three top imperial banners later became the emperor's personal bondservants. Their heirs, working for the Imperial Household, were the salt commissioners of the eighteenth century.

7. Each *gūsa* was divided into two hordes (*geren*), and these were further subdivided into camps (*tatan*) which included a mixture of heavily armed cavalry (*uksin*) and infantry (*yafahan*) at a ratio of one to two. The Mongolian influences on Manchu military organization have been carefully pointed out by David M. Farquhar. See, for example, "Mongolian versus Chinese Elements in the Early Manchu State," *Ch'ing-shih wen-t'i*, 2.6:11–23 (June, 1971).

8. The Ming *wei-so* garrison system, for instance, had originally been copied from Mongol military organizations.

9. The Manchus' first capital was located at Hulan Hada. In 1621 Lioayang became their third capital, succeeded four years later by Shenyang (later renamed Sheng-ching or Mukden by Abahai).

10. According to Manchu legend, Gintaisi's dying curse upon the new khan was that the Aisin Gioro clan would someday be destroyed by a woman of Yehe. This prophecy was supposedly realized three centuries later when Tz'u-hsi's misgovernment helped bring about the fall of the Ch'ing Dynasty. The Empress Dowager Tz'u-hsi, née Yehonala, belonged to the Yehe clan.

11. The name, "Abahai," is never mentioned in the original Manchu texts (*Chiu Man-chou tang*). In those documents he is referred to as *Hung Taiji*, which simply means "Imperial Crown Prince." The name, "Abahai," has become so conventional, however, that I continue to use it for the reader's convenience.

12. The Chinese officials were formed into a Literary Office in 1629 and then later into the Three Courts.

13. The Manchus had learned horseback riding from the steppe Mongols, but they did not fight primarily as a cavalry force, using their horsemen instead as a striking element held in reserve behind armored pikesmen, swordsmen, and archers.

14. This point is strongly emphasized in a recent article by Chou Ch'i-na: "Ch'ing-ch'u pa-ch'i han-chün yen-chiu" [A Study of the Chinese Eight Banner Army of the Early Ch'ing Dynasty], *Ku-kung wen-*

hsien [Ch'ing Documents at the National Palace Museum] 4.2: 55–66.

15. By 1642 there were enough of these adherents to form eight Chinese banner armies, just as Mongol allies of the Manchus had made up their own eight banners several years earlier.

16. Wu San-kuei's father was held prisoner in Peking and also sent a letter, pleading for his surrender. Li Tzu-ch'eng seized Wu's favorite concubine as well, and later poetic and operatic accounts of this famous incident stress that it was Wu's jealous rage which decisively influenced the general's choice of the Manchus over Li.

17. Li Tzu-ch'eng fled to the West and then south. He was later killed by peasants near the Kiangsi border.

18. Cited in Hsiao I-shan, *Ch'ing-tai t'ung-shih* [A Complete History of the Ch'ing Dynasty] (Taipei: Commercial Press, 1963), Vol. 1, p. 279.

VI

Early and High Ch'ing

The Manchu–Chinese Balance

THE CONQUEST of Peking did not end the conflict between Dorgon and the Manchu aristocracy. The struggle between throne and nobles continued to dominate imperial politics until the early eighteenth century, even though the demise of traditional Manchu customs was assured once Shun-chih occupied the Forbidden City. Manchu rule over the Chinese was now a fact, and the eventual sinification of the regime was inevitable. If the Chinese were to be ruled successfully, then their interests ultimately had to be served, and that required no less than the erosion of the Manchu nobles' prerogatives. As Dorgon garnered Chinese support, he diminished the power of the Manchu princes. In 1644 imperial clan leaders were no longer automatically appointed to head the six ministries, and in 1649 Dorgon publicly ordered Chinese officials to cease obeying the Manchu princes' orders. Naturally, Dorgon stood to benefit by these restrictions. After 1647, when his cohort Jirgalang was pushed out of the regency, Dorgon occupied such a supreme position that he was forced to remind Chinese courtiers their nominal master was the Shun-chih Emperor and not himself.

Many Manchus supported this policy, forming a faction around Dorgon which cooperated closely with Chinese bureaucrats to attract former Ming officials to the new dynasty. After Dorgon died in 1650, this faction perpetuated itself by continuing to act in his name, even bestowing upon him the imperial title which he had been denied in his lifetime. But Dorgon's hegemony had angered many other ranking Manchu officials. Jirgalang, still bitter over his defeat in 1647, led a party which supported the young Shun-chih Emperor and decisively defeated the Dorgon faction. Dorgon's imperial title was rescinded, his name was posthumously disgraced, and his followers were removed from office to give the real emperor a better chance to govern independently.

The Shun-chih Reign

The Shun-chih Emperor reigned for only another decade. The first of the Manchu rulers to master classical Chinese, he was more introspective and sensitive than his forebears. His abiding interest in religion aroused hopes of conversion among the Jesuit missionaries at his court, but when Shun-chih eventually did turn seriously to religious devotion, he chose Buddhism over Christianity. In the

TABLE 6–1
RULERS DURING THE CH'ING DYNASTY

Title[a]	Reign
Shun-chih	1644–1661
K'ang-hsi	1662–1722
Yung-cheng	1723–1735
Ch'ien-lung	1736–1795
Chia-ch'ing	1796–1820
Tao-kuang	1821–1850
Hsien-feng	1851–1861
T'ung-chih	1862–1874
Kuang-hsu	1875–1908
Hsuan-t'ung	1909–1912

[a] These are, more properly speaking, reign titles, not rulers' names. "Shun-chih's" proper name was Fu-lin; his Buddhist name, Hsing-ch'ih; his literary names Ch'ih-tao jen, T'ai-ho chu-jen, T'i-yuan-ch'ai chu-jen; his temple name, Shih-tsu; and his canonic name, Chang Huang-ti. Strictly speaking, he should be referred to always as "the Shun-chih Emperor," just as one should say "the K'ang-hsi Emperor." Conventionally, however, I use the reign title to refer to the man, viz. Shun-chih, K'ang-hsi, etc.

last years of his reign, the death of his beloved concubine Donggo almost drove him mad with grief and he repeatedly expressed his wish to take up religious orders as a Ch'an Buddhist monk.

Shun-chih's longing to renounce the throne was understandable, as it was not a placid decade. Ming loyalists thwarted Ch'ing efforts to bring the South under control. In 1659 Coxinga (Cheng Ch'eng-kung), the colorful pirate who dominated Fukien, almost captured Nanking. The gentry of Kiangnan in the lower Yangtze harbored anti-barbarian sentiments and were reluctant to implement necessary tax reforms. In return, the Manchu princes nourished strong anti-Chinese sentiments, believing that the throne had become too ob-sequious toward the haughty Chinese elite. The nobles' reaction only impelled Shun-chih all the more in the direction of Chinese forms of imperial rule. He had always believed in a Confucian dyarchy of Chinese and Manchu bureaucrats, but now he leaned all the way toward the Ming model of emperorship. After abolishing Abahai's private secretariat, Shun-chih revived the old Hanlin Academy, which was staffed by successful examination candidates. And instead of using bondservants of the Imperial Household[1] as his confidential agents, the emperor resorted to the infamous eunuchs carried over from the Ming. Ministry officials and members of the regular bureaucracy were highly offended by having to communicate with the throne through these distrusted castrates, and the Manchu nobles' pride in their martial virility was insultingly demeaned. A few dared speak out but most bided their time.

The Oboi Regency

Their moment came on February 2, 1661, when the Shun-chih Emperor died of smallpox. Then the pendulum swung back from Ming-style government to Manchu aristocratic rule. Four Manchu princes—veterans of the Korean and Mongol campaigns, leaders of the tough bannermen who had fought across central China—assumed charge of the regency for the seven-year-old K'ang-hsi Emperor (reigned 1662–1722). Their first act was to disavow the former regime's policies. The leading regent, Oboi, was helped by the empress dowager to forge a false testament in the dead em-peror's name. Supposedly written on his deathbed, Shun-chih's spurious last words were an abject apology to his courtiers for betraying the Manchu legacy. By trusting sycophantish Chinese courtiers and eunuchs, he had supposedly rejected the advice of his *beile*. His successors were therefore urged to return to a kind of Manchu fundamentalism by awarding the nobility its rightful place in the government.

In the next six years Oboi and the other regents brought about swift and far-reaching changes. They expelled the eunuchs and returned the responsibility for palace administration to officers of the Imperial Household; gave the Collegium of Manchu and Mongol Princes powers to advise on major policy matters; stripped the Chinese censorate of its right to criticize the throne and limited the censors' powers to the impeachment of other bureaucrats; arrested, tortured and painfully executed persons caught expressing anti-Manchu sentiments; instituted a severe system of personnel scrutiny which rewarded local magistrates for the alacrity and efficiency with which they cleared their judicial dockets and fulfilled tax quotas; and arrested over thirteen thousand members of the gentry in Kiangnan and northern Chekiang guilty of tax arrears. After these changes were decreed, no officials dared publicly dispute the new policies. Private dissent grew, however, and even Manchu ministers began to search for a middle way between Shun-chih's sinophilia and the avowedly pro-Manchu stance of the Oboi regency. Some means had to be found to respect the interests of the Manchu princes without sacrificing the support of the Chinese gentry. It was to the everlasting credit of the K'ang-hsi Emperor that such a compromise was devised before public loyalties were altogether lost.

The K'ang-hsi Emperor

The Ch'ing Dynasty's greatest emperor, K'ang-hsi, completed the military conquest of China. As befitted such a glorious ruler, his birth was notably auspicious. Hagiographers later reported that stirring fragrances and vivid colors appeared as splendid omens of his reign-to-come. Yet his selection as heir to the throne was entirely accidental. The third son of Shun-chih by a Liaotung woman who may have been Chinese, K'ang-hsi was fortunate enough to have survived an attack of smallpox as an infant. When his father lay dying of that same disease, only K'ang-hsi of all the emperor's sons could safely be brought into the sickroom to receive Shun-chih's last benediction. At the time he was only seven and thus incapable of ruling for several years. Although the regent Oboi accorded him ceremonial deference and formally enthroned K'ang-hsi at the age of thirteen, real power was still withheld from the monarch. K'ang-hsi was not patient for long, however, and when only fifteen he engineered a plot against Oboi, who was arrested and whose followers were purged. By 1669 K'ang-hsi was in full control of his palace, if not of the realm.

South China, where Ming loyalists had held out for years, was by then ostensibly under Ch'ing rule. The last Ming emperor-in-exile, Yung-li, had been strangled in a Yunnan marketplace seven years earlier. Ming loyalism survived his death, but there were no longer any formal governments to attract supporters of the previous dynasty. Nevertheless, the Ch'ing government in Peking had only the most tenuous of holds over southwestern and southeastern China since the Manchus had been forced to rely upon Chinese adherents to subjugate the South. Wu San-kuei, named a prince after inviting the Manchus over the Great Wall, had gone on to conquer the Southwest in the name of the Ch'ing. Another former Ming general, Shang K'o-hsi, had repaid his Ch'ing princedom by driving the Ming loyalists out of Kwangtung. And up the coast, Fukien had been pacified by a militarist named Keng Ching-chung, the son of yet another Ming general who had been enfeoffed for joining the Ch'ing.

As further rewards for their service in south China, each of these three men had been awarded feudatories (*fan*). Deriving huge incomes from commercial monopolies and constructing magnificent palaces with their booty, the three princes ruled independently. Their armies, which together outnumbered the Ch'ing forces in Peking, represented a kind of frontier feudalism transposed to southern China. Wu San-kuei's military force, for instance, was organized into *niru* like the Manchu banners. Its commanders took personal oaths of loyalty to Wu and received prebends and aristocratic rank in return. Yet the army was not so feudal as to be entirely self-sufficient. Wu initially demanded nine million taels of silver a year from Peking to cover the costs of his soldiers. By the time K'ang-hsi was formally enthroned, these costs had more than doubled, forcing Peking to divert the valuable revenue of Kiangnan to the feudatory's private coffers. Wu San-kuei's power was enormous. Not only did he appoint all Ch'ing officials serving in Yunnan and Kweichow, but he also had the right to approve bureaucrats assigned to four neighboring provinces.

Shang K'o-hsi, the feudatory controlling Kwangtung, was less

extreme in his demands. In fact, he came to feel that the days of
military feudalism were over now that the Ming loyalists had been
dispersed. Against his own son's advice, Shang tendered his resigna-
tion to the K'ang-hsi Emperor. The other two feudatories routinely
followed suit, assuming that K'ang-hsi would dare not affront them
by accepting their pro forma resignations. But the emperor took
their gesture seriously, almost as though he could not foresee their
reaction. Discovering that he was actually expected to give up his
satrapy, Wu San-kuei promptly revolted. In December, 1673, the
Yunnan warlord called upon Shang Chih-hsin[2] and Keng Ching-
chung to help him overthrow the Ch'ing and restore the Ming.

As Wu had invited the Manchus into China ostensibly to help the
falling Ming Dynasty. Offered a princedom by Dorgon, he had
later murdered the last exiled Ming emperor for his new masters.
Now, he was betraying the Ch'ing to restore what he had destroyed.
Many Chinese were still strongly anti-Manchu, but few Ming loyalists were likely to hearken to the cause of such a double turncoat.

As Wu San-kuei marched north against the Ch'ing, he made his
demands known. If the Manchus abandoned Peking and returned to
Liaotung, he would grant them peace and the kingdom of Korea.
K'ang-hsi's counsellors panicked, for Wu's forces held a military
advantage. Yet the emperor stood firm and rejected the offer. For
a few months the fate of the Ch'ing hung in the balance. Had
Wu San-kuei pressed on, the dynasty might have fallen. But when
the feudatories' armies reached Hunan, Wu stayed his progress in
the hope that negotiations were still possible. That delay gave K'ang-
hsi just enough time to mass an army in Hupeh and try to contain
the enemy. As he was to discover, however, the success of the
campaign depended not so much upon Manchu forces as upon
other Chinese armies which had remained loyal to the Ch'ing. To
defeat the feudatories, K'ang-hsi first chose Manchu princes as
generals, "men with the founding emperor's blood in their veins."
But, in his own words,

> year after year, I had to watch them blunder and fail, hesitate to
> advance, stay snug in their base camps; and had to rely—even
> as rebellious Chinese generals cut the Manchus back—on other
> Chinese generals to turn the tide.[3]

The tide finally did turn in the Manchus' favor three years after
the feudatories revolted. The rebel troops were slowly pushed back,
province by province, until by 1681 the Ch'ing truly controlled

mainland China and the remains of Wu San-kuei's corpse had been scattered over the reaches of the empire.

K'ang-hsi's victory over the three feudatories, followed by the subjugation of Taiwan in 1683, his personal campaigns against the Oirat Mongols in 1696–1697, and the conquest of Tibet in 1720, recalled the imperial glories of the T'ang and early Ming when central Asia had been brought to heel and tribal tribute poured into China. The emperor seemed a true heir to the martial spirit of Nurhaci, and K'ang-hsi was plainly not averse to exploiting this image in order to gain the support of the *beile*. His famous hunting parties in Jehol and Manchuria gratified the nobles' pride in their tribal culture, while K'ang-hsi's state policies seemed obviously designed to grant the Manchu elite a favored position apart from Chinese officialdom. The Collegium of Princes was retained, conducting its sessions in the Manchu language, and the banners were carefully separated from the rest of the government as autonomous administrative units whose personnel was supplied by the tribal clan heads (*mokunda*).

K'ang-hsi also reserved top posts within the regular bureaucracy for Manchu officials. Like the Ming government, which Abahai had copied, the Ch'ing administration was organized into six ministries or boards:

Board of Civil Appointments—bureaucratic appointments and sanctions, the sale of offices

Board of Revenue—auditing tax accounts, supervising state welfare, managing state monopolies, allocating provincial revenue

Board of Rites—responsible for imperial Confucian ritual, diplomatic relations with the central Asian tribes, and the examination system

Board of War—routine supervision of the Green Standard armies

Board of Justice—drafting legal provisions, supervising provincial judges, acting as an appeals court

Board of Works—roadworks, water conservation, and flood control

The posts of president and vice-president in charge of each of these boards were divided evenly between Manchu and Chinese bureaucrats, always ensuring a strict racial balance of power at the top levels of the civil service.

A similar balance was decreed for the provinces. Whenever

possible, a Chinese governor was supervised by one of eight vice-roys or governors-general who were usually Manchu, Mongol, or Chinese bannermen. Banner troops stationed in any given province were commanded by their own officer, a tartar-general, who held the same rank as a viceroy and reported directly to the banner ad-ministration in Peking. Provincial governors did control a Chinese constabulary known as the Green Standard (*Lü ying*), but in the event of major military mobilization these troops were either sub-ordinated to the banner generals or placed under the personal command of imperial commissioners. Wu San-kuei had taught K'ang-hsi a bitter lesson—one that later emperors were unlikely to forget. Chinese provincial governors must never again be permitted to acquire independent military forces. To prevent the development of future regional satrapies, strategically located banner garrisons were established, answerable only to Peking and able to intervene decisively against Chinese armies. Banner garrisons were intended to be internal colonies whose Manchu military families lived apart from the indigenous Chinese. They were forbidden intermarriage and urged to take special pride in their own importance for the defense of the dynasty and of the race. Like the Mughals of India, the Manchus sought to dominate a conquered population by preserv-ing a superstratified elite that avoided assimilation.

Yet while K'ang-hsi satisfied some Manchu aspirations, he con-tinued to curb the power of the nobility. Manchu aristocrats were forbidden to appropriate Chinese lands, and members of the royal family were prevented from holding high ministerial posts. Such restraining measures showed how eager K'ang-hsi was to win the Chinese gentry's support. To secure the participation of the genera-tion of literati who had demonstrated their loyalty to the Ming by refusing public service under the Ch'ing, he announced a special examination (*po-hsueh hung-tz'u*) in 1679. Those scholars whose reputation was inextricably linked with Ming loyalism still refused to go to Peking, but even they appreciated the emperor's deference in their direction and encouraged friends and relatives not so sentimentally constrained to enroll for the examination.

Successful candidates were posted to the Hanlin Academy or joined the *nan shu-fang*—the famous study where K'ang-hsi sur-rounded himself with the most eminent scholars of the realm. Under his aegis, philosophers like Chang Ying revied orthodox Neo-Con-fucianism, historians undertook a drafting of the Ming dynastic history, classicists assembled a copious index of literary quotations

(*P'ei-wen yun-fu*), and lexicographers compiled the most complete Chinese character dictionary (*K'ang-hsi tz'u-tien*) ever published.[4] Like the greatest of Confucian monarchs, K'ang-hsi also issued a set of Sacred Edicts, sternly lectured his officials on proper behavior, and earned popular gratitude by freezing the land tax rate in 1713.[5]

Gradually K'ang-hsi came to have more and more confidence in the loyalty he inspired among the Chinese. On his early tours south after the three feudatories were crushed, K'ang-hsi preferred to stay within the Manchu banner garrisons for his own safety. But during his four trips to the Yangtze region after 1699, he felt certain enough of his popularity to attend public banquets and lodge in the residences of Chinese officials. As K'ang-hsi cast himself in the mold of an enlightened Chinese monarch he also consciously contributed to the secular growth of imperial despotism by modeling himself after the early Ming rulers. Like the Hung-Wu Emperor (reigned 1368–1398), K'ang-hsi put himself at the center of all decision making. Arising before dawn to read the memorials sent to the palace from all over the empire, he conceived of the throne as being in direct contact with the entire bureaucracy. Consequently, the administrative boards were sometimes little more than clearing houses for his imperial commands. In the provinces the authority of the governors was diffused among military, fiscal, and judicial officers who reported directly to Peking. Banner generals, Green Standard commanders, circuit intendants, provincial treasurers and censors each had their own chains of command to the metropolitan administration and some even memorialized the emperor on their own.

An additional secret hierarchy, concealed from public view, reported on all these officials and was entirely independent of the regular bureaucracy. Called the Imperial Household (*Nei-wu fu*), this was the apparatus with which Oboi had replaced Shun-chih's eunuchs. K'ang-hsi cleverly altered the Imperial Household to suit his own ends, staffing it with bannermen and bondservants (*pao-i*). The latter were descended from the Chinese prisoners of war captured in the Liaotung campaigns by Nurhaci and Abahai. The most intelligent and enterprising bondservants were rewarded with rank in the Imperial Bodyguard and office in the Imperial Household. They made ideal servants for the emperor. Like eunuchs, they derived their status wholly from attachment to his person and so were unusually loyal functionaries. Yet because the bondservants were not castrati, Chinese sensibilities were not insulted. Further-

more, the bondservants' connection with the Manchu banners kept
them from offending the *beile*. In search of trustworthy officers,
K'ang-hsi naturally turned to this corps of intimates who soon became his confidential agents. Partly because he did not entirely trust
regular officials and partly because all memorials were forwarded
to him through semipublic bureaucratic channels, K'ang-hsi developed a secret memorial system. Bondservants posted to the provinces were ordered to send reports for his eyes only on such matters
as the competence of officials, the mood of the public, and military
affairs. The bondservants were also fairly reliable custodians of the
ruler's privy purse so that state monopolies were routinely supervised by Imperial Household officials. The hoppo in charge of the
Canton customs office was thought by Westerners to represent the
Board of Revenue, but he was actually a servant of the Imperial
Household who made sure that the emperor got his share of tariffs
before the regular quota was filled. Thanks to such private em-
ployees, the emperor's personal treasury sometimes held much more
than the government's coffers in Peking.

The Succession Crisis

K'ang-hsi's many accomplishments were slightly marred by the
succession crisis that broke out near the end of his sixty-year reign.
Chinese rules of imperial succession did not dictate primogeniture.
A monarch picked his heirs from among all the princes, sometimes
on such whimsical grounds as the favoring of a particular concubine. Courtiers and ministers often formed factions around potential
heirs, bitterly supporting the claims of one consort against other
imperial favorites.[6] To avoid this kind of opportunistic squabbling,
rulers were advised to make their selection early. The heir apparent
could then be properly prepared by Confucian tutors to occupy the
throne and, in the event of his father's premature death, be already
designated to conduct the ancestral rites. However, an early selection was not always the best one, since a promising young prince
could easily turn out to be an incompetent adult.

This was precisely the case with K'ang-hsi's choice, Yin-jeng
(second son), who was named heir apparent in 1674 at the age of
two.[7] Lovingly raised by the emperor himself and trained by excellent Confucian tutors, Yin-jeng eventually proved to be an ar-

rogant and brutal prince, fond of intrigue and jealous of his father's power. Worst of all in the virile emperor's eyes, Yin-jeng was also a notorious homosexual—consorting with palace clerks and buying little boys from the slave dealers of Soochow. In 1708, after learning that the prince was physically abusing civil officials, K'ang-hsi finally dismissed Yin-jeng as heir apparent. But the grief-stricken emperor simply could not understand how his favorite son could have betrayed his affection and judgment. So puzzled was K'ang-hsi by this question that he convinced himself Yin-jeng had been possessed by demons, and reinstated the prince the next year after executing several Buddhist lamas supposedly guilty of casting an evil spell.

But nothing had changed. Yin-jeng's outrages continued. In 1711 K'ang-hsi discovered that several of his highest military officials were plotting with Yin-jeng, and by the following winter concluded that "his madness was back and I could bear no more; he spied on people in the privies, he spat and swore at his retinue and his consorts and showed no remorse."[8] Once again K'ang-hsi canceled Yin-jeng's titles and this time placed him under palace guard, warning his officials that any ministers who pleaded for Yin-jeng's reinstatement in the future would be summarily executed.[9]

The consequence of this unfortunate affair was that by 1713 the throne was without a formal heir. Officials repeatedly pleaded with K'ang-hsi to name a new heir apparent, but the emperor was so angered and disappointed by the Yin-jeng episode that he had those memorials returned. However, factions continued to form around those of K'ang-hsi's sons who seemed most likely to inherit the throne, and by 1721 most courtiers believed that Yin-t'i (fourteenth son), the prince who had commanded a victorious expedition to Tibet, would emerge as K'ang-hsi's favorite.

Yet while Yin-t'i was winning military honors, another rival, Yin-chen (fourth son), was laying plans of his own to seize power. Born to a palace maid-servant and repeatedly humiliated by his brothers, Yin-chen had been quietly preparing for his father's death by cultivating allies in the military forces. His two most crucial supporters were Lungkodo, commander of the Peking gendarmerie, and the Chinese bannerman, Nien Keng-yao, who ostensibly served as Yin-t'i's chief strategist.

In May 1722, Yin-t'i returned to the front under the watchful eyes of Nien Keng-yao. That winter K'ang-hsi suddenly fell ill in his country villa west of Peking. As one of the imperial princes,

Yin-chen was at that time supposed to be conducting the winter solstice sacrifices at the Temple of Heaven in Peking. Instead, on December 20, he rode out to his father's villa and entered the emperor's sickroom. He emerged with the claim that K'ang-hsi had made him heir—an assertion that no one could contest because the emperor now lay dead, perhaps even murdered by Yin-chen. While his ally Lungkodo kept order in the Forbidden City, Yin-chen brought his father's corpse back to the capital under the drawn swords of a military escort. Then he sealed his coup d'etat by naming himself Yung-cheng Emperor (reigned 1723–1735), imprisoning or executing the other imperial princes, and purging the court and ministries of Yin-t'i's supporters.

The Yung-cheng Reign

Yung-cheng's ruthless seizure of power has given him the exaggerated reputation of being the harshest and most intolerant of Ch'ing monarchs. Other acts further darken his portrait: Yung-cheng completely censored the historical record of his accession by having his minister Chang T'ing-yü prune the K'ang-hsi archives of documents about his struggle with his brothers. Suspecting veiled anti-Manchuism in portions of an encyclopedia (*Ku-chin t'u-shu chi-ch'eng*) which his father had sponsored, he called in all copies of the work to expunge slighting mention of barbarians. He also encouraged antiforeign polemicists at court and rigidly proscribed Christian missionary work. Not even Buddhist theologians' works were spared if Yung-cheng felt their doctrines to be misguided. His own most famous work, *P'eng-tang lun* (On factions), was the strongest attack on bureaucratic factions written by any Chinese emperor.

Confucian ministers who read *P'eng-tang lun* agreed with his diatribe against selfish coalitions of "petty men," but what they wanted instead was never granted them. That is, Confucianists criticized bureaucratic factionalism because it betrayed the individual relationship that was supposed to exist between a forthright minister and his emperor. In exchange for giving up bureaucratic alliances, they expected a ruler to respect their moral integrity and loyal honesty. However, this was far from Yung-cheng's conception of unquestioning loyalty to the throne's interests. In place of the bilateral

integrity and implicit equality of the Confucian ideal, he preferred
devoted obeisance to the monarch's wishes.

Yung-cheng thus elevated personal fealty above all other bureaucratic desiderata and amply rewarded those who repaid his
trust. His habit was to single out intelligent and ambitious officials,
who were tested by being asked to report on other civil servants.
If they proved reliable, Yung-cheng jumped them rapidly up the
bureaucratic ranks and put them in charge of particularly sensitive
administrative regions of China. For example, Li Wei[10] was dele-
gated to supervise foreign trade and curb piracy in the troublesome
coastal province of Cheking; T'ien Wen-ching[11] to curb gentry
peculation in central China; O-er-t'ai[12] to subjugate the aborigines
of Yunnan. After appointing them to such posts, Yung-cheng remained in constant contact with his protégés, backing up their decisions even when they proved to be unpopular. Like his father
before him, the emperor was a very hard worker, perpetuating
K'ang-hsi's style of personal intervention in the affairs of the realm.
The many volumes of his Vermilion Endorsements (*Yung-cheng
chu-p'i yü-chih*) testify to the avid interest which he took in the
pettiest of matters. Anything might attract his attention: the inter-
rogation of a petty felon, a district tax dispute, the price of grain,
rumors of a deputy magistrate's peculation. Once involved, Yung-
cheng was unrelenting. His red-inked brush would skip down the
margin of the memorialist's page, hectoring, scolding, cajoling,
praising, and criticizing.

Yung-cheng's favorites were all tough, hardnosed administrators.
They were usually effective because they had no reason to fear the
criticisms of injured parties. In fact, denunciations of their policies
by other officials were often proof to Yung-cheng that his protégés
were rooting out entrenched interest groups. By now the dynasty
was over eighty years old. Officials were beginning to grow lax and
clerks were abusing their privileged positions in local yamens. Members of the lower gentry were more and more ensconced in tax
farming. Yung-cheng believed that the empire needed a house
cleaning and so relied upon the kind of officials who were not afraid
to punish underlings or impeach superiors. If toes were stepped on,
that was all the more evidence of genuine administrative reforms.
For, more than any other Manchu emperor, Yung-cheng was resolved to rationalize the fiscal policies and bureaucratic institutions
that had been copied from the late Ming period.

One of his major targets was the lower gentry's abuse of tax remission. Since gentry fees increased the tax burden on the peasants, Yung-cheng ordered officials like T'ien Wen-ching to curtail the petitionary rights and tax exemptions of degree-holders. This attack upon the elite's privileges momentarily diminished the local gentry's social and political influence. But Yung-cheng was not opposed to gentry privilege for its own sake nor was he simply attempting to curtail official misappropriation. Instead he was primarily concerned with formalizing the informal—with forcing private fees into the public sector. Behind his assault on *pao-lan* (proxy remission of taxes) by the gentry, on the customary fees of the clerks, and on the informal salaries (*lo-kuei*) of district magistrates was the rationalizing desire to transform personal surcharges into regular taxes. The *lo-kuei*, for instance, were converted into tax increases which provided salary raises to "nourish incorruption" (*yang-lien*).[13] Inflation during the later eighteenth century forced officials to reintroduce customary fees, but for a while at least the Yung-cheng fiscal reforms were remarkably effective.

Under Yung-cheng, too, the old informal network of imperial agents was made into a regular organ of government. Like his father, Yung-cheng relied heavily on the secret memorials that were his alone to read. As he introduced more officials into that privileged communications network, however, the volume of paper was too much for one pair of imperial eyes. In 1729, therefore, Yung-cheng endorsed the formation of a Grand Council (*Chün-chi ch'u*)[14] to summarize and evaluate this data. Thenceforth, routine administrative memorials were transmitted to the Grand Secretariat (*Nei-ko*), while important policy recommendations and intelligence reports were processed through the Grand Council. This new bureau, for which there was no provision in the Ch'ing statutes, was a much more compact group of officials (five grand councillors, usually headed by a Manchu) than the Grand Secretariat (sixteen Manchu and sixteen Chinese members). Meeting in secret, ready at any moment to attend an imperial audience, the Grand Council soon assumed a decisive role in policy making and controlled higher level appointments in the government.

The formation of the Grand Council sounded the death knell for the old Collegium of Manchu Princes. It also represented a consistent tendency in the later imperial period for Chinese rulers to replace bureaucratically routinized offices with new ad hoc secretariats. Originally the Grand Secretariat had been the Ming emperors' equivalent of Yung-cheng's Grand Council—a kitchen cabinet which deprived the six ministries of decisive powers and restored policy making to the throne and its private advisers. But the cabinet of secretaries gradually became more than an advisory board. It appropriated the emperor's powers of decision, if only because it controlled the flow of documents to and from the throne, suppressing memorials with which it disagreed and drafting edicts for the emperor to sign. When the Grand Secretariat—originally an imperial creation—acquired such independence, a new private council took its place. But the Grand Council, too, would eventually evolve in precisely the same way as its predecessor, forming alliances with bureaucrats in the regular ministries and becoming increasingly difficult for the monarch to override. The Chia-ch'ing Emperor (reigned 1796–1820) even felt constrained in 1799 to order governors to send their confidential reports directly to him, without giving copies to the Grand Council. Nevertheless, the Grand Council retained its strategic importance until the early 1900s when the Manchu Collegium of Princes was revived to discuss important matters of state.

Yung-cheng employed the same autocratic style to resolve the Ch'ing's dynastic succession problem. Pressured early on to name an heir, he summoned the princes and ministers to an audience on September 16, 1723. Announcing that he had made his choice, the emperor flourished a folded piece of paper before the court. On it, he said, was written the name of his successor. Then he sealed the slip in a small casket, which was placed behind a horizontal plaque 25 feet above the floor of the throne room. The casket was not to be opened until his death.

So simple a device worked remarkably well. Yung-cheng could presumably alter the name in secret if the heir he had chosen proved later to be a disappointment. Yet, without breaking into the throne room and risking death, no one could learn the identity of the heir or form a faction around him. Yung-cheng himself singled out none of the princes for special attention. Instead of revealing his choice by having one of them receive special tutoring, he turned K'ang-hsi's former study into schoolrooms where all of the princes were indiscriminately enrolled to study the classics, history, and *belles lettres* under Confucian scholars. The secret was thus preserved until just before Yung-cheng's death in 1735,[15] when it was an-

nounced that his fourth son, Hung-li, would ascend the throne as
the Ch'ien-lung Emperor (reigned 1736–1795).

High Ch'ing: The Ch'ien-lung Period

Thanks to his father's cunning, Ch'ien-lung's coronation was
largely free of the intrigue that characterized earlier Ch'ing acces-
sions. There were clique struggles, notably between Yung-cheng's
former favorites, Chang T'ing-yü and O-er-t'ai, but the former fell
into disfavor after 1743 and the latter died peacefully in 1745.
Partly because the Manchu princes had lost so much power, and
partly because the emperor was 25 when he ascended the throne,
Ch'ien-lung was soon able to rule almost entirely on his own. He
did rely on his brother-in-law, Duke Fu-heng, for military advice.
But, like Louis XIV, Ch'ien-lung was much of the time his own
chief minister, and a grandiose symbol of imperial strength and
plenty to his people. Indeed, Ch'ien-lung was a series of symbols
even to himself. Dorgon, K'ang-hsi, and Yung-cheng were leaders
whose colorful individuality had made policy as much a matter of
personality as of statecraft. Ch'ien-lung's personality, however, was
overwhelmed by imperial stereotypes and fixed Confucian roles:
sage king, filial son, gentleman scholar, military genius, and so forth.
Because he studiously shaped his own historical record to accord
with these paradigms, Ch'ien-lung can be viewed only as a series
of *topoi* which largely conceal the man behind the image.

The Ch'ien-lung reign was the most splendid era of the Ch'ing,
and perhaps the most luxurious in all Chinese history. Yung-cheng's
fiscal reforms had left 24 million taels in the national treasury. The
propitious ration of population to land produced high agricultural
yields, and by 1786 Ch'ien-lung had increased this surplus by another 50 million taels—more than enough to pay for the monumental palaces and ornate pavilions of the Garden of Circular
Clarity (*Yuan-ming yuan*), his summer residence west of Peking.
There, on the Hill of Imperial Longevity, the emperor built a Buddhist temple for his mother in the summer of 1751. His ode for this
monument to filial piety reads:

> This mountain decked with gold is a garden of prayer to Buddha
> to requite such benevolence. The golden dew plate shines in the
> sun, reflecting its light on the clouds. The breeze stirs the wind

bells under the eaves and carries their notes beyond the sky. Everywhere resounds the booming of the drums. Amid these delightful scenes the scriptures are being chanted for the eminent, prolonged, and extensive happiness of my mother and for her long life without measure. From this day on, this temple shall be a pleasant grove, a kingdom of incense. Before the temple spreads a lake, sweet as koumiss. Behind it rises a high green mount protecting it. The monastery is extensive. The pagoda is tall and resplendent with glazed tile. The terrace appears to be of jade. The trees and flowers are brightened by the splendor of the pagoda. Their fragrance is that of costly incense. The friendly breeze brings to our ears the songs of the birds of Ch'ieh Ling. My mother's benevolent heart sincerely honors the doctrines of Buddhism. She is charmed with the scene, she claps her hands in devotion, and her face beams with joy, a joy which comes partly from what I have done for her.[16]

This was the great age of decorative art in China: heavy, intricate cloisonné and multilayered lacquerware; enormous bronze temple bells and polychrome marbles; gilded jade tablets and variegated porcelain. The splendor of the high Ch'ing dazzled foreign visitors to China in the eighteenth century. When Sir George Macartney led an embassy to China in 1793, he presented Ch'ien-lung with the best gifts George III had to offer: Vulliamy clocks, globes, orreries, an elaborate planetarium, and the finest Wedgewood porcelains. But these seemed almost tawdry beside the goods Ch'ien-lung had already accumulated. Taken on a yachting trip around the lake at the emperor's Jehol palace, Lord Macartney stopped to visit forty or fifty pavilions, each

> . . . furnished in the richest manner, with pictures of the Emperor's huntings and progresses; with stupendous vases of jasper and agate; with the finest porcelains and japan, and with every kind of European toys and sing-songs; with spheres, orreries, clocks and musical automatons of such exquisite workmanship, and in such profusion, that our presents must shrink from the comparison and "hide their diminished heads."[17]

Many of the Ch'ien-lung Emperor's possessions were tribute gifts from other countries, and thus commemorated China's continual military expansion during the eighteenth century. Between 1755 and 1792 the Ch'ing subdued, pacified, or conquered the Zungars, the Turkestani, the Chin-ch'uan, the Miao, the Taiwanese, the Burmese, the Annamese, and the Ghurkas. Never had the Chinese empire encompassed so much territory.[18] The conquest of Ili and Turkestan alone added six million square miles to the realm, and awe of Chinese strength brought other states within its tributary orbit.

Yet the gifts of vassal states hardly compensated China for its increased military costs. In 1782 sixty thousand more men were added to the army rolls. Quartermaster expenses soared. Campaign expenditures plus famine relief drained 200,000,000 taels from the once overflowing imperial treasury. Not all these expenses were legitimate, however, and one reason for the high cost of empire was the continual siphoning off of funds by corrupt officers and civil servants. The degree of embezzlement was scandalous, but no one acted to prevent such abuses because the highest minister in the realm, Ho-shen, was totally corrupt himself.

The Ascendancy of Ho-shen

The last 23 years of Ch'ien-lung's reign were dominated by the grand councillor Ho-shen. In 1775 the emperor was 65 years old and tiring of personal administration. One day, passing through the Ch'ien-ch'ing gate of the Forbidden City, his eye was caught by a handsome 22-year-old guardsman. Perhaps because the guardsman resembled a Yung-cheng consort he had once loved, Ch'ien-lung was immediately taken with the young Manchu bannerman. Within a year he had made Ho-shen a grand councillor and showered him with unprecedented gifts and privileges. Ho-shen accepted them greedily and placed his henchmen in key posts throughout the empire. In 1782 censors impeached some of his associates, implicating Ho-shen. But Ch'ien-lung would brook no criticism of his favorite—which amounted to an indictment of himself—and kept Ho-shen in office. Two years later, in fact, Ho-shen gained control of both the boards of civil appointments and of revenue, and in 1790 he was given the emperor's favorite daughter in marriage as a signal honor. Critics were stilled and each looked to his own nest. Corruption spread the length and breadth of the bureaucracy.

Scarcely aware of the rot, Ch'ien-lung reached his sixtieth year of rule in 1795. Consciously wanting to be a paradigm of sagehood, he decided to observe filial piety by abdicating before his natural term exceeded the reign of K'ang-hsi. With great pomp and ceremony his son took the throne as the Chia-ch'ing Emperor (reigned 1796–1820)[19] but governed in name alone. Ch'ien-lung still held the reins of political authority and—sliding into senility—put them in Ho-shen's avid hands. This intolerable situation persisted for three years. Finally on February 7, 1799, the emperor emeritus passed away. Freed from filial deference, Chia-ch'ing waited five days before ordering Ho-shen's arrest. As denunciations of Ho-shen poured in from all sides, the new emperor confiscated the former guardsman's estate. When all the jewels were appraised, the lands evaluated, and the pawnshops tallied, the magnitude of Ho-shen's corruption staggered the court. His movable property alone amounted to 80,000,000 taels, which was even more than the imperial treasury then contained. No doubt assuaged by this sudden boon, the Chia-ch'ing Emperor honored his father's memory by staying the painful execution of Ho-shen who was instead permitted to take his own life. Chia-ch'ing also chose not to widen the purge by indicting Ho-shen's former henchmen. Consequently, it was Ho-shen alone, and neither Ch'ien-lung nor the Grand Councillor's underlings, who took entire blame for the political corruption of the late eighteenth century.[20]

Nevertheless, contemporaries viewed the Ho-shen affair as a symbol of the hollowness behind the sagely façade of Ch'ien-lung's later years. The contrast with the earlier part of his reign was startling. When Ch'ien-lung mounted the throne in 1736 the dynasty was climbing to its zenith. Dominating the middle span of the Ch'ing, his pivotal reign (counting his erstwhile retirement, the longest in Chinese history) saw the dynastic cycle begin its downward swing. In a matter of decades it was descending toward its nadir. Attempting to live up to grandiose ideals, Ch'ien-lung had been too much a captive of the Chinese image of a sage ruler to remember some of the harsher realities his Manchu ancestors had faced. In acting out the role of an ideal Confucian literatus, he had inadvertently become a model of acculturation for the rest of the Manchu elite, which was forgetting its own language almost as quickly as it lost its lands in north China. Ch'ien-lung consciously wished to keep his race apart from the Chinese, but his own behavior helped make assimilation irresistible. By the late eighteenth century the Manchu balance of power was teetering, and when crisis finally struck in the nineteenth century, the banners were to prove so useless that Ch'ien-lung's descendants would have to arm Chinese viceroys for want of Manchu martial vigor.

The White Lotus Rebellion

Ch'ien-lung's reign also marked the Ch'ing's first major loss of control over rural society. The end of the eighteenth century saw the resurgence of White Lotus sectarians in central China. In northwestern Hupei during 1775 a doctor and magician called Liu Sung openly preached of the coming of Maitreya Buddha. When he was arrested, his successor, Liu Chih-hsieh, continued to predict a new kalpa. Seriously alarmed, the authorities seized the second prophet and ordered a general roundup of suspected dissidents in that area. Then, just as panic was spreading, a Ch'ing expeditionary force marched through Hupei to quell a Miao uprising in the Southwest. The undisciplined government troops foraged on the way, looting villages and raping women. "The officials force the people to rebel," said the peasants, and in 1795 the White Lotus movement launched its rebellion against the dynasty.

The government was then in the hands of Ho-shen, who treated this as yet another opportunity to embezzle government appropriations. His commanders padded their army rolls or hired the lame and infirm, reporting every government defeat to the throne as though it were an imperial victory. The rebellion spread from Hsiang-yang to the rest of Hupei. Entire districts slipped under rebel occupation and the government did nothing. Soon Honan and Szechwan were in arms to oppose the regime.

It was only after Ho-shen's disgrace and suicide that Peking fully realized the dimensions of the rebellion and mobilized sufficient forces to suppress it. Chia-ch'ing was fortunate in having generals he could still trust to control the rebellion. The best of these was a semiliterate lieutenant-general named Eldemboo who had devoted a lifetime to the military expansion of the dynasty. A Gualgiya Manchu conscript, he had accumulated a campaign record that extolled the victories of the Ch'ing: the Burmese war of 1768, the suppression of the Chin-ch'uan rebels in 1773–1776, the subjugation of the Kansu Muslims in 1784, the Taiwan expedition of 1787, the Ghurka wars in Tibet in 1791, and the Nepalese war of 1792. By 1797 Eldemboo had crushed the Miao rebels in Kweichow and was transferred to Hupei to fight the White Lotus. Two years later his talents were recognized by Chia-ch'ing, who made him assistant commander, then commander-in-chief, of the entire government campaign.

A new tone of realism pervaded government reports, and unreliable officers were dismissed. As the Ch'ing armies began to contain the rebels, the local gentry rallied to the throne. Militia were enrolled. "Walls were strengthened and the fields cleared." Slowly, district by district, the forces of order cut the core rebel armies off from the peasantry, which was allowed to redeem itself by returning to the land. The White Lotus diehards were then gradually bottled up in Szechwan, where imperial troops disposed of them in 1804.

Population Pressure and the Gentry's Role in Local Defense

In addition to the immediate evils which caused the White Lotus rebellion of 1795–1804, there were other more profound disturbances that defied rectification. The most serious of these was increased population pressure on political and economic resources. A century of Ch'ing peace and prosperity had given the Chinese time to multiply. By 1800 the empire's population was nearing the 400 million mark, making China the most populous nation in the world. However well conceived the Ch'ing system of administrative balances, this demographic factor alone made effective government almost impossible. The average magistrate was now responsible for the welfare of approximately 200,000 residents in his district. Famine relief, local irrigation maintenance, and the preservation of public order were all exceeding the existing government's physical abilities. To suppress the White Lotus rebels, the regime therefore had to rely on aid from the gentry. Eldemboo's troops were decisive in large scale warfare, but pacification really depended on the patient enrollment of the rural population into gentry-run militia and relief organizations. Because the central government still commanded superior strength, this increase in the gentry's influence did not result in its local political hegemony. Once the rebels were expelled from a district, the gentry disbanded the militia and returned its weapons to the local magistrate. But the military expertise that local notables acquired in this period not only aided them later on against Taiping rebels; the experience also prepared them to assume new local defense roles at the dynasty's ultimate expense in the nineteenth century.

The gentry's growing domination of Chinese rural government

was the most consequential internal political development of the late imperial period. In contemporaries' eyes, however, the most significant result was the evolution of the dynastic cycle. Although the Ch'ing had dispelled the White Lotus rebels, it was hard to believe that the dynasty had permanently recuperated from disruption. Too many signs pointed to senescence. The expenses of suppressing its enemies had cost the dynasty 100 million taels between 1796 and 1801. Ho-shen's spirit had not been completely exorcised. Officials insisted on the need to recover moral discipline, but during the Chia-ch'ing reign the Yellow River flooded seventeen times—a sure sign that conservancy officials were pocketing dike repair funds. Chia-ch'ing compensated for his inability to prevent public corruption with personal miserliness. As palace expenses were ruthlessly cut, prebendaries suffered. Bannermen drifted into petty crime and terrorized the inhabitants of Peking. In 1813 *T'ien-li chiao* (Heavenly Principle Sect) rebels, accompanied by eunuchs, actually attacked the palace in an attempt to kill the emperor. Chia-ch'ing was saved, and optimists spoke loosely of an imperial restoration.[21] But gloom and pessimism characterized other officials who thought they saw fresh disasters just over the historical horizon. The Ch'ing Dynasty had accumulated sufficient past glories to make its future days seem numbered.

Yet the familiar dynastic cycle was about to be decisively interrupted by strange and exotic events. The outer world and its own historical conceptions would soon impinge upon China. So far, the mainstreams of Chinese history had been landlocked, occasionally flooding the countryside but never flowing out into the sea. Even external invaders like the Manchus had come from inner Asia to conquer what the Chinese thought of as an empire within the four seas (*ssu-hai chih nei*). But now for the first time the seas would intrude. Macartney's embassy had been the first wave to reach China. Lord Amherst would follow in 1816 and by 1839 the incoming tide would overwhelm the Chinese altogether.

Notes

1. The important bureau that controlled the privy purse and administered the emperor's affairs.

2. Chih-hsin was Shang K'o-hsi's son. He imprisoned his father (who remained loyal to the Ch'ing) and joined Wu San-kuei in 1676.

3. Jonathan D. Spence, *Emperor of China: Self-Portrait of K'ang-hsi* (New York: Alfred A. Knopf, 1974), pp. 38–39.

4. The minor arts flourished as well. Lang T'ing-chi, governor of Kiangsi from 1705–1712, reopened the great kilns of Ching-te-chen, which produced the delicate *sang de boeuf* and apple green porcelains so characteristic of the K'ang-hsi reign.

5. The Chinese land tax by then was levied according to land area, rather than value. K'ang-hsi's *yung pu chia-fu* (never increase the land tax) decree of 1713 forbid any future increase in the rate of taxes per *mou* of land. This eventually set a severe fiscal restraint on the central government's revenue-raising capacities, which crippled it badly at the end of the nineteenth century. Over the course of the next two centuries, the amount of cultivated acreage nearly doubled in China as population grew. But there were no continuing cadastral surveys to keep track of this increase, and local magistrates were often reluctant to report newly cultivated land in their districts because of the constant pressure upon them to meet existing tax quotas. The land tax did in fact double between the time K'ang-hsi issued his edict and the time the dynasty fell, but only because surcharges were added to the prevailing rate. And even that increase was inadequate for the dynasty's monetary needs by 1900.

6. Ch'ing rulers were especially aware of the succession struggles of the late Ming. At the end of the Wan-li reign (1573–1619) the "three cases" (the red pill case, the cudgel case, and the expulsion from the court case) led to bitter denunciations and murders at court.

7. In all K'ang-hsi had 56 children who lived for some time after birth. Of his 36 sons, 20 grew to maturity.

8. Jonathan D. Spence, *Emperor of China*, p. 136.

9. One impetuous young censor did so memorialize in 1717 and was publicly beheaded—an act of relative clemency since K'ang-hsi's first instinct was to order a lingering death by slicing. Lynn Struve and Jonathan D. Spence have suggested, in papers delivered at the A.C.L.S. Conference on the Ming-Ch'ing Transition (Palm Springs, California, November 28–December 2, 1974), that the succession crisis marked a major change in Ch'ing history. Thereafter, K'ang-hsi's harsh policies resembled those of his successor, Yung-cheng.

10. Li bought his first official post and by 1717, at the age of thirty, had become a relatively insignificant department director in the Board of War. In 1723 he was sent by the emperor on a secret mission to Yunnan to spy on officials there. He performed so well that the emperor made him governor of Chekiang two years later. Li can be aptly described as paranoiac in his control methods.

11. T'ien Wen-ching, a Chinese bannerman, had an undistinguished academic record, and was apparently prejudiced against *chü-jen* and *chin-shih* scholars. He was frequently accused of abusing officials serving under him. After a tour of duty in the Board of Justice, he proved himself to be ruthlessly protective of the emperor's interests while serving as financial commissioner (provincial treasurer) of Shansi in 1723. The following year he was sent to Honan in that same capacity, and within months managed to oust the governor and take his place. According to Madeleine Zelin, T'ien was probably once a member of Yung-cheng's princely household.

12. O-er-t'ai, a Manchu bannerman, had been both a member of the Imperial Bodyguard and an assistant department director in the Imperial Household. In 1726 he was made governor of Yunnan and succeeded in putting down several Miao aboriginal revolts and in abolishing hereditary chieftainships. In later years a clique formed around him, directed against Chang T'ing-yü.

13. After this reform the official salaries per annum of a district magistrate and the governor of Kiangsu respectively were 40 taels and 150 taels. Their *yang-lien* additions were 1,800 and 12,000 taels.

14. Because this literally means "bureau of military affairs," and because Yung-cheng was then fighting the Oirat Mongols, historians long assumed that the Grand Council was devised as a kind of national security council. Silas H. L. Wu has recently shown, however, that it evolved out of the palace memorial system, in his *Communication and Imperial Control in China: Evolution of the Palace Memorial System, 1693–1735* (Cambridge: Harvard University Press, 1970).

15. There is some evidence that Yung-cheng was assassinated by the daughter of a Ming loyalist.

16. Carroll Brown Malone, *History of the Peking Summer Palaces under the Ch'ing Dynasty* (Urbana: University of Illinois Press, 1934), p. 111.

17. George Macartney, *An Embassy to China, Being the Journal Kept by Lord Macartney during His Embassy to the Emperor Ch'ien-lung, 1793–1794*, ed. by J. L. Cranmer-Byng (London: Longman's, 1962), p. 125. The lines Macartney quoted are from Milton's *Paradise Lost*, Bk. IV, 35.

18. Until 1328, the Yuan rulers, as *qaghans* (khans), nominally controlled the vast Eurasian empire of the Mongols. However, this was not the same as a Chinese empire. See John W. Dardess, *Conquerors and Confucians: Aspects of Political Change in Late Yuan China* (New York: Columbia University Press, 1973), pp. 157–158.

19. Chia-ch'ing (named Yung-yen) was the son of Ch'ien-lung's favorite concubine, a woman who claimed to be descended from banner

stock but who was probably a Soochow actress in the Imperial Household theater troupe. Chia-ch'ing had been secretly made the heir in 1773.

20. This entire matter is subtly analyzed in David S. Nivison, "Ho-shen and His Accusers: Ideology and Political Behavior in the Eighteenth Century," in David S. Nivison and Arthur F. Wright, eds., *Confucianism in Action* (Stanford: Stanford University Press, 1959), pp. 209–243.

21. The government's suppression of the *T'ien-li-chiao* rebels in Hua-hsien, Honan, did demonstrate continued military vigor. Susan Naquin, "Millenarian Rebellion in China: the Eight Trigrams Uprising of 1813," Ph.D. thesis, Yale University, 1974, p. 354.

VII

The Western Intrusion

The Chinese World Order

THE CHINESE did not stereotype all barbarians in a single undifferentiated category. They were acutely aware of the differences between Mongol khans and Russian tsars or between Javanese tribal chiefs and Dutch merchants. But all barbarians were placed beneath the Chinese in an ideal world order of which their empire was the Central Kingdom (*Chung-kuo*). China alone was thought to represent true civilization; only its ruler, the Son of Heaven, deserved to sit at the apex of the hierarchy of earthly monarchs. Korean kings, Annamese monarchs, and Japanese emperors all ruled in their own right, but within the Confucian hierarchy they were ranked as younger brothers of the Chinese emperor, who was expected to ratify their investitures. Peoples who failed to observe the Confucian rites of monarchy were placed much lower in the hierarchy, so that like a great ladder of being the entire world order descended from higher civilization to the lower rungs of barbarism.

This was an ideal projection since numerous international relationships actually denied China its central place. Japanese emperors were seldom willing to assume a subordinate position, and Mongol khans like Timur the Great (Tamerlane) took murderous umbrage at the condescending tone of Chinese diplomatic despatches. Yet there were enough countries seeking trade and intercourse with China who paid their respects as tributaries to lend credence to the ideal. The Chinese recognized that there were sometimes discrepancies between their idealized hierarchy and the conceptions of

other peoples. Occasionally they adopted a double standard, writing
to bellicose neighbors as equals but inserting the superior form of
address in court versions of such a communiqué. They also learned
to shape their foreign relations according to the cultural amenability
and particular interests of different barbarian groups. Mongols, for
instance, were given preferential treatment by the Manchus who
married into the tribal aristocracy. Envoys from Siam or Cochin
China were handled less familiarly, though they were assumed to
be sensible creatures who understood diplomatic protocol. Maritime
barbarians beyond southeast Asia, on the other hand, were regarded
as the least amenable of all, and were occasionally likened to animals because of their inability to observe the civilities of proper
human intercourse.

China's deprecation of Westerners was understandable, given the
history of its relations with them. Though imperial Romans wore
Han Dynasty silks, the Chinese seldom came into direct contact
with Europeans. Trade was usually conducted through intermediaries: central Asian merchants moving across the steppes from caravanserai to caravanserai, linking China with Persia, or Arab seamen
sailing from Shiraz through the Straits of Malacca to Canton. When
the Mongols unified Eurasia during the Yuan period, it was momentarily possible for merchants like Marco Polo to travel under the
protection of the great khan all the way from the eastern Mediter-
ranean to Peking. But the overland contact was lost under the Ming,
which also refused to admit vessels from abroad unless they were
licensed to carry the tribute of foreign governments. As China sealed
itself off more and more from foreign contacts during the Ming, it
also became increasingly difficult for Europeans even to trade with
China through intermediaries. The Turkish conquest of the Middle
East in the fifteenth century severed relations altogether. With the
Ottoman Empire's navy blocking off the Syrian coastline from European merchantmen, a way would have to be found around that
barrier.

The Turks were the last great wave of conquerors to emerge
from the heartland of Eurasia. After their capture of Constantinople
in 1453, a different sort of military expansion dominated world history. Along the warmer littorals of Eurasia new maritime powers
arose. In the Orient private Chinese traders defied Ming laws to
sail for Japan and Southeast Asia. Sixteen thousand miles away, on
the western margin of that same vast continent, the European mon-
archies began to seek new routes to the East now that the spice

markets of Smyrna were closed to them. The intrepid explorations of the African coastline, the discovery of the Americas, the rounding of the Cape, and eventually the circumnavigation of the globe significantly altered the dimensions of world history.

Portuguese Maritime Power

In this maritime exploration Portugal was the pioneer. Its sturdy carracks outmaneuvered Turkish ships of war, cleared the Indian Ocean of Arab opponents, and soon reached India, searching—in Vasco da Gama's words—for spices and converts. Basing his navy at Goa, Duke Alfonso de Albuquerque proceeded to build a series of impregnable bases along the Asian coastline and from these redoubts dominated Asian waters during the sixteenth century, keeping the sea lanes open for Portuguese merchantmen.

The Portuguese soon found that it was unnecessary for them to press on to the actual Spice Islands of the Molucca chain east of Sumatra. Even before they reached India there already existed an extensive carrying trade between important Asian entrepôts. All the Portuguese had to do was to step into this pre-existing commerce and then use their profits to buy spices from others. When they reached Malacca, for example, they discovered the harbor full of junks laden with Chinese silks and porcelains to be sold for sandalwood, aloe, birds' nests, corymander and other Straits' articles in demand at Canton. Seeing the great profit in this merchandise, the Portuguese followed the junks back to China, sailing with the monsoon to reach the southeastern coast in 1515.

The Ming authorities did not at first accord the Portuguese preferential treatment. Calling the newcomers Franks (*Fo-lang-chi*), imperial officials thought to recognize them as one more species of the familiar freebooters then harrassing the coastline of China from Kwangtung as far north as Shantung. The sixteenth century was the heyday of Asian piracy. Achinese sailors, Japanese *wako* (dwarf bandits), Annamese mercenaries, and Fukienese corsairs preyed upon the sea lanes, occupied island fortresses, issued their own letters of trade, and raided coastal provinces. When Portuguese sailors swooped down upon an undefended Chinese fishing village to loot and pillage like their Frankish namesakes, they appeared no different than Japanese pirates attacking the Yangtze shoreline. The Portuguese did send an embassy to China in 1518, but while the envoy, Tomas Pires, was trying to negotiate a commercial agreement in Peking, the naval commander he had left behind in Canton was proceeding to blockade the port and fire on Chinese warships. The character of these barbarians seemed obvious enough to the irate Ming officials reporting this outrage. The *Fo-lang-chi* were feckless criminals who masqueraded civility while gathering booty.

The Ming met such excesses with severity and firmness. The Portuguese commander had to flee for his life, Pires died in a Chinese prison, and it was decided to refuse the Portuguese trading rights, thereby denying them access to supplies for refurbishing their boats.[1] Driven from the port of Canton, the Portuguese could maintain commercial contact with the Chinese only by setting up illegal camps on tiny islands off the coast. From there they periodically held *leilôes* (fairs), sailing to a deserted stretch of coast and displaying their Straits' goods under a temporary awning for Chinese merchants to come and barter silk. During the next forty years, while the Portuguese perched precariously on the coast, relations with the Ming authorities gradually improved. In 1557 the Portuguese were finally allowed to build a permanent trading post on a tiny finger of land jutting out from Hsiang-shan district south of Canton. This small port eventually became the city of Macao.

The Acquisition of Macao

No one knows why the Chinese decided to let the Portuguese settle Macao. Some sources indicate that the Portuguese were rewarded in this way because they had helped the Chinese combat pirates. Others suggest that the military authorities believed it was preferable to confine these freebooters to a single port, rather than have them ranging up and down the coast as they pleased. The Portuguese may even have bribed the customs officers in Canton. In any case, Macao's territorial status was not clearly defined. The Portuguese colonized the port, but the Chinese did not cede their rights to it and regarded the Macaonese as dwelling there only through Chinese sufferance.[2]

The acquisition of Macao permitted the Portuguese to participate more regularly in the Canton trade fairs. After purchasing a license from the Ming trade superintendent, the Portuguese were allowed to sail up the Pearl River or along the inland waterways once or twice yearly to buy export goods in Canton. The Macaonese slowly prospered from this commerce, and the city became a haven for speculators and adventurers.[3] Ties with the viceroyal administration at Goa in India were tenuous. Macao essentially purchased municipal status and trading rights from the Portuguese crown by supplying Goa with cannons from its foundry, which was one of the best in Asia.

The Japanese Carrying Trade

While the Straits' trade was lucrative, it did not generate the amounts of profit that later built the palatial townhouses of Macao. The Portuguese only struck it rich there when they turned to another kind of carrying trade. For hundreds of years Japanese silver and copper had been imported to China for currency. The Chinese paid for these precious metals with raw silk, which the Japanese bought in large quantities. But formal trading relations between the two countries were severed in the late sixteenth century after the Japanese daimyo Toyotomi Hideyoshi invaded Korea and threatened China. Chinese junks still sailed illegally from Ningpo to Nagasaki and Japanese merchants continued to come to China until 1636, but the prohibition afforded the Portuguese an excellent opportunity. By carrying Cantonese silk to Nagasaki and returning with a cargo of precious metals, a single vessel was able to bring its owners a profit of 250 percent on their capital. Macao immediately prospered. Religious orders invested their endowments in ventures to Japan, and shipowners bid avidly at crown auctions for the right to captain the voyages. Japanese merchants even gave capital to the Portuguese on commission to buy silk for them in Canton, and for several decades money flooded Macao. Then in 1639 the trade was suddenly jeopardized.

In Japan the Tokugawa regime had received reports that the Spanish were planning to attack them from Manila. Dutch Protestant advisers helped convince the Japanese that Spain's imperialism was motivated by its Catholic zeal to convert infidels. The Tokugawa government had already become alarmed by Catholic proselytism in Japan. In 1637, after the Tokugawa proscribed Christianity, native Catholics revolted in Shimabara. The rebellion had been put down with considerable bloodshed and great difficulty, leaving the Japanese government resolved to expel all foreign Catholics from its country. As a result the Portuguese were told in 1639 that their trading rights had been rescinded and were peremptorily ordered to leave Nagasaki.

Macao's Economic Decline

The Macaonese were determined to let the Japanese know that they shared none of Spain's dreams of an East Asian empire. A large embassy was therefore dispatched to Japan to convince the government that the Portuguese were interested only in peaceful trade. But the Tokugawa regime had already proclaimed the expulsion order. When the 61 Portuguese envoys landed at Nagasaki in 1640, they were treated as criminals who had disobeyed the law, and the entire embassy was summarily executed. Thenceforth, the only Europeans allowed to trade with the Japanese were the Dutch, and the Macaonese were forced to give up their carrying trade. As the source of such great profits dried up, Macao slowly lost its commercial luster. Although its merchants returned to the Straits trade and Macao later served as an opium entrepôt, those enterprises failed to compensate for the lost Canton-Nagasaki trade.

Nonetheless, Macao continued to be an important enclave for Westerners, and it was especially crucial as a stepping-off point for missionaries hoping to enter the Central Kingdom. It was in Macao, for example, that Jesuit scholars like Matteo Ricci (1552–1610) studied classical Chinese in order to become mathematicians and astronomers at the Ming and Ch'ing courts. Most of these Catholic missionaries genuinely admired China and tried to make their religion palatable to the Chinese by declaring that ethical Confucianism was compatible with Christianity. Seeing China from the vantage point of Peking, where they were treated as savants by the literati, the Jesuits sent glowing descriptions of Chinese civilization back to Europe. Their image of China greatly influenced the European enlightenment, and philosophers like Quesnay and Voltaire insisted that such a deistic meritocracy should be a model for the West. Macao played an important part in transmitting such news of China to Europe, but its cultural function hardly made up for the city's material losses after the Portuguese were expelled from Japan. Gradually Macao faded into only a shadow of its former self.

The Dutch Challenge

As the Portuguese position in Asia weakened, Dutch fortunes rose. Netherlandish merchants turned to Asian trade during their wars with Spain in the late sixteenth century. After 1580, when Spain annexed Portugal, the Dutch became increasingly restive with the Portuguese spice monopoly and in 1594 they were completely excluded from the Lisbon spice market. Already noted for their maritime skills, the Dutch formed a United Netherlands East India Company in 1600 to challenge the Portuguese domination of Asian waters. As an incorporated company, the Dutch E.I.C. was inclined to pursue profits more consistently than the Portuguese, who sporadically financed individual voyages. Nor were the Dutch interested in sharing the Asian carrying trade. They were determined to reach and dominate the Spice Islands, and once that goal was accomplished they turned to colonization, penetrating inland from the coasts that Portuguese vessels only visited. By 1619 the Dutch had begun to settle the island of Java, establishing their company headquarters at Batavia. Whereas Duke Albuquerque had constructed maritime fortresses a century earlier, Jan Coen founded a Dutch empire in southeast Asia. He and his successors pitted one native prince against another until the Netherlands had colonized the Indonesian archipelago, establishing a dominion that lasted until the end of World War II.

The Dutch were also the only Europeans who continued to trade legally with Japan after the Tokugawa exclusion acts of 1633–1639. From Japan they hoped to establish contacts with China. Formosa (Taiwan) soon attracted their attention, and the Dutch built a fort and trading post called Zeelandia on the southern tip of the island in 1634. The trading factory on Formosa, which was then inhabited by aborigines, tried to trade systematically with the Fukienese at Amoy, but the Manchu conquest of China had disrupted regular commercial relations. As the Manchus moved south, they drove the Ming loyalist and pirate chief Coxinga from his mainland harbors to seek refuge in Formosa. Expelling the Dutch from Zeelandia, Coxinga then made the island his own base. Soon the Dutch turned to the new Ch'ing Dynasty to oppose this mutual enemy, offering their ships to help destroy Coxinga's regime on Formosa. A tentative agreement was reached whereby the Dutch would receive trading rights at Amoy in exchange for military aid to the Ch'ing. But a series of misunderstandings and misfortunes kept the alliance from materializing. The Ch'ing eventually did defeat the pirates' navy and occupied Taiwan in 1683, but they were in no way bound to extend trading rights to the Netherlands. Instead, they compelled the Dutch to approach China on tributary terms, sending missions to the court at Peking in the manner of Korean or Southeast Asian client states. Although the Dutch were extremely successful at this kind of diplomacy, they were never able to establish as extensive and continuous a trading relationship with the Ch'ing as did the English at Canton.

The English East India Company

English seapower emerged from the privateering of Sir Francis Drake and Sir John Hawkins. But its major impetus toward Asia came from the struggles of select groups of merchants to acquire trading monopolies from Queen Elizabeth. After the powerful London Company of Merchant Adventurers lost access to Antwerp during the Netherlands wars and was expelled from the German empire in 1597, the English grew increasingly envious of Dutch mercantile successes. On December 31, 1599, the London merchants received a royal charter from Elizabeth giving them the right to monopolize all trade in the East Indies. The 218 merchants who invested £72,000 in this venture had no way of knowing that their East India Company would eventually become a state within a state, governing India as a company colony. For the moment, they were merely in competition with the Dutch to break the Portuguese spice monopoly.

At first the Protestant Dutch and English cooperated against the Catholic Portuguese, but individual trading interests soon dissolved this confederation. In 1623 English pride and profit in Asia suffered a decisive blow. That year Dutch forces massacred the English East India Company factors on Amboyna Island near Sumatra and sealed off the Spice Islands from English access. The E.I.C. furiously pressed for retaliation by the English government, but their request was rejected by James I who was hoping for a military alliance with the Netherlands.

The East India Company's dependence upon a crown monopoly made it vulnerable to English as well as foreign competitors. During the English civil war period, the E.I.C. found temporary shelter under Cromwell's wing, but other companies, jealous of the London Merchant Adventurers, constantly tried to interlope upon the Asian trade. At times there were even two competing East India companies, each claiming an exclusive monopoly. After 1660, however, the original E.I.C. stabilized its position, thanks to the support of Charles II. In fact, when the Stuart monarch married Catherine of Braganza in 1661, the Portuguese princess' dowry included Bombay, which gave the E.I.C. India's best harbor.

India was a major source of goods for the E.I.C. now that the Dutch had excluded the English from Indonesia. The E.I.C. factory at Surat north of Bombay was also a convenient place to outfit vessels before sending them on speculation to China. But until 1685 England's commercial relations with China were quite irregular. Canton was at first closed to the English because the Macaonese had bribed the customs officials there to turn away competitors.[4] The E.I.C. reception at other entrepôts like Amoy or Ningpo depended upon the corruptibility of port officials. For the Manchus, like the Ming, were determined to extirpate piracy by sealing off the coast and prohibiting foreign trade. Every time an English boat appeared in a Chinese harbor, it was legally regarded to be smuggling, and the local magistrate or prefect had to be bribed to turn his back on the trade.

Commerce was so uncertain that the E.I.C. decided to try to find Chinese silks and porcelains in other Asian ports. Tonkin proved to be an expensive disappointment, and the English turned to Formosa where they supplied Coxinga's heir with supplies and arms in hopes of acquiring trading privileges once his pirates recovered the Fukienese coast. But the English had chosen a loser, and when the Ch'ing navies recovered Taiwan in 1683, they expected to be denied entry to China altogether. They were elated, however, to be told in 1685 that K'ang-hsi had authorized foreign commerce and that E.I.C. vessels could call at Chinese ports along the southern coast.[5]

Multiport Trading

During the multiport trading years from 1685 to 1760, the English purchased mainly silks, porcelains and medicine—all high-cost goods for which there was a luxury market at home. They tried to pay for these items with English woolens, but there was little demand for such cloth by the Chinese, who preferred silk floss insulation even during cold Peking winters. Consequently, the English trade was mainly financed with Indian imports, Straits' goods, and specie.

Multiport trading theoretically provided English buyers with a bargaining edge. If Chinese merchants hiked prices in one port, E.I.C. vessels would call elsewhere. However, this edge was blunted insofar as the English were limited to entrepôts where the Chinese dealers possessed capital enough to stock in a large supply of goods in advance. Moreover, several major Chinese ports were dominated by single monopoly merchants who tried to set prices as high as possible. The English called these brokers "king's merchants" because they were usually speculators who had bought a monopoly trading license from one of K'ang-hsi's many sons. Returning to Ningpo or Amoy, the king's merchant used his license to cow the customs official into recognizing the monopoly. But, having spent most of his money on the royal patent, the king's merchant either lacked the capital to set in goods or else fixed ridiculously high prices in an effort to quickly recover his original investment.

In the early 1700s, when the king's merchants made their appearance, the only city that could resist the monopolists was Canton, where the hoppo (customs officer) had direct access to the emperor and could afford to ignore a princely patent, and where the well established Cohong (foreign trade guild) was wealthy enough to capitalize foreign trade on its own. Thus even though the English had multiport trading rights, they called less and less frequently upon Fukien or Chekiang and gravitated entirely to Canton. Simultaneously, a special set of trading relationships and regulations, known then as the "Canton system," slowly took shape on the Chinese side.

The Canton System

Peculage fees and excise duties were fixed, and their collection was guaranteed by the Cohong merchants. Like the E.I.C., the Cantonese Cohong held a state monopoly in foreign trade. But it lacked the corporate strength and legal protection of the London Merchant Adventurers and was as much designed to ensure tariffs as to serve the guildsmen's economic interests. After 1736 each member of the Cohong was forced to become a government security merchant, which meant assuming responsibility for the foreigners' behavior.[6] If a fracas broke out between E.I.C. sailors and the Cantonese, and the foreigners slipped away on the next tide, the security merchant responsible for that particular vessel had to answer to the authorities. This public security device soon became a way for the hoppo to squeeze money out of Cohong members. Every time a foreigner broke the law, the hapless security merchant was ordered to appear before the hoppo and was fined, perhaps as much as two hundred thousand taels. Pleading bankruptcy, the Chinese merchants could beg the English for help. But if the E.I.C. failed him, his only recourse was the usurer—often an Indian Parsi or Scottish money-lender who was likely to charge stupendous rates of interest. Membership in the Cohong was thus fraught with risk, and some merchants tried to withdraw. The hoppo refused to accept such resignations, and insolvency became more and more common.

The Flint Episode

The English watched these developments with increasing concern. Their only defense against the hoppo was to appeal to the governor or the governor-general to intercede. By the 1740s, however, the emperor had forbidden such officials to challenge the hoppo's management of foreign affairs, and the E.I.C. could turn to no one if a particularly greedy Imperial Household official was appointed chief of the Canton customs.[7] In desperation, the English tried to go back to multiport trading, but merchants elsewhere were short on capital, and the port officials of Ningpo and Amoy turned out to be even more rapacious than the hoppo. The E.I.C. factors seemed to have only one recourse left. Ignorant of the hoppo's position in the Imperial Household, the English decided to appeal to the Ch'ien-lung Emperor himself. Influenced by Chinese diplomatic rhetoric which promised to "nourish the men from afar," a company translator named James Flint sailed to Tientsin in 1759 and handed officials there a painfully written memorial in Chinese to be submitted to Peking.

When Flint's memorial arrived, Ch'ien-lung was aghast at the barbarians' brashness. Foreigners had long been forbidden to learn

Chinese, since classical literacy was itself a form of power—a lesson
the Manchus knew better than anyone. In addition, the right to
memorialize was a jealously guarded prerogative of top officials. To
petition the emperor without permission was proof of how little
the barbarians knew of the necessity for maintaining appropriate
relationships between superior and inferior. Ch'ien-lung consequently ordered that Flint be banished, his Chinese tutors executed,
responsible Cohong merchants interrogated, and all future English
trade restricted to the single port of Canton.

Restriction to Canton

During the period from 1760 to 1833 the E.I.C. traded solely
at Canton, where commerce settled into an even more fixed routine.
Wintering in Macao, the factors returned to Canton when the huge
E.I.C. cargo ships arrived from England or India. During lading
time, the company merchants lived with all the other Western
traders in the "thirteen factories," a row of warehouses, offices, and
residences walled into a thin strip along the Canton waterfront. On
Sundays and holidays the Europeans were permitted brief excursions
to fixed points of interest, but the rest of the time was spent in this
guarded compound southwest of the city walls.

Sheer physical restriction accounted for some of the English
annoyance with the Canton system. But other factors contributed
to the dissatisfaction as well. The Jesuits' glowing image of China
had been colored by the splendor of the Ch'ing court. Company
factors, on the other hand, viewed the Central Kingdom through
the hubbub and squalor of the Cantonese waterfront, where they
had to deal with venal officials and obsequious merchants. There
the factory walls kept them from seeing much more of China than
joss houses and singsong girls. And just as stifling were the administrative restrictions. After the Flint episode the Europeans were
not only denied the right to appeal to higher authorities; they
could not even communicate directly with the hoppo. All requests
had to be phrased deferentially and then tendered to the hoppo
through the Cohong. The Chinese intermediaries then passed back
down an answer, phrased in language the English felt to be depre-
cating. It was bad enough—factors felt—to risk China fever and
the gout by coming to Canton, but it was even worse to be contemp-
tuously called "barbarian headmen" every time they asked for a

tariff reduction. Besides, this sort of indirect communication often meant no real answer at all to serious requests. That was why the Earl of Macartney was sent to Peking in 1793. The E.I.C. hoped that an ambassador from the Court of Saint James would obtain a hearing in Peking to help put English and Chinese relations on a more equal footing.

The Macartney mission was a deep disappointment. Most of the discussion between Macartney and his Chinese hosts concerned protocol. The Ch'ing officials insisted that the English ambassador had to observe tributary ritual by conducting the kowtow (*k'e-t'ou*, three kneelings and nine prostrations) in front of the Ch'ien-lung Emperor. Macartney felt that act would only confirm Chinese prejudices toward the lowly English barbarians and would gravely belittle an envoy from King George III. A compromise was finally reached when Macartney agreed to bend his knee, but both parties were so exhausted by this exchange that other issues were never resolved. The English tried to approach Peking again in 1816, sending Lord Amherst to the Ch'ing court. His embassy did not even get as far as Macartney's. The kowtow dispute became so acrimonious that Amherst left Peking without even seeing the Chia-ch'ing Emperor. Nothing, it appeared, would ever relieve the Company's discomfort in Canton. Yet the E.I.C. could hardly afford to pack up and pull out. By the early nineteenth century the nature of its economic relationship with China had changed in such a way that it was almost impossible to think of ever extricating the company from the Canton trade.

Tea

The reason for this growing entanglement in the Canton system can be summed up in a single word—tea. England's early trade with China had dealt in what were essentially luxury items and medicinal herbs. One of the latter happened to be tea leaves, which appealed to the English taste. In the eighteenth century tea gradually became a national beverage, until the average London worker spent 5 percent of his total household budget to purchase it. Instead of importing Chinese goods which only the wealthy could afford, the E.I.C. found itself merchandising a product comparable to tobacco which everyone consumed.

As the English demand for tea rose, the volume of East India

Company cargoes from China multiplied sevenfold. By 1800 the company was investing £4,000,000 a year in teas, and the China trade had become a major source of revenue for the English government which imposed 100 percent excise duties on the E.I.C. tea imports. The crown was so eager for this revenue that it required the E.I.C. to store a year's supply of tea in case the China trade should be temporarily disturbed. The company itself competed with interlopers and smugglers for the English domestic market, attempting to drive them out of business by cornering as much tea as possible in Canton. Each year before the actual trading season began in Canton, the E.I.C. factors there advanced money to Cohong merchants to secure future tea orders from the wholesalers in Fukien, Kiangsi, and Anhwei. The only collateral which the East India Company had for these advances was the individual security merchant's continued solvency. Having given a Cohong broker tens of thousands of ounces of silver, the company simply could not risk letting that merchant go bankrupt when squeezed by the hoppo. In a sense, then, the Chinese broker was a surrogate for the English monopolists—every fine he paid the hoppo came directly or indirectly out of the E.I.C. treasury.

Yet now more than ever before the E.I.C. could not afford to give up the tea trade. The company's conquest of India, begun at the battle of Plassey in 1757, was a costly venture, financed with loans from the English crown. By the early 1800s the E.I.C. debt had grown to £28,000,000, and the only way to repay these vast sums was by means of a triangular trade between India, China, and England. Twenty-seven million pounds a year of raw Indian cotton were shipped from Calcutta to Canton, where they were used in the cottage textile industry. The cash profits from the sale of Indian cotton were then used by the E.I.C. to buy the tea leaves sold in England. Thus it was the Canton trade which provided a vehicle for conveying the company's profits back to London, where its debts had been incurred.

The E.I.C. was not the sole commercial agent in this triangular trade. Private Indian firms called "agency houses" actually exported the cotton to China. Dominated by Parsi and Scottish financiers, the agency houses had begun by conducting a "country trade" with the Malaysian principalities and then expanded into Cantonese commerce. The Straits' goods, European clockworks (sing-songs), and Indian cotton which they sold to the Chinese netted a considerable profit in silver, but the agency houses were prevented by the E.I.C.

monopoly from investing it in tea themselves. Instead they exchanged their cash in Canton for E.I.C. bills of credit redeemed in London. The E.I.C., in turn, used the specie to buy the teas that were sent back to England. It was the agency houses, therefore, which enabled the E.I.C. to repay its debt to the British crown.

The country trade in Indian cotton did not alone suffice to generate enough cash to buy all the tea the E.I.C. required. The agency houses' cash had to be supplemented by importing silver bullion into China from the mines of Peru and Mexico. During the eighteenth century tens of millions of silver dollars flowed from the dominions of New Spain into China's coastal ports. But ironically the tea trade ended by sabotaging this supply of bullion. In 1773 the E.I.C. overstocked its tea supplies for the domestic English market, and then persuaded Pitt's government to allow it to extend the company monopoly to the American colonies. The ensuing Boston Tea Party helped provoke the American Revolution, which cut England off from the Mexican silver supply. Lacking the bullion to pay for tea, the E.I.C. depended all the more upon the agency houses to provide goods for the Chinese to buy with specie. Yet at the same time, Indian cotton imports began to decline because northern Chinese merchants had begun shipping their cotton south to Canton by sea, underselling the Indian product and forcing the agency houses to seek other Indian goods the Chinese might buy. As it turned out, there was only one item which the Chinese wished to purchase in sufficient quantities to keep the tea trade going, and that was the addictive drug opium.

Opium

Opium had been used as a medicine in China for over a thousand years. When the Dutch introduced tobacco to the Fukienese, the Chinese learned to mix it with opium and smoked crude distillations of the drug. During the eighteenth century a purer form of opium smoking slowly spread through the empire despite official prohibitions of the practice. Then in the later 1700s the use of opium increased sharply. The opium smokers' escape into the dreamy stupor of addiction may have been an evasion from the social pressures of the later Ch'ien-lung reign. But, more decisively no doubt, the increase in demand accompanied a growing availability of the supply, due to the opium monopoly of the East India Company.

Aware that the drug sold well in Malaysia and China, the governor-general of India, Warren Hastings, decided in 1773 to establish an E.I.C. opium monopoly in Bengal. This Patna opium was then the finest quality in the world. Indian peasant tenants were encouraged by the E.I.C. to plant poppies and sell the raw treacle to company refineries outside of Calcutta. Production increased as the Cantonese market for opium expanded, but because the Chinese government reiterated its prohibition of opium smoking in 1796, the E.I.C. was afraid to export it directly to China. Instead the refined opium was sold to the agency houses which marketed the drug in Canton, using their proceeds to fund the company's trade in tea.

During the early nineteenth century opium sales in Canton rose in three dramatic leaps. The first occurred in 1815 when the E.I.C. lowered the price of Patna opium. The second, in 1830, was the result of the company's decision to allow Malwa opium, privately grown in western India, to pass through Bombay to China for a transit fee. The final leap in 1834 was the highest of all because that year the E.I.C. lost its monopoly on the China trade and private investments soared. From 16,000 chests[8] of opium unloaded in Canton, sales jumped the following year to 27,000 chests, worth 17,000,000 silver dollars to the English, Parsis, and Americans[9] who sold the drug. What had begun as a supplement to Indian cotton had now turned into the staple of the country trade. Indeed, opium—the most valuable commercial crop in the world—had become the basis of almost all commerce with China, where demand for the drug was so great that silver bullion began to flow out of the country. During the first decade of the nineteenth century, for instance, China's balance of trade was so favorable that 26,000,000 silver dollars were imported into the empire. As opium consumption rose in the decade of the 1830s, 34,000,000 silver dollars were shipped out of the country to pay for the drug.

These statistics, however important they may be, seem bloodless beside the day-to-day specifics of the trade—specially built and heavily armed agency house ships sailing swiftly toward China from the Calcutta opium auctions, fortified hulks in the mouth of the Pearl River where the drug was transshipped into multi-oared "fast crabs" and "scrambling dragons" crewed by fierce Tanka pirates, upriver landing depots where bribed or cowed police patrols permitted the chests to be unloaded and wholesaled to the opium den owners. By 1835 a vast and illegal distribution network moved the opium from Calcutta up the river and canal networks of China into the heartland of the northern plain.

As their profits soared, Western merchants did have some moral misgivings about the drug traffic. They were also embarrassed by public opinion at home. Missionaries in Canton wrote of emaciated addicts, broken families, and the mortal toll of heavy opium smoking. But in England there were numerous ways of justifying this trade. Apologists insisted that the Western drug dealers were no more reprehensible than gin merchants. They supplied a product which the Chinese wished in the first place. Concealing the fact that they distributed free supplies of the drug to encourage addiction, the dealers insisted that if the Chinese really did not want to have opium sold on their shores, they would do something effective to prevent its entry. The same dealers who bribed Chinese naval patrols to let them unload the drug used the corruption they engendered as an excuse for continuing to flood the central kingdom with Indian opium. And their government continued to support them. For it was opium which bought the tea that serviced the E.I.C.'s debts and paid the duties of the British crown, providing one-sixth of England's national revenue. Moral scruples bent easily before this kind of cost accounting.

Chinese prejudices about the barbarians were confirmed by this vast drug traffic. Its extent was truly staggering. Although no one knew for sure how many people actually smoked opium, the Chinese estimated in 1820 that the city of Soochow alone had 100,000 addicts.[10] Whatever the real figures, opium smoking was a highly visible vice by then—practiced in urban centers by those with enough leisure and income to afford their habits: petty gentry, yamen clerks, even policemen and soldiers. Confucian political writers, alarmed by China's increasing commercial contacts with the West, had already tagged Christianity as a barbarian toxin, spiritually poisoning the body politic. Now opium appeared to materialize that menace, and it was even thought to be designed to weaken the Chinese for foreign conquest.

Opium was also identified with China's increasing economic difficulties. By the early 1800s gentry tax evasion had already increased the financial burdens of the peasantry. The opium trade seemed to exacerbate their economic hardship all the more, because the loss of silver bullion apparently increased the actual amount of taxes which farmers had to pay. Chinese currency was bimetallic, with copper cash used for small payments and silver for larger transactions. Peasants remitted their taxes in copper cash, but the government quota was assessed in silver. Even though the tax quota was reasonably constant, the ratio between the two currencies fluctuated to the taxpayer's detriment, that is, the exchange rate was supposedly 1,000 copper cash for each ounce (tael) of silver, but there were no government controls and the price of silver varied according to demand. In the view of contemporary Chinese economists, the unfavorable balance of trade was making silver scarcer, and therefore dearer, within China. As the exchange rates altered, 1,500 or even 1,600 pieces of copper were needed to buy one ounce of silver.[11] This meant that peasants were paying as much as 50 or 60 percent more copper to meet the same silver tax quota as before. It was thus believed that opium was costing China far more than the health of its addicts—it was undermining the agrarian foundations of the entire society.

Legalization versus Enforcement

Ch'ing officials who had supervised the foreign trade in Canton hoped to remedy this situation by having the drug sold under a government monopoly. After all, they argued, forceful measures to stamp out the opium traffic had already proved to be ineffective. Conscientious governor-generals like Juan Yuan had managed in 1821 to drive the dealers off the streets of Macao and into the fortified opium hulks in the Pearl River delta. But even when Chinese drug dealers were arrested and addicts were threatened with severe punishment, opium imports continued to rise. So much money was involved that it seemed virtually impossible to keep law enforcement officers from becoming corrupted. Why not legalize the drug under government control and prevent silver from being exported by trading Chinese goods in barter for Indian opium? This would redress the currency balance as well as provide a major source of revenue for the regime.

It would not, however, solve the problem of addiction. Knowing the effects of opium smoking on his subjects, the Tao-kuang Emperor (reigned 1821–1850) could not countenance the prospect of government owned divans (opium dens) selling "foreign mud." Other alternatives would have to be explored. Obviously, officials so far had only struck at the nearest branches of the drug trade by arresting Chinese dealers. The trunk would have to be severed at its roots in order to cut off the foreign supply of opium, even if that meant seizing Western merchants and provoking armed resistance. With that strategy in mind, Tao-kuang decided in December, 1838, to dispatch a special commissioner to Canton. Lin Tse-hsu, one of the most capable officials in the realm, was invested as a plenipotentiary and ordered to do whatever he deemed necessary to end the drug traffic forever. When Lin left his sovereign in Peking and departed on the long journey south, neither man could guess that this meant the advent of war.

Notes

1. During the sixteenth-century pirate attacks the government in Peking periodically determined to forbid all foreign trade in the belief that the coast could be sealed off against barbarians. Provincial officials often argued against such a policy on the grounds that the inhabitants of Chekiang, Fukien, and Kwangtung made their living by fishing and trade. The ban on trade and navigation was thus temporarily lifted in 1567, though it was reimposed at the end of the century because of the Japanese attack on Korea.

2. Over three centuries later, at a time when China was beset by many European powers, the Ch'ing government was forced to cede Macao to Portugal. The protocol and treaty were negotiated by J. D. Campbell of the Imperial Maritime Customs in 1887.

3. It was also a haven for religious and political exiles. Macao was off limits to the Inquisition, so that would-be victims of the *auto da fé* found it a congenial part of the Hispanic world to inhabit. Others, like the great poet Luiz de Camões, were exiled there.

4. The first English expedition to China reached Canton in 1637 under the command of Captain John Weddell, who fought his way up the Pearl River.

5. A year earlier the K'ang-hsi Emperor had decided to legalize trade because he believed that the prohibition merely benefitted provincial officials who connived at smuggling for their own profit. He also viewed this commerce as a valuable source of imperial income and made certain that his Imperial Household officials were appointed to customs posts.

6. The security merchant (*fiador*) is first mentioned in the chronicles of the E.I.C. on December 4, 1736, but the security merchant system was not formally spelled out by the hoppo until 1754.

7. Each hoppo had a three-year term of office, for which he paid a large sum in Peking. It was rumored in Canton that it took a hoppo one year's worth of squeeze to recover his investment and a further year to meet the emperor's quota. The final, third year's take was his own to keep.

8. Each chest contained about 145 pounds of the drug.

9. Boston and Salem merchants developed their own source of supply in Smyrna and Anatolia. Turkish opium was not as powerful as Patna, but it was superior to Chinese forms of the drug and usually sold well.

10. Later in the nineteenth century, as much as 10 percent of China's total population may have used the drug. See Jonathan D. Spence, "Opium Smoking in Ch'ing China," in Frederic Wakeman, Jr., and Carolyn Grant, eds., *Conflict and Control in Late Imperial China* (Berkeley and Los Angeles: University of California Press, 1975).

11. This was not the sole cause of inflation. The government began minting cheaper copper currency at this time. Gresham's law prevailed, and the bad money drove out the good which was smelted privately and sold for its real value.

VIII

Invasion and Rebellion

Lin Tse-hsu's Efforts to Halt the Opium Traffic

LIN TSE-HSU—the Tao-kuang Emperor's designee in 1838 to halt the opium traffic—had a morally impeccable and politically brilliant civil service record. A full governor-general by the age of thirty-five, Lin was already laden with honors for his fiscal reforms in Kiangnan and his pacification of rebels in Kiangsi. An acknowledged expert in Chinese statecraft, he moved in the capital's most dazzling cultural circles, and attracted a coterie of promising young re-formers.[1] At the time of the opium legalization debates, it was Lin who grasped the essential points of the controversy most easily and who, in an unusual series of private interviews with the emperor, radiated the most assurance that this poisonous habit could be eradicated from China. His straightforward advice urged the emperor to attack the opium problem on three fronts simultaneously. Addicts had to be threatened with severe penalties until they gave up the habit and were then provided with medical care to ease their withdrawal. Chinese drug dealers had to be rounded up and punished until the domestic distribution network was completely smashed. And foreign suppliers had to be discouraged from smug-gling opium into China by confiscating their stores of the drug and by forcing them to sign bonds of good conduct.

The first two goals were quickly and effectively realized once Lin reached Canton in March, 1839. Addicts in Kwangtung were singled out for drug cures in special sanitariums and, had Lin's policy been continued by his successors, opium consumption would no doubt have declined measurably. At the same time 1,600 violaters were arrested and most Chinese dealers were driven underground. Commissioner Lin's crackdown was so effective, in fact, that foreign dealers found it impossible to sell their stocks of opium, even at extremely low prices. Yet Lin knew that his success would be only temporary if the Western smugglers were not also forced out of business. He was confident of his ability to do just that for three reasons.

First, Lin Tse-hsu—a devoted Confucianist himself—assumed that the Westerners could not fail to recognize the superior moral position of the Chinese on this issue. His famous letter[2] to Queen Victoria demonstrated his belief that the English must be secretly ashamed of their involvement in the drug traffic. Second, Lin realized how distant Europe was, and therefore supposed that by controlling the seacoast the Chinese could force the Westerners either to cooperate in exchange for water and provisions, or else sail back to their faroff lands in defeat.[3] Finally, he knew that the Westerners were all ensconced in a single vulnerable spot on the Cantonese waterfront. Remembering the Napier incident,[4] he was sure that the foreign factories could easily be cut off from allies at sea, turning the English and American merchants into virtual hostages of the Chinese.

The first two of these assumptions were fallacious. English embarrassment over the drug traffic was more than compensated for by their smug nationalism and economic convictions. It was easy for Westerners to deride the Chinese concept of a hierarchical world order under the Son of Heaven as a parochial pretension ill suited to an era of powerful nation states. China's non-negotiable tariffs and protective customs barriers also seemed obscurantist and backward in an age of free trade. The E.I.C. had been content to accept the restrictions of the Canton system because China afforded a valuable supply of goods like tea. But now the E.I.C. monopoly was abolished and China was being viewed by restless country traders and Manchester industrialists as a potential market. To Midlands manufacturers struggling against German competitors for the European market, China seemed to offer boundless economic opportunities. English free traders speculated eagerly about how many English textiles 400 million customers would purchase—certainly enough to keep the looms of Manchester humming for decades. No matter that China was economically autarkic. The image of all those consumers inspired the free traders to urge the English government to break down the tariff barriers at Canton and widen their entryways into this huge potential market. Such economic liberalism was just as morally fervent as Lin Tse-hsu's disgust over the iniquities of the opium trade.

Commissioner Lin's assumption about the maritime barbarians' dependence upon Chinese supplies was equally mistaken. Unlike Portugal in the 1500s, England could rely upon the Indian subcontinent a relatively short sailing distance away. There, garrisons,[5] warships, and provisions could all be mustered in the event of war with China. And while England's strength was obviously sea power, her soldiers, hardened in the Napoleonic Wars, were trained to fight in ways and with weapons that were markedly superior to Chinese military devices.

Despite England's strategical superiority, Lin Tse-hsu did have a momentary tactical advantage in the vulnerability of the foreign factories at Canton. The British superintendent of trade, Captain Charles Elliot, was made painfully aware of this on March 24, 1839, when Lin backed up his demand that the Westerners surrender their opium by surrounding the factories with Ch'ing troops. Without major forces at his command and frightened that the Chinese might massacre the 350 European and American merchants in the factory area, Elliot promised to reimburse the major opium dealers if they turned their drug stocks over to the Chinese commissioner. The country firms had not sold a chest of opium for five months and were thus delighted with the arrangement. Some even sent for more opium from India in order to get as much money as possible out of the British crown. Elliot's expensive capitulation was to anger Queen Victoria, but it earned him the gratitude of the English traders[6] and the momentary respect of Commissioner Lin.

Lin Tse-hsu was elated by his temporary success. Maintaining the blockade until he was satisfied that all the drug supplies had been relinquished, the imperial commissioner had his men destroy the opium in salt-and-lime pits outside of the Bogue entrance to Canton's inner harbors. By June 25, over 21,000 chests (2.6 million pounds) of opium had been washed away. True to his word, Lin pulled back his troops and the Westerners fled from Canton to Macao.

The seizure of the opium stocks was only one aspect of Commissioner Lin's plan to cut off the foreign sources of the drug. To make sure that the country firms refrained from renewing their supplies in the future, Lin proposed to have the foreigners sign bonds promising never to deal in "foreign mud" again. This would render Westerners liable to prosecution under Chinese law if they were caught breaking the guarantee.

While trapped in Canton, Elliot had seen no alternative but to turn over the opium on hand. But, free in Macao, he was not prepared to subject his charges to Chinese law. The Europeans had already experienced legal difficulties with the Cantonese authorities, whose concept of justice seemed based as much on the principle of retribution as on the fixing of guilt. In 1784, for instance, a gunner aboard the naval vessel *Lady Hughes* accidentally killed a Chinese in an artillery salute. Though the Cohong security merchants assured the English that their magistrates would regard the case as one of accidental manslaughter, the sailor was executed after being remanded for punishment. To the Western trading community this smacked of *lex talionis*, an eye for an eye. By signing the opium bonds, the foreigners would be voluntarily submitting to a judicial system in which they all lacked confidence, just at the very moment when many hoped for a consular system of extraterritorial legal jurisdiction to protect their interests.[7] Elliot agreed with these sentiments and so refused Lin Tse-hsu's command to sign the bonds. When the Chinese commissioner retaliated by forbidding all foreign trade, the English decided to boycott the port, expecting that Lin would eventually be replaced by an official more sympathetic to their commercial interests. In the meantime, they would remain in Macao and weather the storm as pleasantly as possible.

Commissioner Lin was obliged to refuse the English that comfort. Personally leading troops to Macao, he convinced the Portuguese governor, Don Adriao Accacio da Silveira Pinto, to expel the English, who took to their boats and anchored offshore of Hong Kong. Lin then proceeded to the next stage of his strategy by ordering his naval forces to keep the English from landing for food and water. This provoked the first shots of the yet undeclared Opium War. When the English ships' stores ran out on September 4, 1839, Elliot ordered a supply party ashore under the guns of the warship *Volage*, which fired on the Chinese forces camped at Kowloon. Less than two months later, on November 3, 1839, the British and Chinese clashed again near the Bogue forts. This engagement was much more serious and cost the Chinese four war junks. The very next day in London, quite ignorant of this latest incident, the English foreign minister, Lord Palmerston, ordered the Admiralty to send a naval expedition to China.

Palmerston's decision was not universally applauded. Public opinion was split by the opium issue, and far from all Englishmen agreed with the Whig government's aggressive policy in China. But there existed a powerful China lobby in London, funded by the Canton country firms and Midlands free traders, which vociferously argued that Chinese arrogance knew no bounds and would have to be severely punished. For them, Lin's blockade of the factories provided a perfect *casus belli* to enable them to win so many of the concessions they had long been demanding from the Chinese: a moderate fixed tariff, diplomatic equality, a territorial base somewhere on the Chinese coastline, new ports of trade, and perhaps even the right to extraterritoriality. All of these goals suited Palmerston's view of imperial England's place in the world, especially when he added to them a stiff indemnity to cover the cost of the opium which Elliot had surrendered. Nevertheless, the Tory opposition continued to bridle at supporting a war fought to defend opium smugglers, and Palmerston and his supporters were able to win only a narrow margin of confidence in Parliament.

The Opium War

The Opium War (1839–1842) passed through two distinct phases. The first, under Captain Elliot's command, lasted until the summer of 1841 and resulted in an abortive peace. The second, begun in the spring of 1842 by a new leader, Henry Pottinger, ended with the defeat of China. During the first phase Elliot sailed north, taking the island of Chusan near Ningpo before reaching the Taku forts not far from Tientsin and the capital. The appearance of enemy vessels in the North China Sea alarmed the court, which until then had been receiving favorable military reports from Canton. Furious at Lin Tse-hsu for misleading him, the Tao-kuang Emperor appointed a new commissioner named Ch'i-shan. Commissioner Ch'i-shan met Elliot at Taku and readily persuaded him that his demands would be granted if the English sailed back to Canton and negotiated with him there. Impressed by Ch'i-shan's amiability, Elliot returned to the South, where the two men agreed upon the Convention of Chuenpi in January, 1841. But their respective masters—Palmerston in England and the Tao-kuang Emperor in Peking—refused to accept the terms of the convention. Palmerston felt that Elliot had failed to obey the spirit of his instructions because he had not received a sufficiently large indemnity from the Chinese, and because he had exchanged Chusan for the rocky and arid island of Hong Kong. Tao-kuang, on the other hand, could not forgive Ch'i-shan for agreeing to cede Chinese territory at all, and readily believed the false rumors from Canton that his commissioner had been bribed by the English. Both officials were punished—Elliot by being stripped of his command and Ch'i-shan by having his fortune confiscated after being brought back to Peking in chains.

The second phase of the war, under Pottinger's command, was a more thoroughly planned military venture. Pottinger's strategy was based on the advice of the London China lobby to cut the empire in two at the Yangtze, sealing off the North from the tribute grain of central and south China. English troops and vessels gathered at Canton during the latter part of 1841, before moving slowly north. After a bloody barrage, Chusan was recaptured, and from there, the major city of Ningpo was seized and occupied. There Pottinger intended to await reinforcements before proceeding up the Yangtze River.

The British occupation of Ningpo gave the Chinese the opportunity they had been awaiting in the expectation that, once ashore, the English soldiers were inferior to imperial Ch'ing infantry. The emperor's cousin, a refined and scholarly gentleman named I-liang, was given the responsibility of coordinating a counter-offensive in the spring of 1842. Troops were brought in from as far as western Szechwan, and marines were drilled in amphibious landings in order to reconquer Chusan Island. But the campaign turned into an unmitigated disaster for the Chinese. I-liang consulted the oracles for an auspicious time to attack, which happened to be at the height of the rainy season. His main forces were thus separated from their supply wagons, which bogged down in muddy roads. The vaunted marines became seasick, so their commanders avoided Chusan to sail up and down the coast reporting fictitious victories. The crack Szechwanese aborigines mistook orders and walked into British cannonades at Ningpo armed only with knives. And, most ironically of all, the reserves meant to back them up were never sent into battle because their terrified commander had smoked himself into an opium stupor lying on his palanquin. As their artillery mowed down the attacking Ch'ing troops, British officers were sickened by the bloodshed, which reminded them of the slaughter of Badajoz during the recent Spanish campaigns.

It was not that the Chinese were altogether incapable of fighting. The previous summer at the village of San-yuan-li near Canton, peasant militia had boldly attacked English troops. Later, in 1842, entire garrisons of Manchu bannermen fought to the death, their wives committing suicide rather than surrender. Although the English did not march into China completely unopposed, the Ch'ing military machine was rusty, its weapons and men no match for England's percussion lock muskets, close order drill, heavy artillery, and paddlewheel gunboats. By the summer of 1842 the Yangtze River lay open to the British as far as Nanking, and in August their vessels reached the outskirts of the old Ming capital and prepared to shell the city.

If so symbolic a city fell to the enemy, Tao-kuang understood that his mandate might be in jeopardy. The emperor felt he had no choice but to accept England's demands and sign a peace agreement. Envoys led by the minister Ch'i-ying indicated China's willingness to surrender before Pottinger could attack the former capital, and the Treaty of Nanking brought an end to the war. This agreement, the first of what came to be known as "the unequal treaties," opened China to the West and marked the beginning of a century of imperialist exploitation.

The Unequal Treaties

The Treaty of Nanking, along with the Supplementary Treaty of the Bogue and two French and American agreements, forced harsh concessions on the defeated Chinese.

1. The cession of Hong Kong to the English.
2. The opening of five treaty ports at Canton, Amoy, Foochow, Ningpo, and Shanghai to foreign consuls, businessmen, and missionaries.
3. The payment of an indemnity of 21 million silver dollars to the British crown.
4. The abolition of the Cohong monopoly.
5. The establishment of a moderate tariff and limitation of inland transit duties.
6. The according of foreign officials with equal status and access to Chinese officials.

7. The recognition of the extraterritorial rights of foreigners to be tried by their own consuls.

8. The adoption of the most-favored nation principle in diplomatic agreements with Western countries.

The war had begun over the opium traffic, but English victory did not actually result in its legalization.[8] Instead, the war provided an opportunity to force China to abandon its traditional tributary diplomacy and deal with Western nations on their own terms. Of all the treaty clauses listed above, the last was the most revealing of this new relationship between China and the West. According to the most-favored nation clause, any concession granted by China to one power automatically extended to other treaty signatories as well. If England acquired the right to open a consulate in Shanghai, then so did France, Russia, and the United States. In principle the Western diplomatic arrangement with the Ch'ing Empire allowed all to share the spoils of victory evenly. Rather than let a single nation become dominant by separately colonizing a portion of China, the unequal treaties opened the five new ports to all, so that commercial rights were equally shared.

The international settlement which rapidly burgeoned in Shanghai was built on this diplomatic principle of joint access to China. Shanghai's Christian missions, extraterritorial law courts, municipal council, Western residential enclaves, Sikh policemen, and foreign customs inspectors were all galling symbols to the Chinese of gunboat diplomacy, and at the same time were very real manifestations of the basic treaty port proviso that of all nations, only China stood to lose by this sharing. Of course, equality among the powers was not always preserved in fact. Russia, for example, seized hundreds of thousands of square miles of Chinese territory by the Treaty of Aigun in 1860, and France secured its own special concession in Shanghai apart from the international settlement. But in general, all of the powers combined to keep China intact so that it did not become a battlefield for competing European armies as had the disintegrating Ottoman Empire. The country was not to be carved into separate and exclusive spheres of influence until the end of the nineteenth century, when a new and different imperialist impetus ended the treaty-port era of equal exploitation.

The spirit behind the reality of gunboat diplomacy defied China's traditional foreign policy prescriptions, and the subtlest Chinese statesmen failed at first to realize that the unequal treaties completely denied their diplomatic assumptions. Even after the Opium War they continued to practice techniques of barbarian management that had evolved over millennia of relations between the Central Kingdom and other countries. And just as Han officials had debated the best ways of confronting the Huns, so did Ch'ing bureaucrats argue over two opposing ways of dealing with the Europeans.

Ch'ing Foreign Policy

The first position held that all concessions should be resisted. Appeasement would bleed China dry, and regular diplomatic relations would give the enemy an opportunity to master the arts of civilization which it needed to conquer the empire. Therefore, the barbarians must be kept at arm's length for as long as it took China to rebuild its military strength and expel the foreigners altogether. It was this hard line which had prevailed at court in the winter of 1841–1842 before the British armies invaded the Yangtze valley. Unfortunately, the policy was crippled by a tragic contradiction. Western steamships and cannons could not be defeated unless the Chinese mastered the techniques and skills of the very civilization which those statesmen wished to repel. Yet conservatives like the grand councillor Wo-jen realized that if the West was studied in earnest, China's own cultural values would be jeopardized. If scientists and soldiers were encouraged to command the empire's defenses, what role would be left for Confucian ritualists and classical scholars? When forced to choose between traditional learning and western studies, men like Wo-jen preferred relatively unchanged military defenses to decisive military strength. And their influence was strong enough to force China to postpone acquiring Western military techniques until it was far too late to resist imperialism.

The conservatives' opponents were no less loyal to Confucianism, but they preferred a more pragmatic and flexible policy of barbarian management. This second position called for diplomatic intercourse with the foreigners in the belief that the Chinese could domesticate the barbarians with the arts of civilization, rendering them more prone to the blandishments of the culturally advanced Central Kingdom. The Chinese could also make use of this opportunity to learn more about the enemy's military techniques while playing off

one Western power against the other (*i i chih i,* "use the barbarians
to control the barbarians"). Such proponents of barbarian management depended on knowing their enemies in order to control them
with a policy of divide-and-rule. Although this policy, which dated
from Han times, had been applied successfully in central Asia by
the Ch'ing to distribute favors among various tribes, it did not yield
comparable results with the Quai d'Orsay and Whitehall. Under
the most-favored nation clause, a favor granted to one country was
given to all. Concessions were incremental, steadily weakening
China instead of selectively strengthening one European power so
that it quarreled with its neighbors. Nevertheless, barbarian management was the only alternative at hand when the hard line of
resisting all concessions failed along with the Chinese counter-
offensive during the spring of 1842.

When Henry Pottinger reached the walls of Nanking, it was a
conciliator, the Manchu Ch'i-ying, who led the negotiations for the
Ch'ing side. The Treaty of Nanking was thus partly Ch'i-ying's
creation, and the foreign policy of the next six years largely his
handiwork. Refined and perceptive, Ch'i-ying seemed the quintes-
sential mandarin to Pottinger, who took his civilities to be a promise
of ongoing Chinese cooperation. Pottinger was unaware, of course,
that many of the Manchu's fellow bureaucrats felt Ch'i-ying was too
polite to the barbarians and perhaps had become a tool of English
interests. To protect himself from the wrath of the conservatives,
Ch'i-ying even had to memorialize the Tao-kuang Emperor, explaining that though repulsed by the barbarians' appearance and manner, he was nonetheless willing to take on the obligation of dealing
with them. Thanks also to the political support of other high officials like Grand Councillor Mu-chang-a, Ch'i-ying was able to wend
his way cautiously between British demands that China live up to
the letter and spirit of the peace settlement, and conservative senti-
ment at court that he—Ch'i-ying—had already given too much
away by signing the Treaty of Nanking.

For the next two years, Ch'i-ying agilely maintained his footing.
Then feelings hardened on both sides. Pottinger was replaced by
much more aggressive officials like Sir John Francis Davis, who
believed that the Chinese would backslide into tributary diplomacy
unless the Westerners insisted rigorously on all the newly won treaty
rights. At the same time, more and more Chinese were coming to
resent and fear the foreign presence in the treaty ports. This was
especially true in Canton, where the Opium War peasant militia

had never really disbanded. Its gentry leaders continued to believe that the people could have driven the British into the sea if the dynasty had not given in so readily at Nanking. The Tao-kuang Emperor was particularly sensitive to these grumblings that the Ch'ing had *mai-kuo* (sold out the country) and encouraged Ch'i-ying not to accede to the English demand to reside in the city of Canton. As popular hostility to the foreigners heightened during 1848, a party of Englishmen picnicking in the countryside near Canton was set upon by villagers and murdered. To appease Davis, Ch'i-ying hastily executed the killers. When news of his decision reached Peking, Tao-kuang decided that the practitioners of barbarian management had become too concessive, threatening to cost the regime its popular support. Ch'i-ying was summarily dismissed, and a much more militant official, Hsu Kuang-chin, was appointed to succeed him as governor-general in Canton. Hsu stolidly ignored English threats and continued to deny them entrance to the city. In fact, his haughty style of address reminded old China hands of the pre-Opium War hoppos. Once more there was a hostile buffer between foreigners and Peking, leading the English to estimate that the diplomatic gains of another short war with China might be sufficient compensation for the momentary loss of trading profits during the hostilities. To British superintendents like George Bonham and Sir John Bowring it seemed as if the first Opium War had produced almost no long term effect on the demeanor of Chinese imperial officials.

The Social Effects of the Opium War

The war did have major social effects, however, provoking a wave of disorder in southeastern China that continued to swell even after the treaty was signed. Triad secret societies recruited widely in the mid-1840s, while the British navy drove pirates away from the coast and up the rivers into the Kwangtung-Kwangsi highlands, whence they descended periodically to raid the wealthy villages of the Canton delta. Former militiamen kept their arms and turned to professional banditry. Clan feuds broke out, and different dialect groups began to wage internecine war. In Canton city itself, urban crime increased in step with unemployment. For, when the Treaty of Nanking opened Shanghai to foreign trade, much of Canton's commerce was diverted north. This shift also affected the hinterland because tens of thousands of boatmen and coolies who had once packed tea and silk down Kiangsi or across the Fukienese mountains found themselves out of work.

All of these symptoms of social pathology accompanied the profound psychological shock of the Opium War defeats in the South. The Cantonese had watched the gunboat *Nemesis* command their waterways with impunity, sinking Chinese naval vessels on all sides. They knew how effective British weapons were against the imperial armies. Most hated the West, but some felt its influence overpoweringly enough to consider new and alien doctrines.

Among the groups susceptible to Western influence were the Hakkas (guest families), northern Chinese immigrants in the South who were treated as an ethnic minority by the original Cantonese settlers (Punti) there. A proud and ambitious people with a high rate of literacy and success in the state examinations, the Hakkas spoke their own dialect and had different customs. Hakka women were much more independent than their Punti counterparts, never binding their feet and discouraging polygamy. They also worked alongside their husbands in the fields, making the Hakkas formidable economic competitors for good farming land. Because suspicion and dislike arose the moment a Hakka lineage moved into a village, the Punti there were likely to abandon their farms and move elsewhere. When the Hakka repaid Punti (native) scorn with contempt and hatred in return, feuds (*hsieh-tou*) broke out between the two groups. During the 1850s these communal wars took hundreds of thousands of lives on both sides.

The tribulations of such a minority, however oppressed, might hardly receive attention in the general sweep of Chinese history if it were not for the Hakkas' role in the Taiping Rebellion (1850–1864). Not only did the Hakkas form the core of the Taiping movement, but it was a Hakka visionary, Hung Hsiu-ch'üan, whose mystical revelations inspired a rebellion which was the major turning point of nineteenth-century Chinese history. After the Taiping Rebellion it was no longer possible to distinguish between hermetic Chinese developments and outer influences. Just as the rebellion itself was an effect of internal social pressures combined with external influences, so did Hung Hsiu-ch'üan's revolutionary doctrines inextricably join classical Chinese ideas with Western religious themes.

Hung Hsiu-ch'üan and the Ideological Origins of the Taiping Rebellion

Hung Hsiu-ch'üan, the future emperor of the Taiping Heavenly Kingdom, was the talented son of a well-to-do Hakka farmer from Hua-hsien just north of Canton. It was the hope of his family that Hung pass the civil service examinations. After arduous tutoring Hung Hsiu-ch'üan did succeed in becoming an aspirant (*t'ung-sheng*) in 1828, when he was sixteen, but during the next several years he repeatedly failed the prefectural examination for the lowest gentry degree (*sheng-yuan*). This was a familiar syndrome in late imperial China, and those who suffered its frustration were sometimes prone to turn against the regime. Trained to classical literacy, they frightened local authorities because their leadership could transform a bandit gang into organized political rebels. Of course, most disappointed examination candidates chose much less dramatic outlets for their discontent, such as Buddhist philosophy and Taoist self-cultivation. Hung Hsiu-ch'üan might himself have taken such a direction had he not been exposed to Christianity.

The exposure was entirely accidental. In 1836 Hung Hsiu-ch'üan went to Canton for yet another try at the examination but failed again. While disappointedly walking in the streets he encountered a black-robed foreign missionary with a long beard, and a middle-aged Chinese convert at his side, preaching and interpreting the Christian Gospel. Listening for a while, Hung was encouraged by the interpreter, Liang A-fa, to accept a set of nine Christian booklets under the general title of *Ch'üan-shih liang-yen* or "Good Words to Exhort the Age." Hung returned to his home in Hua-hsien and put the pamphlets on his bookshelf with hardly a glance. The following year he tried again for the degree. This time news of his failure precipitated a nervous collapse, and he had to be carried home in a rented sedan chair. For over a month he remained in his room, hallucinating, thrashing out at devils, and falling into deep trances. He finally awoke with memories of strange visions. In one dream, for example, he was taken away to a luminous place, a divine realm, where mysterious surgeons replaced all his internal organs. From surgery he was led to a kind of throne room. In that vast hall an old man with a black robe and a golden beard handed

Hung a sword to slay demons. In another hallucination the black-robed man angrily scolded the figure of Confucius, who was made to confess his guilt to some nameless crime.

Although the black-robed man's identity was a mystery to Hung, the punishment of Confucius made some sense in the context of his failure to pass the state examinations. The humiliation of the sage was Hung's own psychic rejection of the system which had refused to recognize his talents. But this was an antinomian act; at the moment Hung conceived of no alternative order to replace the old world he longed to destroy. The forty days' dementia had definitely altered Hung. From a compliant and insecure aspirant he was transformed into a fiercely self-confident leader who visibly swelled in physical stature and spoke with new authority in his community. However, his megalomania lacked positive direction.

Hung Hsiu-ch'üan discovered that direction in 1843, six years after his hallucinations, when a cousin chanced upon the Christian missionary pamphlets stored in Hung's bookcase. The cousin passed on the tracts to Hung, who read them with a growing sense of revelation. Then the elements of his dream suddenly fell into place. The black-robed figure was none other than God, his father. He—Hung—was the younger brother of Christ, sent to earth with his demon-quelling sword to "restore" Christianity to China.

According to Hung's revelations, the religion of the conquering West had originally been a Chinese doctrine, revealed to the Central Kingdom long before the time of Confucius.

> Father had ordained the Heavenly Kingdom to be in China; since China was originally the home of the Heavenly Kingdom, it is therefore also the home of Father. Before Father descended to the earth, China belonged to Father, and yet the barbarian devils stole into Father's Heavenly Kingdom. This is the reason Father decreed that I should come to destroy them.[9]

The foreign devils whom Hung believed himself destined to destroy were not Europeans but Manchus, whom he saw as the latest wave of barbarian invaders to intentionally keep the Chinese from realizing that Christianity was their true creed. Once the Chinese people recovered their original religion by exterminating the Manchu *yao* (demons), an age of great peace (*t'ai-p'ing*) would arrive, uniting the world in universal harmony and brotherhood.

Western missionaries quickly learned that Hung was not a simple convert, for his Christianity signified what he admired or feared in the West. He was not adopting a foreign creed; he was asserting a Chinese right to it. As Christ's younger brother, he declared himself the divine spokesman of world Christianity. He—not a pope or a bible—determined dogma, and the era of universal harmony which he promised had as many Chinese elements as Western ones. The classical *Record of Rites* described a past period of universal harmony (*ta-t'ung*) when property divisions were unknown.[10] And the New Text (*chin-wen*)[11] Kung-yang commentary divided history into three ages: disorder (*shuai-luan*), ascending peace (*sheng-p'ing*), and great peace (*t'ai-p'ing*). Hung may not have drawn the name of his movement (*T'ai-p'ing t'ien-kuo*, the Heavenly Kingdom of Great Peace) from this particular text, but there were sufficient references to the great peace throughout Chinese prose and poetry to certify its native origin.[12]

These Chinese sources alone would not have motivated a revolutionary social movement. The *ta-t'ung* and *t'ai-p'ing* motifs appeared frequently enough in earlier chiliastic movements, but they were usually contained within the millennial promises of Maitreya Buddha, which actually engendered rebellion. Christianity occupied that same function in Hung Hsiu-ch'üan's ideology. As he described the Heavenly Kingdom which would shortly reign on earth, Hung also tapped the anti-Manchu feelings of the southern Chinese. And by postulating tangible barriers—the Manchu *yao*—to this paradisiacal goal, he managed to afford his future followers a militant means of salvation. Armageddon was theirs to fight; they alone could create heaven on earth by destroying a concrete enemy.

Hung Hsiu-ch'üan would have been little more than a mystic, an inspired visionary, if there had not existed social forces ready to respond to his prophecies. These forces were produced by the confluence of inner and outer historical currents analyzed earlier: population growth, official corruption, tax evasion on the one hand; the disruptions of the Opium War on the other. The neighboring province of Kwangsi was especially stricken by these sources of disorder. Added to the influx of bandits and pirates from Kwangtung were unemployed silver miners and charcoal burners, peasants driven off the land by drought, and feuding Punti and Hakka. Because of the public insecurity in Kwangsi, the gentry recruited militia which became strongarm squads for local landlords. Since the militia leaders were usually Punti, communal conflicts became even more polarized, with local magistrates tending to identify Hakkas as criminals opposed to the Punti forces of law and order.

The Hakkas naturally clung together all the more strongly and organized their own villages into embattled self-defense units.

Hung Hsiu-ch'üan became involved in this tumultuous situation because of religious persecution in Kwangtung. After his revelation, he and his cousin had baptized each other and began to proselytize other Hakkas around his hometown. But when Hung attracted the attention of the Hua-hsien magistrate for smashing Confucian idols, he was fired from his job as a local schoolteacher, and he decided to move elsewhere. In 1844 he persuaded one of his converts, Feng Yun-shan, to accompany him to Kwangsi where they lived with relatives. Hung's presence embarrassed his hosts and he returned to Kwangtung that same autumn. Feng remained in Kwangsi and during Hung's absence made astonishing progress in converting Hakka peasants living around Tzu-ching-shan (Thistle Mountain) to Taiping Christianity. It was there that Feng formed the converts into a Society of God Worshippers (*Pai shang-ti hui*), which turned the isolated villages into a self-enclosed religious community, connected by goat trails and hidden behind mountain passes.

The Society of God Worshippers was not yet a militantly rebellious movement. Devoid of political pretensions, the brothers and sisters of the faith were baptized into a sect which as yet only fled society, living apart from the surrounding Punti countryside. Conversions were community affairs. Disciples joined as members of a Hakka defense unit, retaining their familiar primary group identifications as members of a lineage or residents of a village settlement. As individuals, the brethren had not yet been reprocessed into a new kind of social integer. That would have to await the formation of Taiping military society in 1851.

Growth of the Society of God Worshippers

The Society of God Worshippers did not grow quickly. When Hung rejoined Feng at Thistle Mountain in August, 1847, there were only two thousand converts. Yet Hung immediately injected a political tone into the religious life of the community, stressing the coming of the great peace and calling himself *chün wang* (noble king). His arrival also coincided with a rising crescendo of Hakka-Punti conflicts in that area, which had the effect of driving more and more Hakka defense units into the protective embrace of the Society of God Worshippers.[13] Not all who joined were Hakkas. This was a time of growing political tension and disarray in the southern reaches of the empire, and the increasingly militant character of the Society of God Worshippers was bound to attract social dissidents. One of these was an unruly group of charcoal burners and silver miners who were brought to Thistle Mountain early in 1848 by two bravos named Yang Hsiu-ch'ing and Hsiao Ch'ao-kuei.[14] They joined the community of devouts just as the God Worshippers were suffering from a leadership crisis. That January, Feng Yun-shan had been captured by local Punti militia and turned over to the local magistrate. Hung, meanwhile, had gone to Canton in an unsuccessful attempt to negotiate his friend's release. Feng was eventually ransomed from jail by the God Worshippers, but only on the magistrate's condition that he return to his home in Kwangtung. Thus, both founding leaders were absent from the Thistle Mountain encampment throughout most of 1848, and they returned to their followers only to find that Yang and Hsiao, the charcoal burners' chiefs, had usurped much of their authority. Whether by cunning design or genuine belief—or most probably a combination of both in this community of ecstatics for whom spiritual possession (*kuo-shen*) was commonplace—Yang Hsiu-ch'ing had fallen into a two-month trance of his own. When he awoke in the spring of 1848, he spoke in the voice of the Holy Ghost. Less than nine months later, Hsiao Ch'ao-kuei had a religious seizure and completed the trinity by becoming a spokesman for Jesus Christ.[15]

Under other circumstances Hung Hsiu-ch'üan might have been able to refute the encroachers' claim of divine possession, but the God Worshippers' camp was in a state of religious hysteria. As enemies multiplied on all sides of Thistle Mountain, many people spoke in tongues. How could Hung deny the charismatic ecstasy of other prophets when they adopted his rhetoric, inflated his imagery, and enlarged his cult? As more Hakkas, then river pirates and Miao aborigines, joined the camp, bringing the total number up to thirty thousand,[16] he and Feng Yun-shan found themselves losing control of the movement. Perhaps to reassert their authority, Feng called for a political rebellion but Yang Hsiu-ch'ing failed to respond. Instead, Yang had a second, bedridden seizure in May, 1850, which was to last for six months. The movement now fissioned. Hung Hsiu-ch'üan and Feng Yun-shan persuaded some of their followers to leave Thistle Mountain and come with them to nearby

Hua-chou, where a friendly gentryman loaned them his house for their headquarters.

The authorities were growing gravely alarmed by the activities of the God Worshippers. They formally ordered the sect to disperse after a Hakka pawnshop owner, Wei Ch'ang-hui, held a public meeting to discuss military measures, but continuous Hakka-Punti conflict kept the Thistle Mountain God Worshippers together. Finally in the fall of 1850 the local government decided to launch a frontal attack on the society. The Thistle Mountain encampment was too well guarded to be easily taken, but Hung's smaller group at Hua-chou appeared to be doomed.

At this moment Yang Hsiu-ch'ing providentially awoke from his six-month trance. Calling himself a "redeemer from illness" who—Christlike—took on mankind's ills, Yang issued orders to rescue Hung at Hua-chou. The two separate camps were thus reunited at Chin-t'ien, near the foot of Thistle Mountain, and it was there on January 11, 1851, the Hung Hsiu-ch'üan formally inaugurated the Heavenly Kingdom of the Great Peace (*T'ai-p'ing t'ien-kuo*).

Three Paradigms of the Taiping Movement

The Taiping movement was a radical departure from the former Society of God Worshippers. By proclaiming a new dynasty, Hung was announcing the leaders' decision to take the offensive against their enemies. The movement was no longer just an escape from the existing society; it was intended to replace it. The reorganization that followed the January 11th declaration was determined by three different paradigms.

First was the Chinese imperial model, represented by the person of Hung, the Heavenly King (*T'ien-wang*), whose own birthday coincided with the new reign era. However, the Taiping monarchy was not a simple copy of Confucian imperialism. Hung was not striving to take heaven's mandate away from the Ch'ing. Rather, he was devising a new heaven and earth of his own, and investing himself with a transcendental mission because of his divine descent from God. As the prophet who had discovered that God, Hung was partly his own source of authority and could, if the imperial Taiping paradigm prevailed, legitimize himself. From the standpoint of internal Taiping leadership struggles, this heavenly kingship made Hung relatively invulnerable to Yang Hsiu-ch'ing's ploys. Yang was able to appropriate much of Hung's authority, but he could not challenge his legitimacy. From an external viewpoint, the Taiping movement had ceased being merely chiliastic like the White Lotus sect and was establishing a secular claim for the ruler-ship of China based on anti-Confucian sources of legitimacy. That was why, even when the movement later failed to implement a radical social program, it still remained a revolutionary threat to the Confucian political order.

Meanwhile a second communal paradigm was carried over from the former God Worshippers, who were ecstatically joined as one great family, all children of God, living together under the rule of the ten commandments. Like an earthly family, all of the members of the new kingdom were brothers and sisters, observing incest taboos by avoiding sexual intercourse—even between former hus-bands and wives.[17] This stricture, however, was quickly waived for the top leaders. Some brothers, in George Orwell's ironic terms, were more equal than others. Hung Hsiu-ch'üan, Yang Hsiu-ch'ing, Hsiao Ch'ao-kuei, Feng Yun-shan, Shih Ta-k'ai and Wei Ch'ang-hui thus formed a superior fraternity which was partly modeled on the sworn brotherhood of the novel *Shui-hu chuan* (Water Margin) and stood above the rank and file.

The third paradigm was the most radical of all and constituted the organizational form of the Taiping movement. This was the ideal military society described in the classic *Chou-li* (Rites of Chou). The *Rites of Chou* purported to be a blueprint of the in-stitutions of the Chou Dynasty. In fact, the work provided an ideal bureaucratic system which merged civil and military organs into an overarching structure that covered every aspect of human affairs and that turned peasants into farmer-soldiers. This statist ideal was never really carried out in practice during the Chou, but it had inspired Han and Sung reformers who wished to give the state more regulatory powers. Confucianists usually disliked the Legalist im-plications of the *Rites of Chou* and preferred a more relaxed laissez-faire policy of government non-interference in the natural workings of society. To the Taiping leaders, however, the *Rites of Chou* offered an organizational model for transforming the Society of God Worshippers into an army of the faithful, who were now assigned to 25-person squads commanded by sergeants called *liang ssu-ma*.[18] The farmer-soldiers lived and fought together, putting all of their property into a common treasury which was soon to fill with the spoils of conquest.[19] By deliberately assigning people from different places to the same squad, the Taiping leaders were able to replace the old natural Hakka associations (village defense units and lineages) with a new military society determined by bureaucratic ties. However, organization did not displace ideology. Membership in the Taiping Army inspired a disciplined ideological commitment, fashioning soldiers of the faith out of simple peasants. The commitment was so total—demanding the abandonment of property, family, and even the former self—that only one[20] among all the secret societies that originally joined the Taipings remained within the movement. The Heavenly Kingdom thus lost some allies, but through communalism gained so much military cohesion and morale that its armies were almost unbeatable.

The Taiping March North

When the army moved—a new order on the march—it did not compete with existing rural society but ingested the indigenous peasantry. From September 25, 1851 to April 5, 1852, the Taiping forces settled in at Yung-an, grouping themselves for the sweep north. Then, breaking out of the Manchu commander Sai-shang-a's encirclement of the city, they began their sweep up the rivers of Hunan toward central China. Defiant villages and cities were razed to the ground, their inhabitants sometimes massacred. Peasants who submitted to the Taipings watched the longhaired rebels[21] destroy their farmhouses and dwellings, forcibly cutting all their ties with the past, before they were incorporated as regimented recruits in the *liang ssu-ma* squads. The Taiping Army did occasionally meet defeat. When a city like Kweilin proved too difficult to capture, the rebels simply bypassed the obstacle. Even when a defeat at Hsin-ning forced them out of the Hsiang River valley, the Taipings benefitted by picking up a number of new adherents from the tough and impoverished hill farmers of western Hunan. Their siege of Ch'ang-sha (Hunan's capital) from September to November 1852, was a failure, but they soon abandoned the attack and turned eastward, pushing rapidly down the Yangtze. In January, 1853, they scored a stunning victory by taking the city of Wu-ch'ang, whose populace swelled the rebels' ranks to a half million soldiers. Now, facing the Yangtze's middle reaches, the Taiping leaders had to make a fateful choice. The capital of China lay to the north, but downstream was the old Ming capital of Nanking. Should they press on into the central plain, maintaining their initial momentum in hopes of establishing the Heavenly Kingdom in Peking? Or should they follow the Yangtze on down to the fertile delta lands where they could enrich themselves and consolidate their ranks?

The leadership received conflicting advice. The commander of Hung Hsiu-ch'üan's flagship, a spokesman for the rivermen who had joined the Taipings, argued against a foray into Honan, fearing the open plains where Manchu cavalry held the tactical advantage. A gentry military advisor also urged Hung and Yang to head for Nanking because of its wealth and symbolic importance as a site for the imperial capital of the Heavenly Kingdom. After wavering, the Taiping leaders decided to turn to the east and try to take Nanking. No one knows who made that fateful decision, which marked the beginning of a change from the military paradigm of the *Rites of Chou* to Hung Hsiu-ch'üan's imperial mode of rule, but the choice certainly favored Hung's interests in his continuing power struggle with Yang Hsiu-ch'ing.

The competition between the two men had not ended with Hung's assumption of an imperial title in January, 1851. Yang Hsiu-ch'ing's power had continued to grow during the Taiping march north. A better military leader, he was also more rabidly anti-Manchu at a time when the movement was trying to attract Han racists. In addition, Yang exploited his private intelligence system to humiliate Hung and enlarge his own religious claims. During the occupation of Yung-an, for example, Yang's men uncovered a Ch'ing spy in their midst. Yang kept the news to himself until he called a seance, where he identified the agent in God's voice. The man was then brought in front of the other leaders and made to confess his guilt to them. Hung's authority was gravely jeopardized by this dramatic scene.

Since Yang could claim equal, if not superior, access to the godhead, Hung's only recourse was to stress his personal legitimacy as the Heavenly King. Beginning in the fall of 1851, he had talked more and more frequently of the ranks, robes, and titles awaiting all of them when they founded a capital for their Heavenly Kingdom. Yet Yang and Hsiao Ch'ao-kuei continued to speak as God and Christ, vilifying the Manchu swine, the "demons of the eight banners," with Old Testament wrath. They even managed in December, 1851, to force Hung to announce that only God and Jesus were truly holy, placing the Heavenly King on more of a par with the other leaders. Moreover, the military commands were reorganized in such a way as to make each of the major leaders a *wang* (king) in his own right. Each *wang* was allowed to create his own administrative staff, although the largest belonged to Yang (the Eastern King, *Tung-wang*) who controlled all military promotions. This "feudalization" of the original *Chou-li* organization eventually caused the Taiping armies to evolve in the direction of the seventeenth-century warlord armies, providing Hung with an opportunity to divide and rule. But for the moment Yang Hsiu-ch'ing clearly monopolized military decisions, ensuring that Hung would continue to lose importance as long as the Heavenly King lacked a civil setting to assert the imperial paradigm. Nanking provided such a stage for Hung, who must have strongly supported the decision to attack the city.

On February 18, 1853, Chiu-chiang fell to the rebels, who went on to take Anking. Less than a month later, on March 19, the Taiping forces captured the beautiful city of Nanking, which was renamed T'ien-ching (Heavenly Capital) to commemorate the occasion.

The Occupation of Nanking

The occupation of Nanking may have strengthened Hung's position, but it was a strategic mistake for the movement as a whole, which changed—in a contemporary's phrase—from a locomotive to a stationary rebellion. By settling in Nanking the movement lost that initial momentum which had so constantly kept the Ch'ing forces off balance. Yang Hsiu-ch'ing did send two armies into northern China, but they bogged down at the siege of Huai-ch'ing on the Honan-Shansi border and were destroyed by imperial forces just outside Tientsin in March, 1855. As long as the Manchus continued to hold Peking, they retained the Mandate of Heaven in most people's eyes. The Taipings did have their own capital in the South, but their concentration of troops there gave the Ch'ing a chance to lay siege to Nanking from army camps north and south of the Yangtze. At times the Taipings broke out of this containment, but the vise would be retightened, limiting the Taiping armies to horizontal movements up and down the banks of the Yangtze River.

The settlement at Nanking also vitiated the radical social system of the Heavenly Kingdom. *Chou-li* communalism had destroyed the two private pillars—property and the family—of peasant society when the army was on the march, enrolling and molding new recruits. But when the Heavenly Kingdom took in a vast civilian population outside the mobile army, it lacked the cadres and ideological unity to destroy or supplant existing society.[22] In other words, once the Taiping armies stopped moving, they had to come to terms with the resilient and tenacious rural society of central China. This meant accommodating themselves to the local notables who had come to play such an important role in informal district government.

In theory, the Taipings fully intended to apply their communalism to the society at large. In 1854 a special law was promulgated, ordering the appropriation of all cultivable land, which was supposed to be distributed to peasants enrolled in squads composed of 25 families each. Under this system adults would grow their own food and turn over the agricultural surplus to the local *liang ssu-ma* (sergeant) who managed the treasury, adjudicated disputes, and held Taiping religious services. In fact, however, the *Chou-li* land system encouraged outright tax farming. The Nanking regime simply appointed hereditary local generals (*chün-shuai*) from among those gentry who had turned the local tax registers over to the central administration of the Heavenly Kingdom. The gentry and landlords were then given special retinues of henchmen and were equipped with Taiping banners empowering them to collect taxes. At the very lowest level of local government, the *liang ssu-ma* often turned out to be the notables' protégés or bailiffs. The paradox of Taiping local administration was therefore two-fold: a movement directed against the Confucian gentry ended by supporting their local hegemony, and a system of public land tenure turned out to benefit the private sector even more than had the Ch'ing. Desperate for revenue and less aware than regular magistrates of the dangers of gentry economic appropriation, the Taiping leaders ironically permitted the gentry to ensconce themselves in local government more than ever before. The old society absorbed the new, rather than vice-versa.

Within the Taiping movement, too, old and familiar scenes of court intrigue were played. At first Yang Hsiu-ch'ing was more than able to hold his own against Hung, the reigning emperor. Centralizing appointments in the hands of his staff of more than 7,200,

Yang tried to turn the monarch into a rubber stamp for his own decisions, and he developed a powerful city police force of men and women that held Nanking in a tight grip. In the last part of 1853, he even had recourse to a trance again, threatening Hung in God's voice for having been cruel to his concubines. Hung Hsiu-ch'üan accepted the humiliation meekly, but secretly began to play upon the other Taiping kings' jealousy of Yang's position.[23] For Yang had not only arrogated Hung's authority; he had also repudiated the fraternal equality of the original leaders and insulted Shih Ta-k'ai and Wei Ch'ang-hui by forcing them to kneel in his presence. Wei, the more homicidal of the two, was the first to act. Perhaps under the orders of Hung Hsiu-ch'üan, Wei Ch'ang-hui attacked Yang on September 2, 1856, murdering the Eastern King along with twenty thousand of his followers. Shih Ta-k'ai was then campaigning in Hupei, but he returned immediately to stop the bloodbath. After Shih reproached Wei for such needless slaughter, Wei decided to remove this last military rival as well. Shih, however, got wind of the assassination plot in time to flee from Nanking and rally his troops. With Shih's support Hung Hsiu-ch'üan then had Wei murdered and the purge was over.

The Taipings' night of the long knives left Hung in supreme command of a badly scarred regime. A poet of the time summed up the mood of Nanking in the purge's aftermath:

> In the cities few men will venture out, and
> Fowls and hounds have no peaceful retreat.
> Throughout the street is blood,
> The Forbidden Palace has lost its shining glory.[24]

Shih Ta-k'ai had lost most of his faith in Hung's probity and deeply distrusted Jen-ta and Jen-fa, the emperor's constantly plotting brothers. Eight months after Wei's execution, Shih decided to abandon Nanking. Taking several hundred thousand soldiers with him, he first moved south, then west toward Szechwan where he continued to fight the Ch'ing for many years. In the meantime Hung Hsiu-ch'ün was showing signs of greater mental instability, ranting before his courtiers and putting administration in the hands of his harem purveyor, Meng Te-en. Command of the armies, which were now partly composed of adolescent war refugees ignorant of the Taiping creed, fell into the hands of two new generals, Ch'en Yü-ch'eng and Li Hsiu-ch'eng, who held their own strategy conferences in the field without bothering to contact Nanking. Li in particular was a superb tactician and inflicted many defeats upon the Ch'ing, but his independence eventually undid the Taiping reform program initiated by the emperor's cousin, Hung Jen-kan, in 1859.

The three years after 1853 thus saw the turning point of Taiping fortunes. Viewed from within, the movement seemed fatally stricken by 1856. And yet another eight years would pass before the Ch'ing Dynasty's forces recaptured Nanking. Why—if the Heavenly Kingdom was visibly so feeble in the 1850s—did the rebellion last such a long time? Was the Ch'ing Dynasty simply not strong enough to immediately press its advantage?

The Beleaguered Ch'ing Dynasty

The imperial government in Peking had more to contend with than just the Heavenly Kingdom. After the Taipings erupted in Kwangsi, other rebellions flared across the empire. The Small Sword Society momentarily seized the city of Shanghai and, to the south, along the Chekiang-Fukien border, Gold Coin rebels drove out government troops. Triads took the city of Amoy, and the Red Turbans attacked Canton. In the Pearl River delta, a half million Hakka were killed in wars with the Punti. Farther to the west, in Yunnan, miners rebelled, and Panthay Muslims established a separatist government in Tali that reigned for 15 years, costing three hundred thousand lives on both sides before it fell. New Sect Muslims stormed Chinese villages in Shensi; Miao aborigines revolted in Kweichow; salt smugglers arose in Manchuria. And in central China, across the Huai River basin, huge armies of Nien horsemen defied imperial control altogether. The devastation of these years was overwhelming. In some provinces two-thirds of the population was reported dead or missing. One could go for miles along the Yangtze River and see nothing but deserted villages where packs of wild dogs tore at rotting corpses. Conditions worsened as the Taiping Rebellion ground on. Social services broke down. Floods swept over parts of the country. In Kuang-te county, for example, an Anhwei gentryman reported that:

> From 1860 to 1864, for five years, people could not grow food. Toward the end all roots and herbs in the hills were exhausted and cannibalism occurred. Consequently epidemics struck. At that time corpses and human skeletons piled up and thorns and weeds

choked the roads. Within a radius of several tens of *li* (leagues) there was no vestige of humanity. The country's original population was over 300,000. By the time the rebels were cleared only a little over 6,000 survived. This was a catastrophe unique for the locality since the beginnings of the human race.[25]

All told, over thirty million people died from natural and human causes during the fourteen years of the Heavenly Kingdom.

As if this appalling misery were not enough to tax Peking's meager resources, Western imperialism also afflicted China. As in the Opium War years, it was England who took the lead. Fretting over the Canton entry question, convinced that the Chinese were still refusing them proper diplomatic deference, the English seized upon a flimsy pretext in 1856 to declare war on China.[26] This time they demanded eleven new treaty ports, unlimited travel in the interior, the right of envoys to live in Peking, more territory near Hong Kong, the legalization of opium, the protection of missionaries, and the inevitable indemnities. The French promptly joined this adventure, fired by Napoleon III's imperial pretensions and a pretext of their own after a French missionary was murdered by the Chinese.

The Anglo-Chinese War of 1856–1860

Because of the Sepoy mutiny in India, the Allies were unable to attack China in 1857. But the following year an expedition led by Lord Elgin and Baron Gros landed in north China at the Taku forts, which the English and French seized. The Hsien-feng Emperor (reigned 1851–1861) promptly dispatched a party of negotiators accompanied by the foreign affairs specialist, Ch'i-ying. As affable and persuasive as ever, the old gentleman (who had been freed from political prison for the occasion) quickly discovered that British attitudes had hardened considerably since Pottinger's day. The English negotiators included skilled Chinese linguists like Thomas Wade and Horatio Lay, who were very cynical about Ch'i-ying's barbarian management techniques. They were quick to produce copies[27] of Ch'i-ying's correspondence with the emperor a decade earlier when he had described his revulsion from the barbarians' appearance. Shamed and humiliated, Ch'i-ying had no choice but to withdraw from the negotiations—an act for which

Peking condemned him to death. Shortly thereafter, his dispirited colleagues acceded to the allied demands, which were written up as the Treaty of Tientsin.

The Treaty of Tientsin still had to be ratified by the emperor, and provision was made in the original agreement for Western representatives to come to Peking the next year, 1859, and exchange signed copies of the document. Before that happened, however, the Chinese changed their minds. The treaty itself had been negotiated by the Manchu Kuei-liang, who was the father-in-law of Prince Kung, a powerful member of the Council of Princes. Opposed to Kuei-liang and Prince Kung were a group of Chinese officials in the National Academy led by a junior censor named Ying Keng-yun, who enjoyed the protection of Prince I. The Hsien-feng Emperor sympathized openly with the war party, regarding the treaty as the handiwork of one official—Kuei-liang—and therefore as not necessarily binding. The war party, in the meantime, had begun to argue that the Chinese need not give in this time because they possessed sufficient military strength to resist France and England. Above all they believed that one general, Seng-ko-lin-ch'in,[28] stood a good chance of defeating the Westerners on the battlefield. Seng-ko-lin-ch'in was not quite so optimistic, but he did agree to go along with their plans, and the emperor was persuaded to reject the western envoys when they finally did appear.

On June 24, 1859, Lord Elgin's brother, Frederick Bruce, arrived at Taku, planning to proceed routinely up to the capital. To the utter astonishment of his landing party, which was wading across mud flats at the time, the Taku batteries opened fire and routed the English. The allies were enraged. Louis Napoleon and Palmerston, convinced that this was just one more example of Chinese treachery, decided to send an even larger expedition of ten thousand British soldiers and seven thousand French troops armed with the latest Armstrong rifles and breech-loading artillery. The new force landed with care near the Taku forts in July, 1860. After taking the emplacements on August 21, the allies occupied Tientsin. The Chinese tried to halt the invaders by negotiating a ceasefire, but Lord Elgin did not believe that the Ch'ing envoys held plenipotentiary rank. He therefore broke off the discussions and moved the expedition toward Peking, defeating the Chinese on September 21. Once again a truce flag stayed the allied advance at Tungchow, but Seng-ko-lin-ch'in, who was evidently playing for time to ambush the English and French, imprisoned the British negotiators sent to discuss terms. Filled with righteous indignation at what seemed to be arch perfidy, Elgin ordered an all-out attack on October 5. The Mongol general's lines failed to hold, and the allies pushed through Peking's outer defenses. One week later the first allied patrols entered the capital unopposed.

Even that defeat was insufficient punishment in Elgin's eyes for the treachery at Tungchow, and as his army hovered on the outskirts of Peking, he cast about for an even more stunning way to chastise the Hsien-feng emperor into submission. It was Harry Parkes who pointed out to him that a full-scale attack on the capital would really harm only the common people. A better way of punishing the emperor alone would be to destroy the Summer Palace northwest of the city. On October 18, then, Elgin ordered that the torch be put to the two hundred pagodas and pleasure pavilions of *Yuan-ming-yuan*. The fires burned across those ten square miles of the Summer Palace for two days, and the skies over Peking grew black with the pall of smoking lacquer. A British chaplain serving with the expedition justified the desecration.

> Yes, a good work, I repeat it, though I write it with regret, with sorrow, stern and dire was the need that a blow should be struck which should be felt at the very heart's core of the government of China, and it was done. It was a sacrifice of all that was most ancient and most beautiful, but it was offered to the manes of the true, the honest, and the valiant, and it was not too costly, oh, no! One of such lives was worth it all. It is gone, but I do not know how to tear myself from it. I love to linger over the recollection and picture it to myself, but I cannot make you see it. A man must be a poet, a painter, an historian, a virtuoso, a Chinese scholar, and I don't know how many other things besides, to give you even an idea of it, and I am not an approach to any one of them. But whenever I think of beauty and taste, of skill and antiquity, while I live, I shall see before my mind's eye some scene from those grounds, those palaces,[29] and ever regret the stern but just necessity which laid them in ashes.[30]

Hsien-feng, the object of Elgin's barbarity, was spared the sight of such destruction. He had already fled beyond the Great Wall to his hunting lodge in Jehol, leaving behind his brother, Prince Kung, to appease the invaders while eighty thousand leaderless Ch'ing troops rioted in the streets of Peking. On October 24, 1860, Elgin entered the city in military state and was received by Prince Kung in the Hall of Ceremonies of the Imperial Palace. There, before ranks of Chinese civil servants and French and English officers, the Convention of Peking was formally signed. The Treaty of Tientsin was ratified, an additional Shanghai tariff and opium legalization agreement approved, an indemnity promised, and Kowloon opposite Hong Kong ceded to the British crown. The Opium Wars were finally over.

In Jehol the emperor lay ill and was soon to die. While barbarians occupied his capital, the rest of the empire shuddered under rebel attacks. The question was not why the Ch'ing had failed to take advantage of the Taiping's weakness in 1856, but rather how the dynasty managed to survive at all.

Notes

1. For example, Wei Yuan, Ho Ch'ang-ling, and Liang T'ing-nan.
2. Translated in Teng Ssu-yü and John K. Fairbank, eds., *China's Response to the West: A Documentary Survey, 1839–1923* (New York: Atheneum, 1965), pp. 24–28.
3. By typifying the English as maritime invaders like the Japanese *wako*, Lin and his contemporaries underestimated their opponents' military skill. They knew that Westerners had technologically superior navies, but they assumed them to be helpless on land. Some officials even argued that the English soldiers bound their leggings so tightly that they could not bend their knees in combat and were thus no match for Chinese and Manchu infantry.
4. Lord Napier was sent to Canton as superintendent of British trade when the East India Company monopoly ended in 1834. His instructions were to put Sino-English relations on a new footing. When he insisted on addressing communiqués directly to the governor-general, Lu K'un, instead of going through the Cohong, the Chinese authorities refused to have anything to do with him. A crisis ensued, won by Lu K'un who blockaded the factories, closed the river entrance to Canton, and forced Napier to retire ignominiously to Macao where he died of "China fever."
5. Many of the English troops that fought in China during the Opium War were actually Indians.
6. The drug dealers became major capitalists by expanding into banking, insurance, and international finance. Profits from the opium trade built the beautiful residences of Salem, Massachusetts, and helped finance the Union Pacific Railway. The English firm of

Jardine and Matheson came to dominate Shanghai and Hong Kong investments. Its heirs, the Keswicks, today sit on the directing boards of such powerful corporations as the Hongkong and Far Eastern Investment Co., Hongkong and Shanghai Banking Corp., Hongkong Electric Co., Hongkong Land Investment, Lombard Insurance, Mercantile Bank, Barclays Bank, First Empire Bank New York, Hambros Bank, Container Finance, Container Leasing, Western American Bank (Europe), Yorkshire Bank, Sun Alliance, Mercantile Credit Co., and British Petroleum, among others. See Martin Walker, "Open File," *The Guardian,* November 22, 1973.

7. Extraterritoriality was also at stake in an affray at Chen-sha-tsui (Kowloon), where some English and American sailors beat a Chinese named Lin Wei-hsi to death with wooden clubs on July 7, 1839. Lin Tse-hsu demanded the culprits, but Elliot refused to surrender them.

8. That would have to await yet another British victory during the Anglo-Chinese conflict of 1856–1860.

9. Hung Hsiu-ch'üan, decree, cited in Vincent Y. C. Shih, *The Taiping Ideology: Its Sources, Interpretations and Influences* (Seattle: University of Washington Press, 1967), p. 6.

10. Hung cited the relevant passages from this text in his early writings. Later on, Taiping references to the *ta-t'ung* section of the *Record of Rites* were deliberately expunged from his works.

11. See p. 202.

12. For example, in *Shui-hu chuan* (Water Margin). The Taiping specialist, Chien Yu-wen, argues that Hung was directly influenced by Kung-yang Confucianism. See *T'ai-p'ing chün Kuang-hsi shou-i shih* [A History of the Initial Uprising of the Taiping Army in Kwangsi] (Shanghai: Commercial Press, 1946), p. 67. However, another eminent scholar disputes that interpretation. See Vincent Y. C. Shih, *The Taiping Ideology,* pp. 212–214.

13. These were not all poor peasants. Shih Ta-k'ai, who later became an important Taiping general, was a wealthy landlord before joining the society with his relatives and followers.

14. Yang was a charcoal burner who may also have been a professional convoy bodyguard. Hsiao, perhaps a relative of his, had been a farmer.

15. However, the theological trinity of Taiping religion was, and remained, God, Jesus Christ, and his younger brother Hung Hsiu-ch'üan.

16. This figure may be an exaggerated claim made by the Taipings to impress their followers. See Teng Ssu-yü, *The Taiping Rebellion and the Western Powers* (New York: Oxford University Press, 1971), pp. 330–335.

17. The sexes were segregated. Women usually formed a labor corps for military units. Some feminine units, especially those of Miao tribeswomen, went into battle, commanded by their own women officers.

18. This was a rank taken from the *Chou-li*. Other Chou ranks were given to the commanders of the larger units, moving up through platoons, companies, battalions, to an army which supposedly totaled 13,156 soldiers. At the time there were actually only 7,000 formally enrolled in the new army. To centralize command, Hung issued an order in August, 1851, creating a vanguard under Hsiao and Shih, a rearguard under Wei and Feng, and a main unit under Yang, who was clearly paramount.

19. By 1853 the Taiping treasuries reportedly contained 18 million taels: six times the reserves of the Ch'ing Board of Revenue in Peking.

20. That of the pirate chief, Lo Ta-kang.

21. Long hair was a traditional symbol of revolt. For the Taipings it also represented a protest against the shaved forehead and queue of the Manchus.

22. It is hard to avoid comparing the Taiping occupation of the lower Yangtze with the Red Army in Yenan during World War II. Both had been military societies on the march. Indeed, the Chinese Communist general, Chu Teh, was influenced enough as a boy in Szechwan by tales of the Taipings to copy their marching orders. However, once the Long March was over and the Red Army settled in, there ceased to be a similarity between it and the Taipings. In Yenan, the Communists precisely did come to terms with rural society, reshaping it with their cadres into an entirely new and revolutionary form.

23. Feng Yun-shan and Hsiao Ch'ao-kuei were by now both dead, killed in earlier battles. They had been replaced as military leaders by Hu I-kuang and Ch'in Jih-kang, but the most powerful commanders in addition to Yang were Shih Ta-k'ai and Wei Ch'ang-hui, who had his own personal staff of 3,000 men and women.

24. Cited in Franz Michael, *The Taiping Rebellion: History and Documents*, Vol. 1 (Seattle: University of Washington Press, 1966), p. 119.

25. Cited in Ping-ti Ho, *Studies on the Population of China, 1368–1953* (Cambridge: Harvard University Press, 1959), p. 239.

26. This was the Arrow War, named after a Chinese pirate vessel which falsely flew the English flag. When Ch'ing troops arrested the pirates and hauled down the flag, an aggressive English consul named Harry Parkes took this as an affront to the British crown and presented his government with a *casus belli*. Palmerston was again in power, and used this flimsy pretext to "teach the Chinese a lesson."

27. The copies were stolen from the archives of the Canton yamen, which was occupied by the Western allies after they captured the city.

28. Seng-ko-lin-ch'in was a Mongol banner chief from the Borjigit clan. He had been a protégé of the Tao-kuang Emperor and had an excellent military record, having destroyed the northern expedition of the Taipings in 1855.

29. The English and French took care to loot before they set the grounds afire. Though not nearly so great a prize as the Parthenon friezes, the Summer Palace's robes and thrones were brought back to England where they grace that monument to English imperialism, the Victoria and Albert Museum.

30. Cited in Harley Farnsworth MacNair, *Modern Chinese History— Selected Readings* (Shanghai: Commercial Press, 1923), Vol. 1, p. 317.

The Illusion of Restoration
and Self-Strengthening

By 1869, when the great rebellions were over, Ch'ing officials were speaking openly of their regime's "restoration" (*chung-hsing*), a late flowering, just as if the resuscitated imperial government was following the same cycle as the Han, T'ang, and Sung dynasties. In fact, this rebirth was an illusion. Behind the Confucian rhetoric of restoration and beneath the ante bellum facade of civil administration, important social and political transformations had taken place. These changes would eventually destroy both the dynasty and the traditional political system. The Taiping rebels, however revolutionary their intent, had failed to defeat the traditional order. But they had forced the regime to defend itself in ways that disturbed the old balance of power between local and central interests, civil and military wings, and foreign and native ruling elites. It was the reaction to the Taipings, not the rebels themselves, that had the most revolutionary effects in the end.

The Militia Movement

The changes began with the failure of the regular Ch'ing armies to contain the Taiping rebels in Kwangsi. As commanders like Sai-shang-a and Hsiang Jung reported one imperial defeat after another in 1851 and 1852, the court realized that its Green Standard forces and banner troops were unable to withstand the enemy. In 1852, however, more heartening news reached Peking. A private militia force led by a Hunanese gentryman named Chiang Chung-yuan had defeated the Taipings at Kweilin, forcing them to abandon their siege of the city. This same contingent of militiamen joined the fray at Ch'ang-sha where—for the second time—the Taipings were repelled.

Such gentry-led militia—whether peasant minutemen defending their villages, braves (*yung*) paid to serve over a longer period of time, or regular mercenaries—were not a new phenomenon. But their organization and training had become more complex since they had been used to suppress the White Lotus rebels at the end of the eighteenth century. Local defense experts had produced an elaborate body of literature which explained how to mobilize militia (*t'uan-lien*) both to defend a locale and to enroll the peasant population in control units. Although this prescription for creating farmer-soldiers was not taken from the *Chou-li*, it did structurally resemble the Taiping formula for militarizing rural society. But the motivation of the two groups was quite different. Where the Taiping squads had been organized in communal units which negated particularistic ties, the gentry-led *t'uan-lien* were supposed to draw their strength from personal attachments to place, property, and family. The statecraft (*ching-shih*) school of Confucianism that had been championing gentry-led militia since at least the seventeenth century believed that local militiamen fought with more spirit and commitment than disinterested professionals or religious sectarians precisely because they were defending their own personal belongings.[1]

Statecraftsmen did not find it difficult to promote local defense measures among the gentry. But they were hampered by the imperial government's reluctance to sanction paramilitary units which could potentially become landlord vigilantes, like the Punti *t'uan-lien* that had militarized Kwangsi. The sorts of men who took an interest in local militia work were often members of the lower gentry, sometimes even connected with secret societies and gangsters. Drawn from the same social stratum that had produced Hung Hsiu-ch'üan, these militia leaders were less likely to perform responsibly than were members of the higher gentry. Yet the upper gentry, while morally reliable, represented a graver political threat. If the Ch'ing Dynasty ignored its own law of avoidance and named scholar-officials as militia leaders, the upper gentry might transform their *t'uan-lien* into the constituents of a provincial military machine. Remembering the three feudatories' revolt in 1673, the

Manchus easily conceived of such a situation encouraging regional secession from the empire, or even the birth of a rival dynasty headed by some prestigious Chinese official.

Normally such a risk was considered too great. But these were abnormal times, and the Taiping Rebellion was so unusual that the central government believed it could rely on the upper gentry's loyalty. The Taipings were not fighting to restore a Ming or Sung dynasty; they were engaged in a crusade to establish a new order, anti-Confucian and—especially in the early 1850s—anti-gentry. The struggle was not between two rivals for the same throne; it was a contest between a revolutionary social movement dedicated to destroying Confucian culture and a dynasty which claimed to preserve it. Believing that the gentry's allegiance was secure because of these circumstances, the throne decided in December, 1852, to appoint the first of 43 militia commissioners from among high officials home on leave.[2]

The appointment of militia commissioners was both a recognition of the kind of local militarization that had been going on for some time and the first important step toward the formation of regional armies to fight the rebels. These two processes, local militarization and the formation of regional armies, overlapped each other, but they were not identical phenomena. Local militarization, for instance, created a new kind of opportunity for the lower gentry to entrench themselves in local government, and by the 1920s rural affairs were utterly monopolized by an uncontrollable landlord class. Regional armies, on the other hand, evolved into modern warlordism, which completely destroyed the body politic after the Revolution of 1911. Each of these extremely significant developments deserves to be analyzed in detail in this and following chapters.

Local Militarization and Gentry Managers

The recruitment of militia during the Taiping years placed new judicial and fiscal powers in the hands of the local gentry. Exercising the right to punish rebels on the spot, militia leaders often condemned captives to capital punishment and carried out the death sentences themselves. Needing funds for their troops, they also opened taxation bureaus and imposed levies as they wished. Once the war years were over, these bureaucratic functions, nor-

mally the prerogative of the district magistrate, were forbidden the
gentry. But it was not easy to get the local notability to give up
the habit of usurping powers that the government was too weak
to recover. Moreover, the formation of militia tended to throw the
upper and lower gentry together, giving them common interests
and obliterating the political division between the two which had
been so effectively exploited by the Yung-cheng Emperor a century
earlier. The new alliance was difficult to break because the upper
gentry now relied upon gentry-commoners to manage the administrative infrastructure of tax collection offices, famine relief bureaus,
rent control agencies, and quartermaster depots that were needed
to restore law and order to the countryside.

As their informal influence became formally institutionalized
in rural government, the gentry's private economic practices were
also bureaucratized, melding with the public sector. In Kiangsu,
for example, wealthy landlords turned rent collection over to rental
bursaries (*tsu-chan*) whose property managers (often lower gentry)
worked closely with yamen clerks and off-duty policemen to arrest
tenants in arrears. With these duties relieved, the upper gentry
were able to leave their country homes and move into the cities,
living off their rents. The lower gentry managers, on the other hand,
took over more and more functions in the countryside, enriching
themselves from the customary "locust fees" (*huang-ch'ung fei*)
of tax farming which—in south China during the 1870s—ran as
high as 2.7 taels per acre of cultivated land.

The size of this managerial class also increased significantly
during the Taiping period because the Ch'ing government decided
to raise money by selling hundreds of thousands of government
degrees. The distribution between regular and irregular gentry thus
shifted, even in the higher ranks, to absolute parity:

BEFORE THE TAIPING REBELLION

Regular Upper Gentry	80,000	66%
Irregular Upper Gentry	40,000	34%

AFTER THE TAIPING REBELLION

Regular Upper Gentry	100,000	50%
Irregular Upper Gentry	100,000	50%

This enlargement of the official gentry wiped out some of the
cultural distinctions between upper and lower ranks and put a great

strain on the rural economy. By the late nineteenth century the average administrative district contained 1,000 gentrymen, of which approximately 400 were engaged in managerial work or tax remission, nationally collecting nearly 80 million taels a year in fees worth far more than the services actually rendered. It was as though all the fears of the Yung-cheng Emperor had been fully realized. The countryside was slipping out of regular bureaucratic control into the hands of gentry-commoners who mulcted the peasants and drained away what otherwise might be state revenue. And what made matters even worse was that these lower gentrymen were connected through a complex network of militia bureaus and rental agencies with higher gentry patrons in the cities who protected them from the provincial and central government.

In Soochow, for instance, the key political figure was Feng Kuei-fen,[3] a former Hanlin compiler who acquired a large clientele of lower-level gentry managers—some of whom had originally been Taiping tax farmers. It was Feng who pressed for the establishment of a Soochow militia bureau in 1853 and later served as an advisor to the governor of Kiangsu, Li Hung-chang. Feng also provided widely read ideological justifications for this gentry entrenchment in local government. Invoking the famous statecraft writer Ku Yen-wu, Feng argued that the local gentry's informal role in district affairs should be officially recognized despite the law of avoidance. Feng believed that the empire was unable to thwart Western imperialism because the government could not mobilize the population. And that in turn was the result of putting rural administration in the hands of clerks and deputy magistrates who had no personal interest in the economic development, social welfare, or efficient government of a given district. But if the inhabitants—and especially the gentry—of that particular county were allowed to assume some of these responsibilities themselves, then their native pride and involvement would elevate the quality of local government and benefit the country as a whole.

Feng Kuei-fen's writings, which were published posthumously in 1885, profoundly affected reformers at the turn of the century who attributed the West's military strength to constitutional government. As it filtered through statecraft thought, the Western theory of participatory democracy was translated into a doctrine of gentry home rule. This goal was politically expressed in a constitutionalist movement which called for "local self-government" (*ti-fang tzu-chih*) in order to build a new united nation from the ground up. The local self-government movement also united the urban gentry with an emerging bourgeoisie represented by chambers of commerce. Together the two classes formed a new reformist provincial elite which helped precipitate the Revolution of 1911. By then, however, the rural managers who had begun to entrench themselves during the Taiping years no longer needed their urban patrons. As the cities became divorced from the market towns and villages of the hinterland, the landlords and lower gentry of the countryside dominated rural tax and rent collection so completely that the central government's revenue agents could not penetrate through to the peasantry. By the 1930s, in fact, republican magistrates were forced to tolerate a more extreme form of tax farming than had ever before existed because all of the up-to-date land registers were in the possession of the former rural managers.

This continual evolution from the militia leaders and bureau chiefs of the Taiping period to "local bullies and evil gentry" (t'u-hao lieh-shen) of the twentieth century tore the fabric of society in three different ways. First, the link between the higher provincial elite and the state was broken, so that the upper gentry turned away from the central government and allied with merchants and militarists.[4] Second, the balance between regular district administrators and local magnates was completely tilted in the latter's favor, putting rural control in the hands of politically irresponsible landlords. Finally, tax and rent collection became indistinguishable so that the peasantry identified the existing political order with the economic tyranny of petty landlords and usurers. As the preservation of public welfare became confused with the protection of private property, the kan-ch'ing (mutual rapport) which had once mollified class hostilities was replaced by landlord strong-arm squads, euphemistically called "popular militia" (min-t'uan), on the one side, and revolutionary peasant associations on the other. The latter, led by the Chinese Communist Party, would eventually culminate in the greatest social revolution mankind has ever known.

The Formation of Regional Armies

The second process that began with the Taiping period was the formation of regional armies which, in a somewhat different way, also helped destroy the traditional political and social order. Just as the lower-level militia managers were the forerunners of the *t'u-hao lieh-shen* of the 1930s, so were the higher ranking militia commissioners the progenitors of twentieth-century Chinese warlords. Of course, it would be fatuous to argue that a moralistic Confucian statesman like Tseng Kuo-fan (1811–1872) was the direct ancestor of an unscrupulous modern warlord like Sun Ch'uan-fang (1884–1935). If they could have posed side by side—Tseng with thoughtful mien and dressed in flowing Ch'ing robes, Sun's cruder figure constrained in leather boots and khaki uniform—the two would hardly seem related at all. Yet it was Tseng who initiated the process of regional militarization which, through political twists and turns, led to the kind of blunt military power that destroyed the Ch'ing Dynasty and inspired Mao Tse-tung to declare that "all political power grows out of the barrel of a gun."

Obviously, none of these consequences was evident to the Hsien-feng Emperor when he appointed *t'uan-lien ta-ch'en* (militia commissioners) late in 1852. Nevertheless, his decision eventually overturned the old Manchu-Chinese balance in the bureaucracy,[5] permitted horizontal alignments of personal loyalty among high officials to replace a vertical chain of bureaucratic command from the center, and compromised the K'ang-hsi Emperor's system of provincial checks and balances by fusing civil, military, and fiscal powers under each governor-general. Yet no one close to the emperor foresaw these developments because the militia commissioners so chosen were not intended to form regional armies to replace the regular provincial military forces. Rather, they were supposed to mobilize gentry-led *t'uan-lien* (militia) into simple *ad hoc* confederations and coordinate them for local defense against the rebels.

But Tseng Kuo-fan, a board vice-president home on leave in Hunan, had quite a different conception of his role as militia commissioner. Taking the late Ming general, Ch'i Chi-kuang, as his model, Tseng soon made it clear to the court that he was not going to train *t'uan-lien* to supplement the existing imperial armies. Rather, he intended to recruit and organize a much larger force of *yung* (braves) which could be deployed in the field for years at a time away from their native places. This force, which was to be called the Hsiang Army (after Hunan's major river), would be organized through the "old boy" network of gentrymen who held informal power in central China. Tseng, who was widely revered as a Confucian moralist, firmly believed that the scholar-official elite of China had to be aroused to defend its culture against Taiping iconoclasm. More than any other major official, Tseng Kuo-fan regarded the Taipings as a new and revolutionary danger to the existing order, attacking the basic foundations of society (family and property), and replacing the classics with outlandish Christian texts. The duty of the educated elite was to defend and reassert the Confucian way of true civilization. Otherwise, declared Tseng Kuo-fan, mankind would slip back into the darkness from which it had originally come.

In Tseng's view, the force that destroyed the Taiping rebels would have to be consciously organized according to principles completely opposed to the enemy's. It would have to be based on the same Confucian doctrines that he so strongly held in order to stand firm where other armies had fallen apart. If the Taipings' basic cadre was a military overseer (the *liang ssu-ma*), then Tseng's Hsiang Army would be commanded by devoted civilians—scholars as well trained in the classics as they later became skilled in warfare. If Taiping units were communal, antifamilial, and theoretically impersonal, then Tseng's units would be motivated by the particularistic virtues of Confucianism—duty to one's neighbors, piety to one's family, and personal loyalty to one's commander.

Tseng Kuo-fan began with 500 men, divided into companies under the commanders who had recruited them. Four commanders were personally attached to a battalion commander (*ying-kuan*), and up to twenty *ying-kuan* served under a detachment commander (*t'ung-ling*). Finally each detachment commander was selected by the *ta-shuai* (generalissimo), Tseng Kuo-fan himself, who insisted that allegiance be personal at every level of the army. If a commander was dismissed, then his entire detachment was disbanded as well. As one of Tseng's personal secretaries put it, "If the general dies, then his army falls apart. If the general survives, then his army remains intact."

The rank and file were all peasants. A commander was not allowed to recruit city folk, and he was especially encouraged to select sturdy farmers from the same hilly country in western Hunan where the Taipings had secured so many soldiers. An unusually long training period instilled personal loyalty to one's commander. Discipline was harsh. Disobedience meant flogging or worse, and rape was a capital offense. Those who survived this training were paid high wages: 4.5 taels a month, almost twice as much as a regular soldier's earnings. One-third of this amount was sent directly to the brave's family by his individual commander.[6]

As the Hsiang Army grew to number 120,000 soldiers, the appointment of officers and raising of quartermaster funds were co-ordinated by a sophisticated private bureaucracy. Tseng Kuo-fan fashioned this instrument out of the traditional *mu-fu* (literally, offices behind the curtain) or secretariat of aides attached to a major official. The *mu-fu* originally designated a staff for military campaigns. After the Ming government reduced its allocations for clerical personnel, regular officials, including magistrates, hired their own retinues of secretaries (*mu-yu*). Relations between an official and his *mu-yu* (literally, friends behind the curtain) were governed by Confucian protocol, the employer acting as host for his advisers in such a way as to make the occupation of secretary a respectable one for literati. Indeed, by Ch'ing times an eminent official was likely to have some of the most talented scholars in the realm serving on his staff. Just as generals sometimes attribute military success to their skill at selecting aides-de-camp, so did top Ch'ing officials pride themselves on their discrimination of *jen-ts'ai* (men of ability). Tseng Kuo-fan was particularly confident in this regard, as well he had reason to be. By 1856 he had assembled a dazzling array of gifted scholars and officers to help build his military apparatus.

Tseng could reward his *mu-yu* by recommending them for a regular civil service appointment, but he needed cash to pay his troops. At first, when the Taipings still threatened Hunan, members of the gentry volunteered contributions to support Tseng's braves. Tseng also received permission from the central government to raise funds by selling degrees. However, these sources dried up rather quickly when the Taipings ceased to be an immediate local threat. The gentry were becoming exhausted by the militia commissioner's constant request for funds, and surtaxes on landholders were likely to incite them to riot, as they did in Ningpo and Canton. Fortunately, a new fiscal device was conceived at this time by an official in Yangchow. Known as likin (*li-chin*), it was a duty imposed upon commercial goods shipped between market towns.[7] Merchants, rather than peasants or gentry, were most directly affected by likin, which was easily collected by placing customs barriers on major trade routes. At first individual commanders in the Hsiang Army collected likin for their own troops. Later Tseng's *mu-fu* centralized operations and opened up a likin headquarters in Kiangsi province.

Likin did not free Tseng Kuo-fan from his financial dependence on the central government. His military expenses were still higher

than this privately controlled revenue, and he was constantly seeking permission from the capital to tap regular provincial tax sources.
In fact, the government grew impatient with both the money and
time which he said he needed to build a military apparatus in
Hunan. Like many great Chinese generals, Tseng Kuo-fan stressed
the importance of a safe base area. In order to defeat the Taipings,
he needed first to secure his rear lines by restoring stability in rural
Hunan. That meant taking care of the peasants' material needs by
setting up relief bureaus and granaries, and guaranteeing public
security by reinvigorating gentry control mechanisms. Counter-
insurgency would succeed—Tseng believed—if the peasants were
indoctrinated with Confucian values after they had been redeemed
from the rebels' arms and returned to the fold of civilized society.

Defeat of the Taipings

Peking appreciated the need for rural stability, but military
affairs seemed of greater urgency at the moment. Once the Taipings
had settled in Nanking after March, 1853, the regular Ch'ing armies
under Hsiang Jung and Ch'i-shan had moved in from the south and
north to hem in the rebels vertically. The Taiping forces therefore
struck out horizontally along the Yangtze River, taking Wuhan and
northern Hunan at the end of that same year. As their advance
continued, the emperor repeatedly ordered Tseng Kuo-fan to retaliate, but Tseng refused to move until he had consolidated his
control over western Hunan and assembled a naval militia. Then,
in the late spring of 1854, he began to drive the rebels out of his
province. In July the loyalist forces destroyed half the Taiping river
fleet at Yueh-chou, and three months later the Wuhan cities were
recovered. By December the Taiping Army had been expelled from
Hunan and the middle reaches of the Yangtze River lay open to
the Hsiang Army braves. If they advanced along the banks of the
river and took the border city of Chiu-chiang, then Tseng's navy
could push on into Anhwei toward Nanking.

But the Taiping defenses at Chiu-chiang held, and the rebels
counterattacked decisively. In order to save his fleet from annihilation, Tseng Kuo-fan was forced to retreat into Lake Po-yang where
he remained bottled up for the next two years while the Taipings
broke the north-south siege of Nanking and eventually fielded an

army in Hupei. From Tseng's point of view, the only bright point in all this military bleakness was that Peking was now willing to appoint one of his protégés, Hu Lin-i, governor of Hupei. During the next two years, much of Hupei's provincial revenue was diverted to Tseng's commissary, providing him with the means to rebuild and expand the Hsiang Army.

In the spring of 1858 the imperial government launched a second offensive. The siege was reimposed at Nanking, and the Hsiang Army broke the Taiping defenses at Chiu-chiang. But the rebels once again defeated the Ch'ing forces by crushing the northern camp outside Nanking and wiping out the Anhwei detachment of the Hsiang Army under Tseng's brother, Kuo-hua, who was killed in battle. This time, however, Tseng Kuo-fan managed to retain control of the middle reaches of the Yangtze, forcing the Taiping commanders to plan a concerted counteroffensive in 1860 to retake Anking. Although the rebels' main mission was foiled, their general, Li Hsiu-ch'eng, did capture several major cities in eastern Kiangsu.

The Taiping victories of 1859–1860 forced the Ch'ing Dynasty to grant more authority to Tseng Kuo-fan, who was finally named governor-general of Kiangsu, Kiangsi, and Anhwei. From this position he was able to commandeer the revenue sources of the entire Yangtze valley, as well as secure the appointment of his protégés to governorships in the region. By now, in fact, Tseng had used his *mu-yu* to create ancillary armies, outfitted with more modern weapons and modeled upon the original Hsiang Army. The two most important of these new armies were Tso Tsung-t'ang's unit in Chekiang and an army in Anhwei commanded by Li Hung-chang, Tseng's former student. Thus in less than a decade Tseng Kuo-fan had built an entirely new military apparatus of his own to replace the old Green Standard armies in central China, and he was now prepared to commit his forces to a final attack upon the Nanking headquarters of the Heavenly Kingdom. In 1862 he ordered Tso and Li to close upon Nanking from the northwest and south, while the Hsiang Army, commanded by another of Tseng's brothers, Kuo-ch'üan, drove in frontally along the Yangtze.

The Taiping commander, Li Hsiu-ch'eng, realized that his only hope was to stop Tseng's main force at Anking. But the Heavenly King, Hung Hsiu-ch'üan, was frightened by the auxiliary armies and ordered Li back to Nanking. As the vise tightened, Li Hung-chang captured Soochow, Tso Tsung-t'ang occupied Hangchow, and Tseng Kuo-ch'üan drew near the walls of Nanking. By the summer

of 1864, it was obvious that the Heavenly Kingdom was lost. On
June 1, Hung Hsiu-ch'üan died of illness and an heir named Hung
Fu was placed on the doomed Taiping throne. On July 19, 1864,
Tseng Kuo-ch'üan's army attacked and burned the city. No quarter
was given to the rebels, who suffered one hundred thousand dead.

The Nien Rebellion

Not all of the Taipings were killed when Nanking fell. Many
units moved south, resisting the imperial forces for another year
along the Fukien-Kwangtung border. Others fled north to join the
Nien rebels in the Huai River basin.

The multitude of Nien rebels did not form a coherent ideological
movement like the Taipings. They included White Lotus sectarians,
salt smugglers, and bandit gangs which combined in temporary confederations against the imperial forces led by Seng-ko-lin-ch'in after
1860. The advent of the Taiping remnants did not change the nature
of the Nien revolt, but it did enhance the rebels' military ranks, which
defeated and killed Seng-ko-lin-ch'in in western Shantung in 1865.
The throne was gravely alarmed by this Nien victory. Originally
the court had planned to disband Tseng Kuo-fan's irregular army
after the fall of Nanking. Now it seemed one of the few forces in
the empire capable of destroying the Nien.

Tseng tackled the Nien rebellion with some the same techniques
used to pacify Hunan. Whenever possible, the gentry were encouraged to return to their villages and restore civil order. The
pao-chia control system was reconstituted, and the authority of rural
headmen and elders was enforced by Tseng's soldiers. Relief bureaus and self-defense leagues were organized. Above all, an effort
was made to cut the rebels off from their peasant supporters by
physically isolating the villages from the countryside.[8] The policy
of hua-ho ch'üan-ti (making rivers the boundaries and encircling
limited areas) called for dikes and trenches to seal off scorched
earth areas where the Nien cavalry's mobility could be restricted
and supplies curtailed. But the Nien were too many to be so easily
contained, bursting forth in one quarter while Tseng's troops camped
elsewhere. Moreover, Tseng found that his absence from the Yangtze area was jeopardizing his personal grip on the revenue sources

that had financed the Hsiang Army. Individual likin bureaus were escaping from the control of his *mu-fu*. Other provincial command-ers in Hunan, Kiangsu, and Anhwei were diverting taxes to their military coffers. The sinews of his own army were weakening, and Tseng welcomed his transfer away from the Huai basin in 1867 before the task of destroying the Nien was completed. His suc-cessor was Li Hung-chang—a man whom he had elevated to com-mand, and who was to advance military regionalism several steps closer to twentieth-century warlordism.

Li Hung-chang and the Huai Army

Li Hung-chang was the son of a politically prominent Anhwei scholar, Li Wen-an, who had been Tseng Kuo-fan's classmate. After Li Hung-chang acquired the provincial degree, his father sent him to Peking to study with Tseng, who was doubly pleased by Li's success in the *chin-shih* examinations and his subsequent appoint-ment to the Hanlin Academy. When the Taiping Rebellion broke out, Li returned home with his father to raise militia and then joined the staff of the Anhwei governor, Fu-chi. Shortly after that he became a secretary in Tseng Kuo-fan's *mu-fu*.

In spite of his close personal relationship with Tseng, Li did not adjust easily to being a secretary. He was headstrong and opin-ionated, and when his recommendations were ignored he was quick to resign in protest. Repeated invitations always drew him back, but Li really longed for his own command and for the chance to decide rather than merely to advise. His opportunity came in 1861 when Li Hsiu-ch'eng's Taiping Army in Kiangsu threatened the treaty port of Shanghai. Responding to pleas for military aid, Tseng Kuo-fan used his influence to get Li appointed acting governor of Kiangsu, a post which at last made it possible for Li to form his own Huai Army.

The Huai Army (named after the major river of Anhwei) con-sisted of seventy thousand personally recruited, well trained, highly paid braves. Like the Hsiang Army, it was coordinated by a private *mu-fu*. What made it unique was its financial base. As we shall see, Li Hung-chang was to move beyond Tseng's simple likin taxes and develop a new source of revenue from Shanghai's foreign trade.

Shanghai and the Customs Tariffs

After the Treaty of Nanking, Shanghai had become China's major port. Cantonese compradores, Fukienese junk merchants, and Ningpo bankers opened branch offices in the city and soon developed common commercial interests with the Western merchants trading there. After the Small Sword Society[9] seized part of Shanghai in September, 1853, and disturbed international trade, this Sino-Western business community began to cooperate in the city's defense. New social allies appeared in the late 1850s, when the Kiangnan gentry fled to the treaty port from the Taipings, who were then occupying the lower Yangtze cities and drawing near Shanghai. Because the business community wanted to protect their entrepôt and the gentry wished to recover their homes in Kiangnan, it was agreed to hire mercenaries to fight the rebels. The merchants thus financed a flamboyant American adventurer named Frederick Townsend Ward to recruit foreign soldiers of fortune into a private force called the Ever-Victorious Army. Despite its name and the exaggerated accounts of its exploits in the Shanghai press, the army was neither always victorious nor that crucial to the Ch'ing cause. Under a later commander, Major Charles George "China" Gordon (the English officer who later died gloriously at Khartoum), the mercenaries did play a part in Li Hung-chang's campaigns; but the Ever-Victorious Army was mainly important as a symbol of the Chinese and Western authorities' new eagerness to collaborate against the Taiping rebels. Until the spring of 1860, the foreign powers had overtly observed a policy of neutrality in the civil war. But when General Li Hsiu-ch'eng and his Taiping soldiers approached Shanghai, the British and French consuls made it clear that they would fight the rebels with their own troops if necessary. The powers became even more markedly pro-Ch'ing after the Convention of Peking was signed in October, 1860. The English especially believed that they now had a stake in preserving the ruling dynasty that had conceded them so many privileges in the Treaty of Tientsin. Moreover, they were afraid that a continually divided China would "create a fresh Eastern Question in those seas"[10]—that is, invite the same kind of Russian intervention that had led to the Crimean War over the collapsing Ottoman Empire. By December, 1861, when the Taipings sacked the treaty port of Ningpo, British diplomats were solidly on the side of the Ch'ing, and by the following spring they had committed themselves openly to upholding the dynasty.

Formal diplomatic collaboration between the Ch'ing Dynasty and the Western powers was embodied in the Imperial Maritime Customs, which developed out of the foreign consuls' temporary arrangements in 1853 and 1854 to collect Shanghai's customs tariffs on behalf of the Chinese government. As it was finally constituted, the Imperial Maritime Customs was a professional corps of foreign bureaucrats who served the Chinese government as customs officers. Under the incorruptible leadership of an Englishman, Sir Robert Hart, the Imperial Maritime Customs eventually proved to be a financial mainstay of the Chinese government. The duties which it collected were usually well accounted for and kept immune from the peculation characteristic of most other sources of government income. However, this was not true in 1861, when Li Hung-chang arrived in Shanghai. At that point the Shanghai revenues were still being diverted into the hands of the Soochow Circuit Intendant, Wu Hsu, who was supposedly paying for Ch'ing military costs in Kiangnan. In fact, Wu Hsu and his colleagues were raking more than 20 percent of the total right off the top of the customs receipts.

Li quickly realized that this revenue could make his Huai Army financially independent. Feigning friendship with Wu Hsu, he therefore carefully placed his own men in the lower echelons of the Shanghai bureaucracy and began to create shadow offices in his *mu-fu* to assume some of the fiscal duties of the circuit intendant's office. Only when he was sure that his takeover would succeed did Li finally move, accusing Wu Hsu of corruption and of appropriating the Shanghai customs revenue for his own military purposes.

At first glance, the Shanghai customs revenue does not appear that much different from likin—both were taxes on goods in transit. But in the short run there was an obvious and very important distinction between the two. Likin was a series of small taxes gathered over a wide expanse of territory. To keep his collectors from withholding the likin on the spot, Tseng Kuo-fan therefore had to retain administrative control of the territory. Once transferred to a governorship or viceroyalty elsewhere, an official like Tseng had difficulty tapping that revenue at a distance. The Shanghai tariffs, on the other hand, were a large sum gathered at a single spot. By getting one or two of his most trusted protégés placed in charge of the Shanghai receipts, Li Hung-chang could be much more certain in the short run of continuing to receive the revenue even after he left Shanghai.

Yet in the long run his financial security would depend very much on retaining the favor of Peking. For, there was another major difference between the two kinds of revenue that became obvious as time passed. Likin was an inefficient way of collecting extra taxes because there were too many opportunities for revenue agents to keep some of the funds themselves. But precisely because likin collection could not easily be centralized under a provincial administration, it defied Peking's expropriation as well. Even though the Ch'ing government nationalized likin later on, provincial governors continued to collect the transit duties without reporting the proceeds to the Board of Revenue. Yet while this represented a considerable aggregate loss of revenue to the dynasty, it did not amount to a particularly high level of income for individual provincial administrations. Likin provided a measure of fiscal independence for lower-level military governors in the later Ch'ing, but it did not guarantee them enough economic support to build powerful military machines on their own.

The Shanghai tariffs, in contrast, were substantial enough to make Li Hung-chang far more than a mere provincial governor. However, the customs tariffs could not be concealed from Peking because they were eventually collected by the foreign-staffed Imperial Maritime Customs Service. Therefore, in spite of his early sequestering of this revenue, Li Hung-chang had to acquire the central government's permission to continue using these funds. For the moment, the war against the Taipings justified his appropriations. Once Nanking fell, the Nien Rebellion served the same function. But Li could only lay a special claim on foreign trade proceeds by arguing that his military expenditures were more important than those of other officials.

His argument for this was very simple. The funds he was given did not just pay for Huai Army salaries; they were devoted to the "self-strengthening" of the entire nation. By copying foreign military techniques and adopting modern weapons, Li's armies would strengthen the empire against internal rebels and foreign aggressors. It was his leadership in modernizing China that justified taking what would otherwise be national revenue, though of course he used these moneys to personally create bureaus, mines, factories, railroads, armies, navies, and transport companies which eventually competed with the central government. Thus, while the provincial bureaucrats evolved into military satraps partly because of likin, regional viceroys like Li Hung-chang transformed the administrative system at a much higher level. Because they depended on the central government's permission to use national income for their projects, the self-strengtheners were not directly challenging Peking's hegemony. But as their complicated military and industrial machines displaced the national government on a larger scale, the traditional bureaucracy crumbled and a new cadre of professional soldiers and technical experts assumed power. Self-strengthening, then, was both an immediate rationalization for Li Hung-chang to retain his claim upon the public fisc and the harbinger of future revolutionary change as it created entirely new sources of military and economic power.

The self-strengthening movement that Li Hung-chang pioneered received the blessing of foreign diplomats who believed that a strong and unified China best suited their collective interests. In England a less aggressive air swept through Whitehall, where Lord Clarendon was now foreign minister. And in China sinophiles like the American minister Anson Burlingame and the British ambassador Rutherford Alcock pleaded that the Ch'ing be treated fairly according to international law. The years from 1862 to 1869, in other words, were a time of conscious cooperation between China and the Great Powers, with foreign sympathizers zealously trying to convince the Ch'ing authorities of the need for institutional and educational reforms to modernize the country. Their suggestions fell upon reasonably receptive ears for the political climate in Peking had changed a great deal since the last Opium War, and there were now many at court who wished to encourage self-strengthening.

The Balance of Political Power in Peking

Opinions had altered in the capital partly as a reaction to the debacle of 1860 and partly because a new imperial regime occupied the throne. The Hsien-feng Emperor had died in his palace at Jehol on August 22, 1861. At the very end he was virtually the captive of a circle of eight Manchu adjutant generals and grand councillors, headed by the imperial clansman, Su-shun. The latter, though a supporter of Tseng Kuo-fan and Li Hung-chang, was also the proponent of a firm policy against the West and was probably best known to the public for his draconian monetary reforms in 1859.[11]

Like the seventeenth-century regent Oboi, Su-shun believed in
Manchu princely rule and distrusted many of the emperor's Chinese
advisors. There was no problem of succession in this case, because
there was only one heir to the throne—the five year-old son of the
Empress Hsiao-ch'in. But there was a conflict over the regency.
The dying emperor's dictated testament named the eight adjutants
and councillors all co-regents, but it stipulated that edicts had to
be endorsed by his two empresses, Hsiao-ch'in and another favorite
named Tz'u-an. The first of these was the most formidable obstacle
to the co-regents' autonomy. Hsiao-ch'in, later known as Tz'u-hsi,
was a woman of the Yehe clan[12] who commanded the support of
the chief palace eunuch An Te-hai, and who was rumored to have
had a love affair with the commander of the Peking Field Force,
Jung-lu.[13] She was also in close touch with her brother-in-law,
Prince Kung, who had been left in charge of the Peking diplomatic
negotiations when the emperor fled to Jehol. Prince Kung had
developed strong alliances within the higher Peking bureaucracy
and was highly regarded by prominent Chinese officials.

As relations between the co-regents and the two empress dow-
agers grew acrimonious and suspicious, the time came to accompany
the Hsien-feng Emperor's funeral cortege back to Peking. Befitting
his paramount position in the regency, Su-shun was placed in
personal charge of the catafalque. The Empress Dowager Tz'u-hsi
was thus able to reach Peking a day in advance of the procession,
and—guarded by Jung-lu's men—quickly gathered allies against
Su-shun. That night, November 1, while camped outside the capital,
Su-shun was surprised in his tent by the imperial prince I-huan,[14]
who had led a party of guardsmen forth from the capital to arrest
him. The other co-regents were also seized and accused of plotting
to usurp the throne. Several of them were allowed the privilege of
committing suicide. Su-shun, however, was disgraced with the
heavier sentence of a public beheading before the populace of
Peking.

Tz'u-hsi's success showed how much more sinified the Ch'ing
Dynasty was then than it had been in Oboi's days. Consort rule,
which was a frequent aberration during the Han and T'ang periods,
had never before occurred in the Ch'ing. Now an Empress Dowager
had managed to defeat a concerted attempt to restore the old
Manchu collegium. Of course, Tz'u-hsi was not acting alone. The
form of rule that emerged from the 1861 coup was a relatively
stable alliance among herself, the other dowager Tz'u-an, and Prince

Kung. The boy emperor sat on the throne, but from behind a screen in the audience room of the palace the two women conducted "joint rule"—the very name of this reign era (T'ung-chih, 1862–1874). Between them and the outer bureaucracy stood Kung, the "prince advisor" who worked closely with Wen-hsiang and Shen Kuei-fen on the Grand Council and supported the self-strengthening programs of Tseng Kuo-fan and Li Hung-chang.

Self-Strengthening

Feng Kuei-fen, the prominent advocate of gentry self-rule, was also a spokesman for the self-strengthening movement. He was one of the first to point out the failures of the traditional barbarian management experts by showing that the Western nations were not a host of disunited tribesmen but rather a united front whose military superiority would destroy China unless the empire strengthened itself. China was not weak because it lacked men of ability (*jen-ts'ai*) or because it was morally corrupt. The country was unable to defend itself because it refused to change its institutions. The educational system above all needed to be reformed. Officials had to be encouraged to learn about the West. More modern schools like the *T'ung-wen kuan*[15] should be opened to train translators and specialists, and the examination system should be brought up to date.

Li Hung-chang approved of these suggestions and added several of his own, especially stressing military modernization. In spite of the diplomatic cooperation of the 1860s, Li feared that when the chips were down foreigners yielded to power, not to international law. The Chinese desperately needed to train new officers in the use of modern weapons and to replace their unwieldy provincial garrisons with smaller, more mobile armies. Coastal defenses had to be strengthened along the North China Sea and around the Yangtze. Arsenals needed to be constructed so that the country did not have to depend upon foreigners for guns and warships.

Li and his patron, Tseng Kuo-fan, had already opened small arsenals to outfit their armies fighting the Taipings. In 1865, after their victory, they used 20 percent of the Shanghai revenue to build the Kiangnan arsenal near Shanghai. The arsenal grew to include 32 buildings which produced 1,000 pounds of gunpowder a day and eventually turned out 8 warships for the Chinese. In 1866 Tseng Kuo-fan's other protégé, Tso Tsung-t'ang, founded his own arsenal in Foochow, but the following year it slipped out of his control and was put under the management of one of Li Hung-chang's *mu-yu*, Shen Pao-chen. It was thus the regional viceroys who took the initiative in self-strengthening, and acquired a virtual monopoly in a sector which the central government might well have been expected to guard jealously for itself. Peking must surely have foreseen the danger of these administrative satrapies expanding to the dynasty's detriment. Why did the throne permit the process to continue?

At first, because of the civil war, it had no choice. The self-strengthening projects began before Nanking was conquered. And then, as we have seen, Li Hung-chang and Tso Tsung-t'ang had to combat the Nien rebels in north China in 1867–1868. Li Hung-chang managed to contain some of them in Shantung by excavating a hundred-mile trench across the peninsula, and he scored a major victory in December, 1867, but then other Nien units descended upon Chihli from the west. Finally, late in the summer of 1868, Li and Tso's forces combined to defeat the enemy decisively. Tso Tsung-t'ang had yet five more years to spend in Shensi and Kansu fighting the New Sect Muslims, but Li's years as a counterinsurgent were over. Shortly after the Nien rebels' final defeat, pressure therefore began to build in Peking to demobilize the Huai forces. Li's army, and the Kiangnan Arsenal that supplied it, might well have been dismantled if China's foreign relations had not taken a sharp turn for the worse.

Foreign Relations

The era of diplomatic cooperation between 1862 and 1869 was marred by the growing dissatisfaction of Western businessmen who failed to develop markets for their goods in China. Economists insisted that Chinese consumption levels were not high enough to justify the merchants' dreams of four hundred million new customers, but the myth of the China market was hard to dispel. And when that market failed to materialize, foreign merchants did exactly what they had done in 1839 and 1856—they found a scapegoat for their disappointment by blaming the Chinese authorities. This time they were convinced that the new likin tax was hampering commerce and demanded that the Ch'ing government exempt all goods which had already been taxed at the treaty ports from payment of internal transit duties. There were fresh demands as well because the treaty ports' business communities were coming to see new and quite different economic possibilities in China. The development of Shanghai in particular had shown how profitable it might be for Westerners to use cheap Chinese labor in their textile mills, undercutting foreign competitors' manufactured imports. The Ch'ing empire was still basically viewed as an outlet for Midlands or New England products, but by the 1860s investors were beginning to contemplate extending the principle of Shanghai's international concession to the entire country, building factories inland to manufacture inexpensive clothing and tools for the Chinese peasantry. They were also becoming aware for the first time of China's rich mineral resources. How much more there was to exploit—if only Westerners were allowed to reside in the interior, send steamships up China's inland waterways, open more treaty ports, build telegraphs and railways, and insist on the right to mine coal, iron, and precious metals!

Yet at the very moment these claims were voiced most loudly, Chinese public opinion began to harden against the Western presence. The Tientsin Treaty had opened the interior to Christian missionaries. They and their converts were becoming a familiar sight in provinces which, until that time, foreigners had hardly visited. The sight was not a pleasing one to most Chinese. Already during the eighteenth century stories of the strange and frightening religious practices of Christians had circulated in China. Taiping excesses did not improve that image of Christianity. In 1861 an anonymous anti-foreign tract, the *Pi-hsieh chi-shih* (Record of Facts to Ward off Heterodoxy) appeared throughout the empire, detailing the salacious and repugnant practices of the Christians: women drinking their own menses, men kidnapping and sexually deforming children. Lurid prints depicted the Christians as pig-like beasts torturing the Chinese, and broadsheets called for the gentry's militia to track down and destroy these loathsome creatures. The warnings and appeals fell on ready ears. The lower gentry were especially angered by the way in which missionaries quickly gained a local influence more powerful even than their own. As a British military attaché reported later in the century from Manchuria:

The mass of the upper classes regard the missionaries as political agents and fear them. The poor know this, and look, in many cases, to the missionary—the honest for protection, the dishonest to further their own ends. These ends may be the evasion of recovery of a debt, or some similar dispute, in which they know that their connections with the Church will influence the Magistrate.[16]

For example, tenants involved in rent disputes with their landlords sometimes converted to the Western religion and then complained to the missionary that they were receiving discriminatory treatment from the gentry because they were Christians. The missionary was more likely than not to protest to the magistrate in the name of religious toleration. This put the magistrate in an impossible position. If he placated the missionary by ruling in favor of the Christian converts, then the local gentry would accuse him of "selling out the country" to foreigners. Yet if he rejected the Christians' case, the missionary was just as liable to complain of prejudice to his consul and try to have the magistrate removed from office. Prevarication only made matters worse because resentment then spread among the populace and antiforeign tracts were passed from hand to hand until demagogues (often aspiring examination candidates) drummed up a mob and physically attacked the converts or even killed the missionary himself. In that event the magistrate and his superiors had no choice but to punish the rioters in hopes of averting a major diplomatic incident or the arrival of a vengeful Western gunboat. The Ch'ing authorities' reaction to anti-Christian outbursts in Hunan and Kiangsi in 1862, Kweichow in 1865, and central China and Taiwan in 1869, thus appeared to confirm the popular rumors of insidious missionary influence and exacerbated fears that the government was too weak to protect its subjects' interests.

Although many high Ch'ing officials sympathized with the anti-Christian movement, most realized that China was not yet strong enough to risk another confrontation with the West. Instead, they determined to respect international law and abide by the Treaty of Tientsin, which contained a clause calling for limited revision of the agreement by 1870. For the first time in its modern diplomatic history, the Chinese government was willing to entertain, and then to ratify, treaty revisions in order to perpetuate the cooperative spirit of 1862. In fact, when high Ch'ing officials formally debated the matter in 1867, it was clear that men who had opposed any concessions at all in 1858 were now prepared to respond much more flexibly to Western demands. In 1868, therefore, the Tsungli Yamen began to negotiate amicably with the British ambassador, Alcock, and on October 23, 1869, signed an agreement which opened Lake Po-yang to steam navigation and commuted likin on foreign goods for slightly higher silk and opium tariffs.

The British were not nearly so complaisant. Alcock had negotiated the revisions in good faith, but his efforts were undone by the foreign business community. English merchants felt the agreement was "retrograde" because it failed to secure the railway, mining, and residence rights that they had expected. At home Clarendon supported his ambassador against hostile public opinion, but the foreign secretary's death in June, 1870, dashed any hope of ratification by London. Puzzled and disappointed by this lack of cooperation, the Chinese ministry of foreign affairs was about to readdress itself to the question of treaty revision when a new crisis suddenly erupted.

The Tientsin Massacre and Li Hung-chang's Indispensability

While the Alcock negotiations had been taking place in an atmosphere of official cordiality, popular Chinese xenophobia had become more intense. During 1869 there was a veritable crescendo of anti-Christian incidents. The following year rumors circulated in Tientsin, where an epidemic raged, that Catholic priests and nuns were kidnapping children to be ritually sacrificed. In June, 1870, these rumors appeared to be verified when magistrates produced depositions from criminals who had sold children to the orphanage of St. Vincent de Paul.[17] City leaders demanded an immediate investigation, and on June 21 judicial officials asked to be allowed to inspect the premises of the French cathedral. The French consul, M. Fontanier, chose to regard this as a national insult and stormed into the yamen of the city prefect, Ch'ung-hou, who tried to calm the excited man. But Fontanier completely lost control of himself, drawing a sword and revolver which he fired at Ch'ung-hou. The bullet missed the prefect. Fontanier then rushed out the yamen gates, but his exit was impeded by a crowd of curious onlookers who fell back as he began to lay about him with his sword. At that moment the district magistrate and his police aide stepped forward, intending to place themselves between the crowd and the Frenchman.[18] The consul raised his pistol to fire again, and this time his shot found its mark, killing the policeman. The crowd went mad. Within moments Fontanier had been torn to pieces and rioting spread across the city. The French consulate was burned, the cathedral's orphanage razed; and ten nuns, two priests, and seven French residents were killed and mutilated.

When reports of the Tientsin massacre reached Peking, court officials immediately expected the worst and began preparations to defend the country against a French attack. It was at this point that all talk of disbanding Li Hung-chang's army ceased and the government turned to him again for military help. On July 26, 1870, Li Hung-chang was ordered to bring 25,000 men of his Huai Army to Chihli, the province surrounding the capital. There he was named viceroy, put in charge of the regular imperial armies around the capital, and allowed to open an intendant's office in Tientsin to funnel that port's tariffs into his self-strengthening projects.

As it turned out, France did not go to war with China because it was already entering into hostilities with Prussia. But the era of cooperation was definitely over, and Li Hung-chang's importance to the regime was enhanced. As imperialism intensified after 1870, Li's willingness to undertake the refurbishing of the Chinese army was deeply appreciated by the throne. There was, after all, a more fundamental reason for Peking's willingness to place the responsibility for modernization upon the regional viceroys. If the central government was going to directly supervise self-strengthening, then it would have to revamp the entire bureaucracy and follow Feng Kuei-fen's recommendations by altering the civil service examination system. This meant telling over a million literati that their years of classical training had been wasted and that the Confucian canon had no functional place in the modern world. Not only were the Manchus (who ruled China in the name of a Confucian mandate) incapable at that point of making such a radical decision; the mandarinate was still basically confident that the Confucian classics were a better guide to government than gunnery manuals. And the most conservative among them insisted that even studying about the West corrupted the intellectual substance of their culture. Officials like Wo-jen held Li Hung-chang in scorn for what seemed almost a cultural betrayal, and they were quick to oppose dynastic programs of modernization.

The Empress Dowager's Politics of Compromise

The conservatives kept their influence in the government because of the politics of balance and compromise adopted by the Empress Dowager Tz'u-hsi. The alliance between her, Tz'u-an, and Prince Kung had become quite strained in the last years of the regency, with each warily checking the others' attempts to gain a decisive advantage. By 1873 when the T'ung-chih Emperor attained his majority, many officials were relieved to have the regency end and hoped to see an era free of intrigues ahead. But T'ung-chih's health failed[19] and his death the following year provoked a major succession crisis which Tz'u-hsi narrowly won. Instead of appointing a direct heir to T'ung-chih, she wished to put her infant nephew on the throne, thus perpetuating the regency for another fifteen years. Prince Kung opposed this move, but he could not risk open defiance because Tz'u-hsi had already mobilized Jung-lu's field force and apparently had the support of Li Hung-chang's army. The naming of her nephew as the Kuang-hsu Emperor in 1874 scandalized many officials because it contravened the Confucian rule of direct filial succession, but Tz'u-hsi weathered the storm and consolidated her power over the throne. In 1881 Tz'u-an died mysteriously, and three years later Prince Kung was dismissed. The "Old Buddha" (as contemporaries sometimes called Tz'u-hsi) was in complete control of the court. However, she also had to rely upon support from the outer bureaucracy so as to prevent ministerial coalitions from forming against her. One way of doing this was to split the bureaucracy along the major ideological cleavage between cultural conservatives and pragmatic self-strengtheners. On the one hand, Tz'u-hsi kept the central government weighted toward the side of Wo-jen and never entirely condemned the conservative opponents of reform to loyal silence. Yet at the same time she refused to reject the proponents of modernization and encouraged self-strengthening projects in the provinces. In fact, she even earned the gratitude of viceroys like Li Hung-chang (who treated her as his patron after Tseng Kuo-fan died in 1872) for protecting him from the conservatives' vocal attacks on western learning.

Conservatives, too, were grateful to her because she insulated the seat of government in Peking from the immediate consequences of all these new military and industrial projects. Self-strengthening was segregated outside the traditional bureaucracy which observed the same procedures, the same routines, the same rituals as it had for centuries. Interestingly enough, precisely an identical kind of segregation occurred within the modernizing sector as well. This was because all of the new projects were managed by the informal secretariats (mu-fu) of the regional viceroys. A man like Li Hung-chang was thus able to open an arsenal without having to know very much about weapons manufacture himself. His mu-yu—students trained abroad, compradores, naval experts, even foreign advisers—handled those details for him and relied on their patron to provide the financial means to complete their projects: the Kiangnan arsenal, the China Steam Merchants Navigation Company, a railroad, a textile plant, and the Kaiping coal mines.

As Li Hung-chang's conglomerate grew, he participated more and more visibly in international affairs. After Prince Kung was dismissed in 1884, Li acted as a foreign minister without portfolio. He seemed so powerful that foreign diplomats sometimes thought that he could afford to disregard Peking entirely. This was untrue. Li Hung-chang continued to depend on the empress dowager's central government for both patronage and revenue. His mu-yu, for instance, expected to be rewarded eventually with a regular civil service appointment in the bureaucracy. A mandarin's badge still commanded the highest respect in the land, and Li could not provide that for his followers without the help of the bureaus of rites and civil appointments in the capital. Then, too, the major sources of revenue for his projects continued to be the Shanghai and Tientsin tariffs, plus national defense allocations. The purse strings that tied him to Tz'u-hsi and Peking were impossible to cut.

Nor did Li Hung-chang have a personal monopoly on military and industrial activities. Other viceroys competed with him for the same revenues. His first major rival was Tso Tsung-t'ang,[20] who had also earned his reputation under Tseng Kuo-fan. After the Taiping and Nien forces were defeated, Tso was asked by the empress dowager if he could recover China's northwestern provinces from the New Sect Muslims. He rashly promised Tz'u-hsi he would complete the job in five years and, somewhat to his own surprise, finished on schedule. That brought him face to face with the Russians who had illegally seized territory in Sinkiang while Ch'ing forces were occupied elsewhere. The stakes in this encounter were control of Central Asia, and Tso insisted that China could not risk abandoning this strategic zone. He was thus constantly requesting military funds that would otherwise have gone to Li Hung-chang, who believed that the empire's coastal defenses were much more critical than a few mountain passes at the other end of the country.

Another one of Li Hung-chang's major rivals, especially during the 1880s, was Chang Chih-tung. Chang was a younger man, born on the eve of the first Opium War, who came of age as a bold militia leader during the Taiping Rebellion. A brilliant scholar, he rose rapidly in the civil service and acquired an excellent administrative reputation as governor of Shansi. In 1884 Chang was promoted to the viceroyalty (governor-generalship) of Kwangtung and Kwangsi, just as south China was gearing up for a war to dispute France's colonization of Vietnam (Annam). In 1874 France had established a protectorate over the Vietnamese monarchy. The king of Annam, evoking his tributary relationship to the Ch'ing Emperor, asked the Chinese to intervene and help him escape from French bondage. The Ch'ing government was then too distracted by the conflict with Russia over Sinkiang to offer aid, but Chinese irregulars known as the Black Flags[21] began to attack French outposts in northern Vietnam (Tonkin). To expel these irregulars, Commander Henri Rivière occupied Hanoi in April, 1882, drawing dangerously close to the Chinese border.

The Sino–French War of 1884–1885

By now China had had almost twenty years in which to strengthen and modernize its military forces. The Sinkiang crisis had just been resolved by a treaty acceptable to both sides, and for the moment there were no pressing military obligations elsewhere.[22] French colonialism in Indochina was not only a halfway house to the penetration of southwestern China; it was also the domination of a country formerly within China's traditional sphere of influence. To Chang Chih-tung and a clique of younger Hanlin scholars known as the *ch'ing-i* (pure talk) group, the French gauntlet simply could not be ignored. Rivière's occupation of Hanoi had to be contested.

Yet the leader of the self-strengthening movement, Li Hung-chang, was opposed to war with France—partly because he did not assess China's military capability so highly, and partly because he was unwilling to commit his armies to a war outside his northern bailiwick. But the climate of opinion in the capital was so strong that the dynasty went to war in Vietnam, sending in regular troops which were partly provisioned by Chang Chih-tung in Kwangtung and Kwangsi. Li immediately tried to arrange a truce with the French, but neither Paris nor Peking appreciated his effort and the fighting raged on. In 1884 the French tried to conclude the conflict by carrying the war into Chinese waters. French marines landed on Taiwan, and their navy blockaded the southeastern coast. Alarmed for the safety of Canton, Chang Chih-tung quickly blocked the port's approaches, leaving one other major target for the French to attack if they wished to drive China to the conference table. This target was the main arsenal at Foochow, which was not so easily defended. Observing its vulnerability, the official in charge there, Chang P'ei-lun,[23] pleaded with Peking for reinforcements. Chang Chih-tung did send a couple of warships to Foochow, but Li Hung-chang ignored requests to dispatch his fleet south. Consequently, the French easily rammed through Chang P'ei-lun's defenses and destroyed the arsenal. One of the prices of military regionalism, it would appear, was the jealousy with which each major viceroy guarded his own men and weapons, withholding them from campaigns outside his own theater of war. Such parochialism was not quickly forgotten, and others would repay Li Hung-chang for his possessiveness a decade later.

Despite their victory at Foochow, the French did not gain much more from the war of 1884–1885 than treaty recognition of their suzerainty over Vietnam. In the last days of the war, a minor Chinese infantry victory gave the right wing in France an opportunity to overthrow Jules Ferry's cabinet and steer the government back to its *revanchiste* obsession with the recovery of Alsace-Lorraine from Germany. The most astute Ch'ing officials appreciated China's good fortune that France was momentarily distracted by continental diplomacy, but they also recognized the phenomenon of modern imperialism for the first time, and perceived with growing alarm the almost mechanical implacability of European expansion. Kuo Sung-t'ao, Li Hung-chang's former *mu-yu* who became China's first foreign ambassador, wrote in 1884:

> At first [the European nations] had no intention of resorting to war, but after [the local people] had repeatedly gone back on their promises, the foreigners inevitably took offense and so used military force. Nor had they any preconceived idea of fighting for territory; but the more they fought, the further they advanced and thereupon they took the opportunity to usurp territory.[24]

The lesson of the Sino-French War seemed clear enough to the Chinese. There would be no subsequent era of cooperation this time. However unpleasant the prospect, China was faced with a continuing struggle to survive, and that meant renewing the self-strengthening efforts of the previous two decades. The government had also learned to its grief how important it was to have a unified military command. In 1885, therefore, the throne appointed Prince Ch'un, the emperor's uncle, to head a new admiralty which would theoretically draw all of the regional navies together. But the office was actually administered by Li Hung-chang, and the navy divided into northern and southern fleets which desultorily gathered once or twice a year for formal maneuvers. Moreover, each fleet had its own peculiar ordinance because the ships were constructed in different arsenals or bought by individual viceroys. These weaknesses were not immediately discernible to contemporaries. Foreign observers were, in fact, quite impressed by China's spate of naval building after 1885 and actually ranked the two fleets as stronger than the Japanese navy.

The Sino–Japanese War of 1894–1895

The comparison between China and Japan was an unavoidable one at the time, because those two countries were increasingly at loggerheads over the future of Korea. Like Vietnam, Korea was a former vassal state of the Ch'ing Dynasty. It was also a country which many Japanese coveted for their own emperor. In 1876 a struggle had broken out at the Korean court between conservative and reformist factions. Each side invited foreign intervention, with the conservatives turning to China and the reformers to Japan. In 1884 the latter revolted against the monarchy with Tokyo's encouragement and aid. The conservatives promptly appealed to China, whose representative, Yuan Shih-k'ai, helped suppress the revolt. Some Japanese officials wished to retaliate immediately, but the Meiji foreign minister, Itō Hirobumi, agreed to meet Li Hung-chang at Tientsin. There the two men managed to negotiate a convention of neutrality for Korea, pledging that neither China nor Japan would intervene in the future without the other's permission.

The Tientsin Convention was put to the test in 1894. A rebellion similar to the Taiping movement tried to overthrow the Korean monarch, who again requested Chinese help. While Ch'ing officials pondered their alternatives, the Japanese decided to move first, sending in troops to support their faction. Chinese military units engaged the Japanese in July, and on August 1, 1894, war was formally declared.

The naval issue was rapidly and humiliatingly decided in Japan's favor. On September 17, each country's fleet of 12 modern warships engaged in a major battle off the mouth of the Yalu River. The Chinese squadron was commanded by Li's protégé, Admiral Ting Ju-ch'ang. His performance was lamentable. Battle orders were countermanded by one of his captains, his ships wasted their ammunition before the enemy was even within range, and the concussion from the flagship's first major salvo demolished Ting's own flying bridge. Minutes after the Japanese fleet began raking the Ch'ing battleships and cruisers with deadly accurate fire, two Chinese vessels were on fire, two others had been sunk, two had refused to engage, and two more were steaming hastily away from the battle. Of the 12 warships that began the battle on the Chinese side, only 4 had acquitted themselves well and managed to survive.

The land war was no less a defeat for the Chinese. By mid-September 1894, Pyongyang had fallen to the Japanese, and Li Hung-chang's soldiers began to retreat behind the Yalu River into Manchuria. In October, Japanese marines landed on the Liaotung peninsula and seized Dairen, and less than two months after that the Chinese garrison at Port Arthur surrendered. The one remaining hope was the heavily fortified redoubt of Weihaiwei on the Shantung peninsula. But on February 12, 1895, it too fell into Japanese hands. China had no alternative now but to sue for peace on Japanese terms, which included the territorial cession of Taiwan and Liaotung, and a 200 million tael indemnity.

The surrender of so much Chinese territory was humiliating, but what distressed the Chinese even more was having to turn it over to the Japanese. It was bad enough to be defeated by European nations—countries whose civilization was so different from China's. But to see the "dwarf bandits" who had once copied their culture from the Chinese now humble the Ch'ing empire was a cruel blow to national self-esteem. Because it was such a profound psychological shock, the Sino-Japanese War of 1894–1895 did more than any other crisis to force the Chinese to evaluate their own strengths and weaknesses. What had gone wrong? How could Chinese self-strengthening have turned out in the end to be such an illusion?

The Failure of Self–Strengthening

Most of the self-strengthening projects were coordinated by individual viceroys' private *mu-fu*. The old Confucian bureaucracy thus preserved its inner "essence" (*t'i*) intact by assigning the techniques or "functions" (*yung*) of modernization to a nominally extrabureaucratic institution. The specialists were not formally rewarded for their activities at the time. Although the importance of their function was recognized, their rewards were the familiar status symbols of a regular civil service post after they had completed their ungentlemanly tasks in the modern sector. Indeed, Admiral Ting's own naval officers had spent most of their time before the battle of the Yalu River waiting for their enlistments to run out so that they could claim their rewards ashore by donning scholars' robes and mandarins' caps. No one was completely engaged by his specialized mission, since everyone involved in self-strengthening projects preferred to be doing something else, and the projects consequently suffered.

The *mu-fu* also blurred the private and public sectors of a bureaucrat's responsibility. Just as a secretary's loyalty to Li Hungchang sometimes overrode the public interest, so was each *mu-yu* often overcome by personal venality. Public office had always been a major source of private income in late imperial China. How much more so was private office, especially when it included such lucrative pursuits as arms-buying with accompanying salesmen's rebates, or railway building with accompanying contractors' kickbacks. Governor-General Li Hung-chang, for example, amassed hundreds of thousands of acres of land, innumerable silk stores, and pawnshops across the empire. A common saying at the time alleged that "every dog that barks for Li is fat."[25] This degree of corruption was what really condemned the *mu-fu* in idealistic contemporaries' eyes. It was learned, for instance, that the Chinese warships in the Yalu River battle had lacked explosive warheads for their naval shells, because Li's purveyor, his son-in-law Chang P'ei-lun, had pocketed the money and bought hollow warheads from Krupp instead. Other associates had taken similar liberties. Torpedoes turned out to be filled with scrap iron instead of gunpowder and the munitions bags of Weihaiwei with sand instead of explosives. In fact, Li and his cohorts had personally profited so much from military preparations that when the war finally came it was deemed theirs alone to fight. The southern fleet refused to budge and Li was later heard to bitterly remark that it was "left up to the province of Chihli to fight Japan."

While the *mu-fu* was not a formal bureaucratic organ, it was official enough to discourage private capitalism from developing at the same time. One of the most important self-strengthening projects was Li Hung-chang's China Steam Merchants Navigation Company. It and the 15 or 20 other major industrial enterprises undertaken then were run, like the salt monopoly, according to the principle of *kuan-tu shang-pan* (official supervision and merchant management). Having secured a maritime monopoly on grain transport, Li Hung-chang endeavored to encourage merchants to invest their capital in the new steamship company. But just as eighteenth-century salt merchants were wary of official squeeze, so were nineteenth-century investors afraid that Li and his supervisors would not redeem their shares. They would have been even more reluctant to underwrite the China Steam Merchants Navigation Company (*Chao-shang chü*, literally, bureau to invite merchants) if they had been privy to Li's secret reports to the throne.

> We are uncertain whether business will be good or bad. Even if business should not be good, the only ones who will suffer will be the merchant stockholders. I plan to make the repayment of official loans a steady practice and to exhaust the capacity of the merchants to support the company.[26]

Li eventually did attract investors, but only by promising dividends as high as 20 percent per annum. That deprived the company of reinvestment capital once the original shares were subscribed, and the corporation simply ceased growing after 1887. Furthermore, Li's *mu-yu* continuously raided the company's stocks for other projects, giving all such state-supported enterprises a bad reputation for years to come.

Ironically, the *mu-fu* system did in the end alter the system it was designed to protect. The specialists had not functioned well, but even their minor efforts had begun to erode the ancient system of government. Wo-jen had been absolutely correct in 1867—even so limited and circumscribed a form of technocracy would inevitably affect China's sealed-off cultural essence. Within the *mu-fu* there did eventually develop an independent professionalism, scornful of classics-quoting Confucianists, eager to enlarge its own expertise. Out of the secretariats of the late 1800s came two new kinds of leaders: a body of technocrats who would run the railroads and steel mills of the early twentieth century, and a corps of militarists who would become the first warlords of the 1900s. The historical extension of Li's *mu-fu* was thus the Peiyang Army's Bureau for Supervision of Training under Yuan Shih-k'ai, the man who seized what remained of the polity after the dynasty finally fell.

But little of this was apparent to the alarmed scholars and officials who learned of the surrender of Weihaiwei in 1895. At the time they only felt in the most general way that the system they knew had failed their country. More radical steps had to be taken if China was to survive the future. As the imperialist powers gathered for spoils in the twilight of the century, the first of many loyal voices was heard crying out at last for revolutionary change.

Notes

1. The statecraft school, which hearkened back to Ku Yen-wu (1613–1682) and Ch'en Tzu-lung (1608–1647) stressed the importance of district government and the upper gentry's responsibility for local administration. Its best known nineteenth-century advocate was Feng Kuei-fen (1809–1874) who believed that the most vigorous defenders of the established order were those who had an important stake in preserving their own private property. For Feng's role in Soochow politics, see p. 167.

2. According to Confucian propriety, an official had to take three years of mourning leave when either one of his parents died.

3. See note 1 *infra.*

4. When the civil service examination system was abolished in 1905, the gentry no longer drew its status solely from the imperial government, and so gradually sought new ways of maintaining its position by developing modern schools, provincial industries, and so forth. (See Chapter XI.)

5. By the end of the Taiping wars, most of the important governors-general were Chinese.

6. The loyalty of the commanders was secured through the network of elite gentry connections. There are suggestions in some sources that Tseng used the same kind of personal connections for non-elite members of his army by encouraging the formation of an Elder Brothers Society (*Ko-lao-hui*). This was a famous secret society

during the post-Taiping period, after the Hsiang army disbanded,
which played an important role in some of the revolts preceding the
Revolution of 1911.

7. There were actually three kinds of likin: likin levied at the place of
   production, likin levied at the market place, and transit likin. The
   last of these was the most productive. Yeh-chien Wang, *Land Taxation in Imperial China, 1750–1911* (Cambridge: Harvard University
   Press, 1973), p. 11.

8. Readers may detect a similarity to the strategic hamlet program
   adopted by the United States military command in South Vietnam.
   Although that policy was begun by Ngo Dinh Diem and partly
   copied from British tactics in Malaya, it was also directly influenced
   by Chinese counter-insurgency techniques. Tseng Kuo-fan's pacification methods were carefully noted by the twentieth-century scholar,
   Ts'ao O, whose writings in turn inspired Chiang Kai-shek's encirclement campaigns against the Kiangsi Soviet in 1931–1934. Those
   campaigns became the basis for Kuomintang military staff college
   courses on counter-insurgency, which were attended on Taiwan in
   the 1960s by United States Army officers who were later to serve in
   Vietnam.

9. The Small Sword Society (*Hsiao-tao hui*) was founded in Amoy
   about 1850 by an overseas Chinese. An offshoot of the Triads, the
   society soon shifted its base of operations to Shanghai, where many
   seamen and riverboat operators joined. Inspired by the Taiping
   capture of Nanking, the society's leaders prepared to revolt in 1853.
   On September 7, the Shanghai Small Sword Society chief, Liu Li-
   ch'uan, rebelled, seizing the Chinese portion of the city of Shanghai.
   His soldiers were quickly put on the defensive, and imperial troops
   (backed up by French army units) besieged the society inside the
   walled city. Although nearby peasants smuggled food into the city,
   the insurgents eventually began to succumb to starvation. On September 17, 1855, they tried to force a sortie, but were defeated by
   the government troops, Liu Li-ch'uan being killed in the battle. The
   Small Sword Society originally spoke of restoring the Ming Dynasty,
   or so at least decreed Liu on September 1, 1853, before the revolt
   actually broke out. This decree is reprinted in *Shanghai hsiao-tao hui
   ch'i-i shih-liao hui-pien* [A Compilation of Historical Documents on
   the Uprising of the Small Sword Society in Shanghai] (Shanghai:
   Shang-hai jen-min ch'u-pan she, 1958), p. 4. On September 18, however, Liu wrote to Hung Hsiu-ch'üan declaring that he was a subject
   of the Taiping Emperor. I have seen the original version of this letter
   in the Small Sword Society museum at Yü-yuan in Shanghai. A copy
   is reprinted in the source collection mentioned just above (p. 11).
   The insurrection is also analyzed in Joseph Fass, "L'Insurrection du

Xiaodaohui à Shanghai (1853–1855)," in Jean Chesneaux et al., eds., *Mouvements populaires et sociétés secrètes en Chine aux XIXe et XXe siècles* (Paris: François Maspéro, 1970), pp. 178–195.

10. Frederick Bruce, cited in J. S. Gregory, *Great Britain and the Taipings* (New York: Praeger, 1969), p. 112.

11. Su-shun was an adjutant banner general and an important member of the Imperial Household. As president of the Censorate he had condemned Ch'i-ying to death in 1858, and as president of the Board of Revenue in 1859 he had countered inflation by arresting bank managers and clerks.

12. The reader will remember Prince Gintaisi's curse on Nurhaci that a woman of Yehe would destroy his house.

13. The Peking Field Force, organized in 1861, was the first army corps in China fully equipped with Western firearms.

14. Prince Ch'un, father of the future Kuang-hsu Emperor.

15. This was a special institute for foreign learning, run by the new Tsungli Yamen (the yamen in general control of matters concerning foreign nations) which was opened in 1861. Though widely hailed by foreign sympathizers as an institutional source of innovation, the Tsungli Yamen was a weak appendage to the unchanged Peking bureaucracy. It was supposed to be a temporary office, and at the emperor's insistence its memorials had to go first through the conservative Board of Rites. The only way any of its ministers had any influence was by holding concurrent posts on the Grand Council.

16. Cited in Victor Purcell, *The Boxer Uprising: A Background Study* (Cambridge: Cambridge University Press, 1963), p. 124.

17. The unwitting nuns thought that they were simply paying cash rewards to kindly souls who directed orphans their way.

18. Fontanier later insisted that they meant to attack him.

19. Though officially dead of smallpox, T'ung-chih was said by some to have contracted a venereal disease in the brothels of Peking. Arthur W. Hummel, comp., *Eminent Chinese of the Ch'ing Period* (Washington, D. C.: Government Printing Office, 1944), p. 731.

20. Tso's family was minor Hunanese gentry without the important metropolitan connections that Li Hung-chang had inherited. Nor did Tso have the literary polish to pass the metropolitan examinations; when the Taiping Rebellion began he had actually retired from public life to become a gentleman-farmer and pursue his reading interests in military geography.

21. The Black Flags were the private army of a former Taiping adherent and Hakka Triad named Liu Yung-fu. After fleeing China in 1865, Liu had created his own frontier military regime along the Sino-

Vietnamese border. Since he cooperated with Vietnamese resistants to French rule, he was formally recognized as an ally by the Annamese king in 1869.

22. However, the Korean question would soon vex Peking.

23. Chang was a leading member of the hawkish *ch'ing-i* group. He also happened to be Li Hung-chang's son-in-law.

24. Teng Ssu-yü and John K. Fairbanks, eds., *China's Response to the West: A Documentary Survey, 1839–1923* (New York: Atheneum, 1965), p. 121. Or as de Tocqueville once said of the French in Algeria, "There is no halfway house between evacuation and full dominion."

25. J. M. Miller, *China: Ancient and Modern* (Chicago: J. M. Miller, 1900), p. 321.

26. Li Hung-chang, cited in Stanley Spector, *Li Hung-chang and the Huai Army: A Study in Nineteenth-Century Chinese Regionalism* (Seattle: University of Washington Press, 1964), p. 255. It should be pointed out, however, that between 1882 and 1885 there was a great deal of merchant capital forthcoming, especially from compradore circles. This was because the company was actually run by compradores under the nominal leadership of Sheng Hsuan-huai. After 1885, when Sheng took over management in person, the merchants lost their trust, and demand for company shares dropped significantly. Wellington K. K. Chan, "Chou Hsueh-hsi and Late Ch'ing Bureaucratic Capitalism," paper delivered at the Association for Asian Studies, April, 1974.

Dynastic Reform and Reaction

Formation of Study Societies

THE TREATY OF Shimonoseki, ending the war between China and Japan, was signed on April 17, 1895. Public agitation over its provisions for the cession of Chinese territory immediately spread throughout the Ch'ing empire. Despite the official ban on political organizations, students, aspirants, and degree-holders began to form associations to mobilize public opinion. On May 2, 1895, twelve hundred provincial graduates (*chü-jen*) from all over China signed a "Ten Thousand Word Memorial" denouncing the Shimonoseki agreement and petitioning for political reforms. The leader of this campaign was a Cantonese scholar named K'ang Yu-wei, who simultaneously founded a [National] Rejuvenation Study Society (*Ch'iang hsueh-hui*) to alert the Chinese that their race was threatened with extinction.

> The Russians are spying on us in the north and the English are peeping at us in the west, the French are staring at us in the south and the Japanese are watching us in the east. . . . Our enfeebled China has been lying in the midst of a group of strong powers and soundly sleeping on the top of a pile of kindling.[1]

Unless the country awoke in time, he declared, the Chinese would be transformed into beasts of burden, herded about like cattle by the imperialists who had already destroyed the Indian people. His society planned to publish a newspaper in Peking to arouse the public and to sponsor provincial branches to unite "scholars of resolve" (*chih-shih*) whose Confucian fervor would allegedly save the empire.

The *Ch'iang hsueh-hui* was only one of many patriotic societies founded after 1895. These elite associations immediately reminded contemporaries of late Ming scholarly clubs whose involvement in the anti-Manchu resistance had provoked a ban on political groups after 1652. In fact, the study societies of the 1890s were an important departure from seventeenth-century literary and philosophical associations—however deeply involved the latter had been in dynastic politics. The post-Shimonoseki groups were not just intent upon influencing the throne to reform the central government, they were also pledged to carry out concrete measures at the provincial level. The most energetic local branches were formed in Hunan, a province whose gentry had attained great metropolitan influence thanks to leaders like Tseng Kuo-fan and Tso Tsung-t'ang.[2] A visionary young Hunanese scholar named T'an Ssu-t'ung followed K'ang Yu-wei's example by organizing a Southern Study Society (*Nan hsueh-hui*) in Ch'ang-sha in 1897. Branch offices were soon established throughout the province, sponsoring radical curriculum reforms in district schools, urban economic enterprises, and improvements in local administration. These activities were the first step toward a politicized provincial gentry. The impatient and sometimes radical leaders of the Southern Study Society were not the same types of people as the reformist gentry of the early 1900s, but T'an Ssu-t'ung and his followers did set an example of local political engagement that was imitated by other members of the gentry a decade later.

Another novel characteristic of the study societies was their emphasis upon the principle of voluntary association. Because of the divisive factionalism of bureaucratic politics during the late Ming, even the most outspoken proponents of local gentry power under the Ch'ing had steered away from endorsing the principle of voluntary political association. Confucian political ethics treated parties or cliques in government as an infringement upon the integrity of the sacred one-to-one relationship between a ruler and a conscientious minister. Imperial despots like the Yung-cheng Emperor had enthusiastically approved this idea because they wished to prevent bureaucratic leagues from hampering the throne's power. Now, in the name of racial survival, younger literati were banding together throughout the empire, not just to form coalitions with officials within the government, but also to mobilize voluntarily around a common program. These transitional societies, which were neither leader-oriented factions nor modern political parties, were as important for their principle of formation as for their programmatic content.

Seeking classical models for such voluntary associations, reformers like Liang Ch'i-ch'ao recalled that the ancient Chinese philosopher Hsun-tzu had distinguished man from other creatures by virtue of his ability to create voluntary communities. If all social units were thus a consequence of human effort to band together, then no single unit was more "natural" (i.e., legitimate) than any other. Confucianists had long argued against social organizations that "unnaturally" transcended particular units like the family or village. Now writers like Liang Ch'i-ch'ao felt justified in arguing that clubs, societies, and parties were all just as necessary to human development as lineage or neighborhood solidarity.[3] Hence, the study societies' justification for their voluntary association necessarily unveiled an entirely new conception of the body politic. China was not only a cultural entity defined by the Mandate of Heaven. It was as well a national territory created by the communities that clustered within it. Man could, in other words, construct a polity. This definition was not far from the democratic theory that sovereignty resided in the people, joined in social contract, and Liang Ch'i-ch'ao was soon to link those two ideas in his own writings.

Although many of these radical ideas were available to the literate public in study society newspapers like Liang's *Shih-wu pao* (Current News) and T'an Ssu-t'ung's *Hsiang-hsueh hsin-pao* (Hsiang River Newspaper), the reform effort was not a popular or mass movement. It enlisted the support of commoners, but the overwhelming majority of the participants, and all of its leaders, were members of the scholar-official elite. Nevertheless, the reformers did not conceive of themselves as intellectuals estranged from popular opinion and unable to gather public support. The "scholars of resolve" believed that they could create a new ideological coherence for the Chinese by transforming Confucianism from a personal moral ethic into a religion, proclaiming it among the world's peoples just as Western missionaries preached Christianity. This new Confucianism[4] would have a social program as well, encouraging the Chinese to abolish opium smoking, footbinding, and other manifestations of the country's backwardness.

However, such hopes were shortlived; one of the many disappointments of the reform movement's leaders was their awareness that a vast gap separated them from the bulk of the Chinese peasantry. In fact, the study societies' major accomplishments depended heavily upon official sponsorship. The *Ch'iang hsueh-hui* in Peking would not have been permitted to hold meetings if it had not gained the support of influential officials like Yuan Shih-k'ai and Chang Chih-tung, who was elected honorary president of the society. Official backing was also important in the provinces. One reason for T'an Ssu-t'ung's success in Hunan was the provincial governor's willingness to entertain the idea of institutional reforms. When these officials withdrew their support, the societies were disbanded and their newspaper offices closed, for opposition developed very quickly to the "scholars of resolve." In Hunan conservative gentrymen opposed the reformers' educational programs and urged that the Southern Study Society be suppressed, while officials in the capital were alarmed by Liang Ch'i-ch'ao's potential political subversion of imperial legitimacy. Most of all, the original sponsors of the *Ch'iang hsueh-hui*, including Chang Chih-tung, felt that the reformers' leader, K'ang Yu-wei, was a dangerous fanatic whose ideas were outrageous and heretical. K'ang Yu-wei frightened defenders of the status quo because he depicted Confucius, the upholder of tradition, as a revolutionary prophet. Many high officials felt that it was rash for Chinese scholars to dabble in foreign political theories. How much more dangerous was it for someone like K'ang Yu-wei to argue that the true Confucius was an innovative reformer, rather than a conservative.

K'ang Yu-wei's Philosophy

K'ang's theories stemmed in part from the New Text (*chin-wen*) writings of the Han period. This was the same esoteric doctrine of the three ages (*shuai-luan, sheng-p'ing,* and *t'ai-p'ing*) which may have influenced the Taiping emperor, Hung Hsiu-ch'üan. The distinction between New and Old Text interpretations of Confucianism initially occurred because there existed two different commentaries for some of the classics. The New Text commentaries pretended to find oracular meanings in the cursive chronicles known as the *Spring and Autumn Annals* and attributed to Confucius. Where the Old Text scholars interpreted the *Annals* as a sage's moral commentary on his times, the New Text followers insisted that these writings represented a paradigm for all human history—just as though Confucius were a seer who could predict the future.

By the third century A.D. the Old Text versions were commonly accepted as authentic, and Confucius lost the characteristics of a demiurge. In fact, little more was heard of the New Text doctrines for fifteen centuries. In the 1700s, however, Ch'ing philologists skillfully showed that certain Old Text versions of the classics were spurious, rearousing interest in the New Text glosses and especially in the Kung-yang commentary to the *Spring and Autumn Annals*. By the 1820s one could almost speak of a New Text "school," prominent especially in the Canton area. The tenets of the school varied from disciple to disciple, but most agreed that unscrupulous Han bibliographers had forged the Old Text versions for political reasons, concealing the true image of Confucius from later generations. It was this original image that K'ang Yu-wei claimed to have uncovered through his own researches. In 1891 he completed a startling work called *Hsien-hsueh wei-ching k'ao* (A Study of the Classics Forged during the Hsin Period) which explained that the Old Texts had been forged because the despotic usurper Wang Mang (reigned 9–24 A.D.) had wanted to keep scholars from realizing that Confucius was not a traditionalist. According to K'ang's conspiracy theory,[5] the Old Text philosophers subsequently concealed Confucius' true creed, condemning China to centuries of backwardness. K'ang then went on to reveal in *K'ung-tzu kai-chih k'ao* (A Study of Confucius the Reformer) that the "true" Confucius was a heaven-sent sage king, "a teacher for his age, a bulwark for all men, and a religious leader for the whole world." Descended to earth in an age of disorder (*shuai-luan*), Confucius' foresight had allowed him to predict:

> the pattern of the Three Ages, progressing with increasing refinement until they arrive at Universal Peace (*t'ai-p'ing*). He established the institutions of these Three Ages, basing himself initially on those of his native state [of Lu, which was described in the *Spring and Autumn Annals*], but stressing the idea of the one great unity that would ultimately bind together all parts of the great earth, far and near, large and small.[6]

The static historiography of later Chinese philosophers was thus in K'ang's eyes a betrayal of Confucius, who was erroneously made to seem a conservative. The real Confucius, claimed K'ang, had developed a theory of progress every bit as vigorous as Western civilization's philosophy of history. Were Confucius alive today, in fact, he would be the first person to give up past institutions and urge fundamental reform. K'ang thus argued that conservatives who cited Confucius to oppose such changes misunderstood the genuine intent of the sage and were his worst enemies.

If these assertions were not enough to shock orthodox contemporaries, then K'ang had other theories—less openly expressed but implicit in his better known works—which were even more radical. These ideas went far beyond the tenets of the New Text school by fusing Western science with Chinese ethics into an iconoclastic utopianism. Having read about Euclid's theorems in missionary explanations of geometry, K'ang Yu-wei searched for a similar set of universal principles in Chinese moral philosophy so that he would have a "scientific" basis for constructing a new social system. His analytic equivalent was the Confucian virtue *jen* (humaneness, benevolence, kindness), which orthodox philosophers believed to be an expression of man's essential goodness as well as the moral inspiration to regulate one's relations with others. Those relations were prescribed by the particular *li* (rites, proprieties) of Confucian ethics, which one's sense of duty (*i*, lit. "righteousness") obliged one to observe in the form of filial piety toward one's parents, loyalty to one's ruler, and so forth. What K'ang Yu-wei did was to make the single concept of *jen* a human universal, overriding all of the other virtues which together made up the functioning whole of Confucian moral philosophy. *Jen* itself became a primal force, equated by K'ang with electricity (about which he also read in western books), that suffused all being. It was, in fact, the essence of being—not just humaneness, but humankindness—obliterating the artificial political distinctions and social hierarchies that otherwise kept human beings apart and unequal. Since K'ang concluded from this that the scientific basis of an ideal society was equality, he felt that no man deserved to be elevated above anyone else. In the name of *jen*, therefore, K'ang struck down those hierarchical values of subordination which orthodox Confucianists revered, and boldly declared that duty (*i*) and propriety (*li*) were customary values devised by Confucius' distorters to justify the authority of the patriarchal family and the patrimonial state.

> China's customs that exalt the ruler and demean his subjects, that favor the male over the female, and that honor the "worthy" while repressing the "worthless"—these are what we mean by "righteousness." Once popular practices and customs become fixed, they are held to be the epitome of "righteous principles." Down to the present day, subjects prostrate themselves in awe of

the ruler's majesty and dare not speak out; wives are held down as inferiors and, being uneducated, are kept in ignorance. These are most oppressive ways to treat subjects or wives. I fear that they are not really the epitome of "righteous principles," but have only become so through popular custom.[7]

K'ang Yu-wei was the first Chinese political philosopher to argue that orthodox Confucianism was merely an ideology, a manner of thinking characteristic of a class.[8] In his view, all of those virtues—such as filial piety and loyalty—which the Chinese had thought to be the bonds of civilized society, separating men from beasts and culture from barbarism, were the instruments of traditional tyranny. Ultimately, then, fundamental political reform depended upon cultural revolution. Precisely because Chinese society was so permeated by Confucian norms, political methods alone were insufficient to wreak basic changes. That was why the cultural iconoclasm of the May Fourth Movement of 1919 was to have more revolutionary significance than the overthrow of the imperial government in 1912. And that is also why Chairman Mao Tse-tung today speaks of a continuing cultural revolution in the People's Republic of China.

Just as Liang Ch'i-ch'ao's principle of voluntary association suggested that a people might create its own nation, so did K'ang Yu-wei's social calculus free his imagination to devise a new society. By combining the equality principle of *jen* and the New Text's prophesy of a great peace (*t'ai-p'ing*) with the arcadian ideal of great harmony (*ta-t'ung*),[9] K'ang predicted a future world liberated from social and political distinctions. His *Ta-t'ung shu* (Book of Great Harmony), written about 1902, described a utopia achievable in two or three centuries. Then the word "nation" would have ceased to exist because the world would be amalgamated into a single race, speaking the same language and sharing the same customs. Property would be communized and all work would be performed with machines, while electric airships darted across the skies. Human suffering would be completely eased by a priesthood of doctors, and all class distinctions would have disappeared. Women would have the same status and clothing as men, and the nuclear family would give way to one-year marriage contracts and communal nurseries.

K'ang Yu-wei's *Book of Great Harmony* later established his reputation as a Chinese utopian socialist like Fourier or Saint-Simon. But he had not made these fanciful projections at the time of the reform movement, so that it was really his theory about Confucius that earned him the sobriquet "wild fox" and made higher officials leery of sponsoring his reform proposals. Yet those proposals as such were not very radical. As he explained them in a series of seven memorials to the Kuang-hsu Emperor, the reformers wished their monarch to follow the example of the Meiji Emperor in Japan and Peter the Great in Russia by replacing the traditional bureaucracy and examination system with Western-style ministries and schools to modernize the country. But these memorials were not even delivered to the emperor because senior bureaucrats feared the implications of any change whatsoever, as well as the zeal of the study societies and the eccentricity of K'ang's views. Indeed, it was not until another national crisis occurred that their opposition to *pien-cheng* (reforming the government) would be overcome.

The Scramble for Concessions

The Treaty of Shimonoseki had significantly altered the balance of power in East Asia—a factor which Li Hung-chang had taken into account during his negotiations with the Japanese. Reviled by his fellow countrymen for the concessions he made at the conference table, Li had harbored no illusions about China's bargaining strength. But he had counted on later using the other Great Powers, especially Russia, to mitigate some of the Japanese demands. By the Treaty of Shimonoseki Japan had gained a number of exclusive rights in China that seriously challenged the treaty port principle of equal exploitation. Above all, she had acquired possession of the Liaotung peninsula, with the warm water harbor of Port Arthur which Russia had long been eyeing as a suitable naval supplement to Vladivostok. The Russians were therefore most receptive to Li Hung-chang's appeals for help and engineered a diplomatic démarche with Germany and France that forced Japan to return Liaotung to the Chinese. The Russians then promptly presented their bill to Peking in the form of a request to extend the Trans-Siberian railway through Manchuria. Partly to protect him from hostile public opinion in the capital, the Kuang-hsu Emperor sent Li Hung-chang to Moscow to settle this matter. There he agreed in 1896 to grant the Russians an eighty-year railroad concession in exchange for a defense treaty (and, it was credibly rumored, a $1,500,000 bribe).

The Russo-Chinese Treaty of 1896 had immediate repercussions. Coming on the heels of the diplomatic démarche, the railway concession infuriated the Japanese, who stepped up military preparations for a showdown with Russia over Korea and Manchuria. That conflict would not erupt for eight more years, but when war did come, Japan would be the first Asian country in modern history to defeat a European power.

Great Britain was also upset by the treaty. The English had long feared Russian expansion and now felt that China was no longer a bulwark against the Tsar's imperialist aims in Asia. Moreover, this new Russian advance threatened to upset the balance of power in Europe, where English policy was to keep the continental nations divided into two relatively equal blocs: a Triple Alliance between Germany, Italy, and Austria, and a Dual Alliance between France and Russia. It is certainly debatable whether Russia's new railway rights appreciably altered the military situation in Europe, but there is no doubt that balance-of-power diplomacy was now transferred to the Far East. When France, Russia's ally, sought its own railway and mining rights in south China in June, 1897, Britain was unable to prevent the concessions because of Russia's firm support for these demands. To balance her own power in Asia, England then began to seriously contemplate a naval alliance with Japan—an arrangement that was eventually sealed in 1902.

Germany, too, was alarmed by signs that Russia was on its way to establishing a protectorate over Manchuria and north China. Kaiser Wilhelm immediately began to contemplate countermeasures, hoping for an opportunity to take his admirals' advice and secure a German naval base in China. On November 1, 1897, that opportunity was granted him by an anti-Christian mob in Shantung, forerunners of the Boxers, who murdered two German missionaries. Wilhelm was euphoric when he received news of this provocation and cabled Tsar Nicholas his intention to seize the Shantung harbor of Kiaochow Bay (already carefully surveyed by German officers) in retaliation. Nicholas would neither "approve nor disapprove," and on November 7, Admiral Diedrichs of the Imperial German Navy occupied Kiaochow with his ships and men. Four months later, after fruitless diplomatic resistance, the Chinese Ministry of Foreign Affairs reluctantly agreed to lease the bay for 99 years, as well as to let the Germans build two railroads and exploit the mines of Shantung.

This was the signal that every chancellery in Europe had been awaiting to start the "scramble for concessions." Tsar Nicholas promptly had his ambassador in Peking present a similar demand for Port Arthur and Dairen in Liaotung. France requested Kwang-chow Bay in the south. Italy declared that it must have San-men Bay in Chekiang. And Great Britain asked for the naval fortress of Weihaiwei as well as for recognition of its special interests in the Yangtze valley. One request triggered the next; each concession seemed to sharpen the other powers' appetites to "carve up China like a melon." The Chinese were helpless in the face of this on-slaught. In less than a year the country was divided into foreign spheres of interest dominated from national leaseholds which were administered by foreign officials, exploited by foreign investors, and policed by foreign troops.[10]

Internal Demands for Reform

Germany's seizure of Kiaochow Bay had reinvigorated the reform movement. By the winter of 1897–1898 a number of reform pro-posals, including K'ang Yu-wei's memorials, were being circulated in the capital. Some of these ironically came from the very treaty ports they were designed to combat, because Western social and political theories were most readily available to the Chinese who lived in cities like Hong Kong or Tientsin. Shanghai even nurtured a kind of treaty-port intelligentsia. The city had boomed after the open-ing of the Suez Canal in 1869, doubling its import and export figures over the next 25 years. By the time of the scramble for concessions, over 17,000 foreigners lived there, enjoying their own law courts, municipal government, modern utility plants, newspa-pers, publishing houses, theaters, and schools. The Chinese sections of the city expanded as well into a squalid, bustling ferment of compradores, coolies, gangsters, shopkeepers, and petty industrialists.

It was there and in the international settlement that the first political refugees from Ch'ing control sought a somewhat ambiv-alent shelter, and there too that the first modern Chinese news-papers were founded in the 1870s. The leading journalist of Shanghai was Wang T'ao, who had gotten his start as an editorial assistant in the Shanghai office of the London Missionary Society after fail-ing to pass the civil service examinations in 1846. During the Tai-ping troubles Wang had been denounced as a rebel spy and was obliged to flee to Hong Kong, where he worked for James Legge, the missionary who was then translating the Chinese classics. Wang T'ao's part in the project was so important that Legge took him back to Scotland to help complete the translation. This gave Wang an excellent opportunity to observe European politics firsthand, and he returned to Shanghai in 1870 to publish a popular account of the Franco-Prussian War. This was one of the first treatises to depict the struggles of modern nation-states. International law to the contrary, the world—said Wang—was ruled by power and force, not by reason or propriety. The globe was in a state of anarchy, and China was only one among many beleaguered countries. Attempts to use foreign techniques to defend China's traditional culture were doomed to fail, because there no longer existed a stable *t'ien-hsia* (under-heaven) surrounded by the four seas of barbarism. Rather, China had entered a new stage of history which she shared with the rest of the world. By awakening to the fact that the barrier between inner and outer had been breached, the Chinese could fundamentally change their political system and combine East and West to create an entirely new *Tao* for humanity, bringing peace to the entire world.

Cheng Kuan-ying, another Shanghai essayist, also pleaded for fundamental reforms. A comprador employed by the treaty-port firm of Dent and Company,[11] Cheng served as one of Li Hung-chang's *mu-yu*, directing the China Steam Merchants Navigation Company after 1892. His *Sheng-shih wei-yen* (Words of Warning in a Seemingly Prosperous Age) contained many dire predictions that were eventually realized in 1897–1898. To avert these catastrophes, Cheng had suggested changing China's traditional form of government. In fact, he even refuted doctrines of unlimited imperial sovereignty, writing in 1893 that:

> Heaven gave birth to the people and established a ruler for them. The ruler is like a boat; the people are like the water. The water can support the boat; it can also overturn the boat.[12]

This populism was not entirely novel. The classical philosopher Mencius (372–289 B.C.) had long before argued for the peasants' right to rebel, and the seventeenth-century writer, Huang Tsung-hsi, had inveighed against despots who forgot their obligation to serve the people and treated the empire as their private estate. But Cheng Kuan-ying's intent was more pointed. If the ship of state capsized, it was because its helmsman had forgotten that the people were his *raison d'être*. Other writers, like the Hong Kong physician, Ho Kai, carried this logic even further, dispensing with heaven altogether. As Ho Kai unequivocally wrote in 1894,

> Government is an affair of the people and managed by the ruler; it is not an affair of the ruler and managed by the people. Since affairs belong to the people, sovereignty also belongs to the people.[13]

Ho Kai also clearly articulated the political implications of this belief, alleging that if sovereignty belonged to the people, the monarch should share his power with a Western-style parliament.

Ideas like these were too radical to be transmitted directly to the official world. Intermediaries who were connected with the bureaucracy, although influenced by treaty-port critics of the government, passed on a more subdued set of suggestions. T'ang Chen, for instance, was the first metropolitan degree-holder to seriously propose that a parliament (*i-yuan*) be convened to "widen the pathway of words" between the gentry and the throne. This proposal was seconded by Ch'en Ch'iu, a provincial degree-holder who had served in the capital and was a close friend of Ho Kai. Ch'en's widely read *Yung-shu* (Concerning Practical Matters) emphasized the importance of creating a parliament to represent the people and bind the country more closely together.

The Political Struggle Between Emperor Kuang-hsu and Tz'u-hsi

Still, none of these declarations would have reached the Kuang-hsu Emperor had they not received the approval of the most senior officials at court. That support was forthcoming partly because of the political struggle then taking place between the emperor and his aunt, Tz'u-hsi. In 1887 the empress dowager supposedly "returned rulership" (*kuei-cheng*) to the emperor, ending her long regency. In fact, Tz'u-hsi continued to issue her own instructions until 1889, the year of her formal retirement, and even afterwards cowed the emperor with her indomitable personality and familial authority. Her own supporters—a "northern" faction of conservatives like Wo-jen and Hsu T'ung, General Jung-lu, and the chief eunuch Li Lien-ying—formed a *hou-tang* (the dowager's clique). Their official rivals, a "southern" faction led by the emperor's tutor,

Weng T'ung-ho, and several influential Chinese members of the Grand Council, were thought of as a *ti-tang* (the emperor's clique). It was they who in 1895 secretly encouraged censorial complaints about Tz'u-hsi's interference in administration, and they who took cheer the following year when Kuang-hsu's mother (Tz'u-hsi's sister) died, loosening the tie between the emperor and the old empress dowager. But the "emperor's clique" was by no means prepared to sponsor wholesale reform. Weng T'ung-ho was quite conservative and genuinely alarmed by what he knew of K'ang Yu-wei's Confucian theories. Nevertheless, he had long shared K'ang's concern over China's weakness and had begun to consider institutional modifications as early as 1889, when he brought Feng Kuei-fen's political essays to the emperor's attention.

Weng T'ung-ho's tolerance for reform proposals continued to increase as China's international position grew weaker. After the 1895 defeat by Japan, for example, Weng mentioned K'ang Yu-wei to the emperor and introduced the writings of T'ang Chen and Ch'en Ch'iu to some of his colleagues. The German seizure of Kiao-chow Bay aroused him even more. By now the reform movement was again gathering momentum. K'ang Yu-wei had formed a new organization (*Pao-kuo hui*, the Society to Preserve the Nation), and many influential literati were openly sympathetic to his cause. What may actually have impelled Weng T'ung-ho to support K'ang and the reformers was the realization that their program would strengthen the throne. K'ang proposed to replace the hidebound six boards with twelve new administrative agencies staffed by specialists and coordinated by a central executive, the Bureau of Government Institutions, directly under the throne. By abolishing sinecures, trimming administrative deadweight, and cutting bureaucratic red tape, he hoped to streamline the government and free the executive capacities of the emperor to make other necessary changes in the military and educational systems. From Weng T'ung-ho's point of view, all these measures would have the additional advantage of reducing the power of the empress dowager and bypassing those ministers that made up her clique. Although palace politics were not the only reason Weng chose to sponsor K'ang, the rift between the emperor and Tz'u-hsi did provide the reformers with an immediate opportunity to carry out their proposals. Unfortunately, it also meant that there existed an alternative source of authority in the form of the empress dowager to whom embattled conservatives could turn for help.

The Hundred Days of Reform

Urged on by his tutor and deeply alarmed by China's diplomatic defeats, the Kuang-hsu Emperor issued an edict on June 11, 1898, announcing his intention to reform the government. That same day K'ang Yu-wei's government sponsors persuaded the supervising censor, Kao Hsieh-tseng, to bring K'ang's seven earlier memorials to the emperor's attention. Kuang-hsu's immediate reaction was shock and even outrage. In one 1897 memorial, K'ang Yu-wei had written that he "could not bear to see such an event recur as when the last emperor of the Ming had to hang himself." This unpleasant allusion to dynastic extinction would normally have been regarded as an unspeakable act of sedition. But these were times to speak the unspeakable, and the sincerity of K'ang's candor persuaded the emperor of his good intent. There was no doubt that K'ang truly believed that his emperor could, by turning his hand, resuscitate the dynasty and save China. On June 16, therefore, Kuang-hsu summoned K'ang Yu-wei to his palace for an imperial audience. The hundred days of reform had begun.[14]

In the space of that summer the entire government was revamped—on paper. An avalanche of edicts, decrees, and rescripts was prepared by K'ang Yu-wei and his young followers for the emperor to sign. Manchu sinecures were abolished in the Imperial Household; redundant governorships eliminated; bureaus of commerce, industry, and agriculture established; Buddhist monasteries nationalized and converted into public schools; the examination system changed to test a knowledge of current affairs rather than the classics; and suggestions made to replace the army and civil ministries with new institutions.

Conservative Reaction

It was hard to find a single group in the bureaucracy that was not somehow threatened and offended by these fiats. Ideological resistance began to accumulate among military officers, Manchu aristocrats, Chinese ritualists, even the million or more gentry aspirants who had, it would seem, prepared for the wrong examinations. Manchu councillors could be heard accusing the emperor of filial impiety because he was tampering with the sacred institutions of his ancestors. Chinese ministers fell back on culturalist arguments. The traditional Way of Chinese civilization was manifestly superior to these barbarous customs copied from the West. Better men, not laws, would save the empire; moral improvement, not institutional tinkering, would guarantee good government. Officials like Ch'u Cheng-po even insisted that the Japanese victory over China had proved that self-strengthening was a mistake in the first place and should never have been approved. Chu I-hsin, another conservative, developed a more subtle argument. According to him, the clumsy and wasteful implementation of self-strengthening measures had already demonstrated that Western techniques, adopted piecemeal, were worse than no improvements at all. The reason for this was simply that barbarian institutions were based upon barbarian cultural principles and Chinese institutions founded on the Chinese Way. It was impossible to graft one culture's products on another society. Officials must therefore identify China's "national essence" (*kuo-ts'ui*), and then hold to its fixed cultural principles unswervingly.

Thus, where K'ang Yu-wei had insisted on the universal relevance of Confucius to world history, the conservatives made Confucianism a particular attribute of Chinese culture. Although this particularism proved fatal to Confucian political theory insofar as the latter pretended to be a universal prescription for government, the national essence argument was frequently used by reactionaries to buttress their defenses against Westernization. Conservatives like the Hunanese Yeh Te-hui believed that the reformers ultimately planned to destroy China's culture by obliterating the distinctions between their race and other peoples. Yeh wrote of the reformers that:

> If they say there can be no distinction between the Chinese and the foreigners, can they also say there is no east and west? . . . Westerners have distinguished the Chinese as a yellow race, which implies that from the beginning, when the heaven and earth were created, the Chinese were given a central position.[15]

Arguments like these helped persuade most officials to drag their feet during the hundred days of reform, so that few of the emperor's fiats were actually implemented. The frustrated reformers quickly conveyed their anger over bureaucratic inertia to Kuang-hsu himself, who was ready to believe the worst of his conservative ministers.

Kuang-hsu's Attack on the Bureaucracy

The Board of Rites was particularly suspect as a conservative stronghold and was apparently doing its best to keep the civil service examinations from being changed. The reformers therefore eagerly seized upon a pretext to remove that obstruction when it was discovered that the ministry had refused to transmit a proposal by one of its junior secretaries that the emperor and empress dowager travel abroad. Kuang-hsu was told, quite correctly, that this action amounted to disobedience of his personal instructions, and he in turn summarily dismissed six conservative board members. One of the dismissed men was a bannerman whose wife was a confidante of the empress dowager. The bannerman thus conveyed to Tz'u-hsi his conviction that K'ang Yu-wei was violently anti-Manchu and a dangerous threat to that ruling elite's survival.[16]

The Board of Rites purge, which shocked many Chinese as well, was soon followed by another bureaucratic scandal which further alarmed the Peking bureaucracy. This involved the policy-making Grand Council, whose senior members were delaying reform measures. Lacking an excuse to dismiss the officials, K'ang Yu-wei arranged in August to have four of his followers, including T'an Ssu-t'ung, appointed probationary secretaries to the council. Since the emperor and K'ang obviously planned to use these junior secretaries to bypass the senior councillors, most bureaucrats regarded the appointments as a thinly veiled attack upon the integrity of officialdom. The action also spread panic among the conservatives. If they waited much longer, there would be no institutions left to defend.

Tz'u-hsi's Coup

In the meantime, pressure had begun to grow for the empress dowager to intervene and stop the reform movement. Tz'u-hsi had originally favored the idea of an imperial reform, but she became more and more skeptical as the hundred days wore on. News of K'ang Yu-wei's alarming innovations was brought to her by group after group of officials who rode out to the rebuilt Summer Palace[17]

with the request that she take back the reins of power before it
was too late.

Rumors of these private audiences soon reached the reformers,
who began to suspect that Tz'u-hsi was conspiring with her old
standby, General Jung-lu, to depose Kuang-hsu. T'an Ssu-t'ung
therefore secretly approached Yuan Shih-k'ai, deputy minister of
war, on the night of September 18, 1898, and asked him on behalf
of the emperor to mobilize his 7,000 soldiers, kill Jung-lu, and be-
siege the empress dowager at the Summer Palace. Yuan Shih-k'ai
agreed. Two days later he left for Tientsin where Jung-lu was garrisoned, but instead of killing the Manchu general, Yuan informed
him of the reformers' plans to stage a preemptive coup.[18]

In the meantime, Tz'u-hsi acted swiftly on her own. After sum-
moning her most trusted officials to the Summer Palace and inform-
ing them of her plans, she hurried to the Forbidden City and
accosted the emperor. "I have been feeding you and taking care of
you for more than twenty years," she raged, "and yet you listen to
the words of these churls to plot against me." And she added, in a
calculated effort to force a filial submission from her nephew:
"Stupid son! If I do not exist today, how can you exist tomorrow?"[19]
Kuang-hsu's resolve broke. Devastated by her anger, he allowed
himself to be led away by her eunuchs, who jailed him in an island
pavilion on K'un-ming Lake beneath the Summer Palace. Tz'u-hsi
then announced that the emperor had fallen ill, leaving her to
govern in his place. The first act of her new regency was to order
the arrest of the reform movement leaders. Six of the reformers,
including T'an Ssu-t'ung and K'ang Yu-wei's brother, were immediately captured and executed. K'ang himself, as well as Liang
Ch'i-ch'ao, were warned in time to escape abroad—K'ang with the
help of the British consul-general in Shanghai, and Liang aboard a
Japanese warship. Yet, the two men's careers were hardly over.
K'ang Yu-wei went on to found an important political party, the
Pao-huang hui (Society to Preserve the Emperor), and Liang became the most influential political writer of his day. But for the moment their activities in China were at an end, and the reform
movement had utterly expired.

The empress dowager was enraged to learn that the leading
members of the reform movement had escaped arrest; she especially
blamed the English and Japanese for helping them flee. The foreign
powers infuriated her even more when they let it be known that
they would not tolerate her killing the Kuang-hsu Emperor and

placing the son of the conservative Prince Tuan on the throne.[20]
The reaction to the reform movement quickly swelled into a general
antiforeignism on the part of the Ch'ing government, which identified subversion with Westernization. Nor were Tz'u-hsi and her close
supporters the only ones to feel that way. Much more tolerant officials also shared the belief that Chinese who adopted foreign ways
were betraying the traditional political order. Weng T'ung-ho, for
instance, thought of Chinese converts to Christianity as "jackals
and wolves that infested the capital,"[21] and felt that the dynasty's
use of steamships and railways had jeopardized the Mandate of
Heaven, causing a spate of natural calamities. For, parts of the
empire had suffered either severe drought or floods every year since
1875, and some provinces like Shantung had experienced repeated
famine.

The Boxer Movement

Shantung was hard hit again in August, 1898, when the Yellow
River spilled over its banks, flooding five thousand square miles of
the northern plain. The province faced other difficulties as well.
Demobilized Green Standard soldiers formed armed bands that
swept across the countryside, looting and pillaging. Professional con-
voymen, skilled in the martial arts of boxing and swordfighting,
supplemented their income as drayers of foreign goods like yarn or
paraffin by turning to banditry or by setting up illegal customs
barriers. Taoist magicians took over temple courtyards to train militiamen and enrolled women in Red Lantern (*Hung-teng*) paramilitary units. Sometimes these sectarians even received official encouragement by violently antiforeign administrators. Li Ping-heng,
governor of Shantung in 1895, for example, had encouraged Small
Sword Society members to attack Christian missions, and it was
here that two German missionaries had been murdered in 1897. But
most Ch'ing officials were very ambivalent about such activities.
Like the governors of Kwangtung during the Opium War, they had
great faith in the ability of armed and aroused peasants to drive
out the barbarians if all else failed. Yet they also realized that such
activities easily got out of hand. Shantung, after all, was a province
noted for its long history of sectarian rebellions, and officials who
recalled the White Lotus revolt of the 1630s, the *Pa-kua* (Eight

Trigrams) uprising of 1786, or the *T'ien-li chiao* movement of 1813, were wary of sanctioning such a militia force.

The populace was so alarmed by the combination of natural calamities and imperialist aggression that it did not need official encouragement to form antiforeign self-defense units. In fact, the German occupation of Kiaochow Bay and news of other foreign incursions brought the peasantry of Shantung to a state of near panic. Secret society chieftains and traveling shamans foretold imminent doom, even the end of the world. Printed prophecies passed from village to village, apocryphally announcing calamities ahead. Hupei and Hunan would soon flood, war would break out in Szechwan, all of south China would be plunged into chaos, more than half the population of the empire would die, foreigners would devastate Chihli, and the people of Shantung would soon disappear. Unlike the predictions of the coming of Maitreya, these portents were concretely linked with the foreign presence in China. Magicians promised salvation to those who stopped using foreign paraffin to light their lamps. Geomancers blamed the climatic disorders on the railway lines and telegraph cables stretching between Tientsin and Peking. In response to these warnings bands of believers began to tear up rail ties and cut down wire poles, while others hinted of magic spells that would "block the foreigners' gun barrels." Thousands of young men began to practice the stylized exercises of Shaolin and Pa-kua boxing—exercises that were supposed to release their *ch'i* (pneuma) and invest them with strength so awesome that it repelled foreign bullets.

Gradually these activities coalesced around the masters of the martial arts in Shantung. Professional boxers like the convoy specialist Chang Te-cheng were selected by village youths to be their leaders. Although the boxing masters were in communication with each other at the head of this spontaneous movement, there was no single commander-in-chief. The most notorious leader, and the person reputed to have given the Boxer movement its name (*i-ho ch'üan*, righteous and harmonious fist), became a projection of his followers' charismatic yearnings.[22] He was called by many names, each of which symbolized a different kind of appeal and affiliation. Some called him Chu Hung-teng, "Chu" being the surname of the Ming royal house and "hung-teng" meaning the Taoist red lamp of the women boxers. Others said he was named T'ien Lung (dragon of heaven), which was a Great Sword Society title. And still others referred to him as Li Wen-ch'eng, which was the name of an earlier

White Lotus rebel, long dead. Whichever his true title, this semi-mythical figure was captured and decapitated by the provincial governor, Yü-hsien, on November 22, 1899. But that did not by any means signal the end of the Boxer movement. For, Yü-hsien (a close friend of Li Ping-heng) was extremely xenophobic and believed that the Boxers could be turned to good use against the foreigners. He thus arranged an alliance with the boxing masters, who changed their anti-Ch'ing slogans to antiforeign ones[23] in return for being recognized as a regular militia organization (*t'uan*).

This was an extraordinary act for any Ch'ing official to take. Under normal conditions a popular movement of this sort would have been regarded as a dangerous threat to public security and dynastic survival. These, after all, were descendants of the White Lotus bands which had driven the Mongols out of north China five hundred years before and in 1813 attacked the Forbidden City. In fact, many responsible officials like Li Hung-chang, Liu K'un-i, and Yuan Shih-k'ai deemed them common rebels who deserved to be bloodily suppressed. Others, like General Ch'eng Wen-ping in Chihli, simply scoffed at their claims of invulnerability to firearms. Yet when General Ch'eng put 50 Boxers of the Golden Belt Society to the test by lining them up against a wall and shooting them, his reports of their mortality were dismissed by the court in Peking.

In the capital, and especially among Manchus like Prince Tuan and the empress dowager, there was a terrific will to believe both that the Boxers were endowed with magical powers, and that they represented a popular force which would save the dynasty and drive out the foreigners. The court's credulousness partly stemmed from the persistent connection between the Confucian Mandate of Heaven theory and the common religious beliefs of the people. Furthermore, Chinese were widely familiar from childhood with the miraculous tales of *ch'i-hsia wu-i* (chivalric) fiction, which described kung-fu experts and fantastic feats of magic. *Hsi-yu chi* (Monkey), the great novel whose superhuman hero defeated armies of demons single-handedly, was also enjoying unprecedented popularity at this time. Such examples must have come hopefully to mind when the court heard tales of the marital experts' exploits or watched acrobatic teams of Boxers perform elaborate sword and knife tricks at Prince Tuan's invitation.

Many officials, and even Tz'u-hsi herself, did remain skeptical about the Boxers. But the throne was willing to override these hesitations because it desperately needed to feel that it had not lost popular support. There were signs of anti-Manchu sentiments on all sides, even among literati who had been disappointed by the empress dowager's coup. In a way, the dynasty now found itself in the same position as a local magistrate handling missionary complaints in the 1860s. Every time the government was forced to concede to the imperialists, Han Chinese grew more and more convinced that the dynasty was simply trying to stay in power at all costs, even if that meant relinquishing Chinese national sovereignty to the enemy. Knowing how vulnerable the Manchus were to this criticism, Tz'u-hsi seized upon any evidence whatsoever that the common people were willing to sacrifice themselves to "support the Ch'ing and exterminate the foreigners." She thus confessed to her court that even though she could not believe entirely in the Boxer's magic powers, she did know that they represented the patriotic feelings of the people. Conventional weapons had already failed to defend her realm. What else did she have to fall back on but the hearts and minds of her subjects?

By the early days of June, 1900, Boxer bands had entered Peking from the east. Antiforeign riots broke out immediately. On June 11, a Japanese diplomat was caught and murdered by the mob, and two days later the Christian churches of Peking were burned, their worshippers slaughtered. Fearing that the next step was an attack on the Legation Quarter, British diplomats managed to get a message through to Admiral Seymour in Tientsin. He immediately set out with almost two thousand men, but the road to Peking was barred by Boxers and he was forced back into Tientsin. His attempt to fight his way to the capital did, however, prompt an emergency session of the Council of Princes and High Officials on June 16 to debate alternatives. Some Chinese officials counseled restraint and urged Tz'u-hsi to suppress the Boxers, but Prince Tuan (who had been named head of the Tsungli Yamen on June 10) took a violently pro-Boxer stance and shouted them down.[24] Still Tz'u-hsi could not be entirely persuaded that China should go to war with the West. Then, on June 17, Prince Tuan handed her a note which he said had been received from the foreigners. It presented an ultimatum, demanding that Tz'u-hsi return the Kuang-hsu Emperor to the throne and declaring that the Great Powers intended in the future to turn China into a military and financial protectorate. The note was probably forged by Tuan, but it appeared substantiated two days later when news reached the court that the Allies had seized the Taku forts. On June 21, therefore, the empress dowager formally declared war against the powers. Still uncertain that China could win such a conflict, she felt that her dynasty, and the country, should at least go down fighting.

Ch'ing soldiers then set siege to the Legation Quarter, joining the 200,000 Boxers who were now nominally enrolled in the imperial army. So vast a force, if disciplined, could easily have crushed the resistance of 450 embassy guards, but the Boxers consisted of thousands of small bands which soon threw the capital into social chaos. The homes of the wealthy were pillaged, Chinese officials were seized by the mob, and the streets became littered with corpses. Fierce Kansu troops got out of control and joined the Boxers to murder the German ambassador, Baron von Ketteler. Cut off from Peking altogether, the outside world imagined the worst of the Chinese. All of the West's "yellow peril" fears were invoked by European and American journalists, who luridly described homicidal hatchet-wielding fanatics butchering diplomats.[25] The Great Powers feverishly prepared an expeditionary force to rescue the trapped foreigners, whom many believed to be already dead. By the end of June, 14,000 foreign troops had been assembled at Taku, and in July another 17,000 German, French, English, American, Russian, and Japanese soldiers arrived under the command of Field Marshal Count von Waldersee. On July 13 this combined force captured Tientsin and began to move up the Peking railway line into Chihli. Four weeks later a decisive battle was fought near Tungchow where the Ch'ing commander, Li Ping-heng, was defeated and committed suicide. On August 11, realizing that her armies would not hold, the empress dowager fled Peking for the northwest, and on August 14 the expeditionary force entered the capital to lift the siege of the legations.

Forty years had passed since foreign troops had occupied the capital, and once again, there were ample reasons to fear for the dynasty's survival. Yet this time, as before, the mutual suspicions of the Great Powers kept China from being dismembered. Britain and Japan were above all distrustful of Russia, whose Admiral Alexeieff had used the opportunity provided by these hostilities to seize China's three northeastern provinces and was preparing to turn Manchuria into a client state of his tsar. The Russians would not be dislodged from Manchuria until their defeat by Japan in 1905, but Anglo-Japanese support at least kept the Chinese from recognizing this annexation. All of the powers, thus negotiating with Li Hung-chang, then managed to hammer out a protocol that kept the Ch'ing Dynasty on the throne.

The Boxer Protocol that was signed on September 7, 1901, forced the Chinese to make public apologies for the Boxer incidents; dismantle the fortifications between Taku and Peking; punish by exiling, executing, or ordering the suicide of nine top officials (including Prince Tuan); convict 119 provincial officials of pro-Boxer acts; and pay staggering reparations that amounted, with interest, to 982,238,150 taels ($738,820,707).[26] The Chinese government had no choice but to comply with these demands, as well as respond to foreign diplomatic pressure to Westernize the government.

On January 8, 1901, even before the protocol was signed, Tz'u-hsi had already issued a reform decree from her temporary abode in Sian, following that with a penitential edict on February 13 which disavowed the Boxer attacks and confessed the need for fundamental institutional changes. Tz'u-hsi's decrees made a special point of distinguishing her new orientation from the 1898 reform movement, and she insisted that K'ang Yu-wei had been as detrimental as the Boxers to the future of the Chinese race. But the fact remained that by appointing a reform commission on April 23, 1901, the empress dowager was apparently making a complete turnabout. Less than three years after executing reformers like T'an Ssu-t'ung, Tz'u-hsi had begun to implement a series of institutional changes that would go even further than the Kuang-hsu's Emperor's proposals toward changing China's government.

To be sure, there was now continuing foreign pressure to transform the bureaucracy, but Tz'u-hsi did not pursue the path of reform without a certain enthusiasm of her own. In fact, she quickly came to believe that parliamentary assemblies and chambers of commerce would strengthen and widen the connection between the throne and the masses. In that sense, the antiforeign measures of 1900 and the Western-style reforms of 1901–1911 were both inspired by the same desire to consolidate the dynasty's popular base. The first policy, urged by desperation in the face of modern imperialism, was an obvious miscalculation. The subsequent reform movement was a much more methodical attempt to win the approval of the people. But ultimately it too proved to be based on political misunderstanding, and this time brought the dynasty to its final end.

Notes

1. Teng Ssu-yü and John K. Fairbank, eds., *China's Response to the West: A Documentary Survey, 1839–1923* (New York: Atheneum, 1965), p. 152.

2. Indeed, Hunan experienced a provincial renaissance after the Taiping period and produced many of the leaders of modern China, including Mao Tse-tung, who deeply admired Tseng Kuo-fan and T'an Ssu-t'ung.

3. The reformers were also particularly conscious of the parliament (diet) in Japan, attributing that country's military strength to an assembly which effectively united the will of the people into a single nation.

4. The word "Confucianism" (*K'ung-chiao*) was coined at this time. Previously Confucianists referred to themselves as members of specific philosophical schools. Although the social welfare program of the new Confucianism was inspired by missionaries like Timothy Richard, whose works in Chinese encouraged reform, the study societies' plans for proselytization were intended to combat the inroads of Christianity.

5. K'ang's account—like Hung Hsiu-ch'üan's insistence that China had been deprived of Christianity by barbarian rulers—allowed him to explain why China was benighted at present, without forfeiting his self-esteem and pride as a Chinese. It also had the same claims to universality. By rediscovering Confucius' hidden teachings, the Chinese would be able to create a new *Tao* to "ultimately bind together all parts of the great earth."

6. Cited in Feng Yu-lan, *A History of Chinese Philosophy*, trans. Derk Bodde (Princeton: Princeton University Press, 1953), Vol. 2, p. 675.

7. K'ang Yu-wei, cited in Richard Howard, "K'ang Yu-wei," in Arthur Wright and Denis Twitchett, eds., *Confucian Personalities* (Stanford: Stanford University Press, 1962), p. 309.

8. Tai Chen had argued in the eighteenth century that principles (*li*) had become instruments of social and political tyranny. But his argument was a functional one which did not put a universal principle like *jen* in the place of regularly accepted social obligations.

9. See p. 145. The parallel with Hung Hsiu-ch'üan is remarkable. For, he too combined the *t'ai-p'ing* and *ta-t'ung* in his early revelatory writings. In a certain sense, K'ang Yu-wei simply fabricated a Confucian theodicy to replace Christian eschatology. There is no evidence that K'ang (whose grandfather and uncles commanded anti-Taiping militia in Kwangtung) was directly influenced by Hung's doctrine. Rather, in another fascinating combination of inner and outer confluences, he applied Western scientistic theories of progress to Chinese arcadian ideals, creating a future utopia where Hung announced an imminent paradise on earth.

10. Only Italy's demand was rejected by the Chinese. There was considerable talk in Europe of the imminent partition of China. On September 6, 1899, the United States secretary of state, John Hay, circulated

an "Open Door" note to the powers. Although this and later notes referred to the preservation of China's territorial integrity, they were essentially designed to maintain the old treaty-port principle of equal access and non-exclusive privileges. Hay requested the powers not to interfere with the treaty-port rights or vested interests of other nations within each new sphere of interest. The leaseholds, of course, remained.

11. The founder of the firm had been a major opium trader in Canton.

12. Cited in Chien Po-tsan et al., eds., *Wu-hsu pien-fa* [The Reform Movement of 1898] (Shanghai: Shen-chou kuo-kuang she, 1955), Vol. 1, p. 56.

13. *Ibid.*, Vol. 1, p. 200.

14. However, the "hundred days" are usually dated from the emperor's edict five days before his audience with K'ang.

15. Cited in Li Chien-nung, *The Political History of China, 1840–1928*, trans. by Teng Ssu-yü (Princeton: Van Nostrand, 1956), p. 165. Yeh's justification for the central position of the Chinese was based upon the observation that yellow was a perfect racial color, falling between the extremes of black and white.

16. This was an unconfirmed rumor at the time. It is definitely known, though, that the Manchu in question, Huai-t'a-pu, along with a Tumet Mongol, Li-shan, told the empress dowager then that Kuang-hsu was changing the ancestral laws. At that time, Tz'u-hsi rejected their pleas that she intervene. Sue Fawn Chung, "Tz'u-hsi and the Reform Movement," Ph.D. dissertation, Berkeley, 1975.

17. Tz'u-hsi had rebuilt the burned Summer Palace with funds originally subscribed for naval development. Patriots blamed the useless ordnance used in the Yalu River battle on this folly. She had retired there after turning over the government to the Kuang-hsu Emperor.

18. Yuan Shih-k'ai's role in the coup has aroused much historical controversy. According to Yuan's diary, which was probably written after the event to justify his actions, T'an met with him the night of September 18th. That same day, however, Jung-lu had already summoned Yuan to Tientsin. Yuan's own military strength (as provincial judge of Chihli, he controlled a contingent of 7,000 troops at Hsiao-chan near Tientsin) was quite inferior to the forces of Jung-lu, who mobilized a portion of his army. Yuan reached Tientsin on the 20th, and told Jung-lu of the plot. He then returned to Peking that same day and asked Prince Ch'ing, head of the Tsungli Yamen, to pass on the news to the empress dowager. Yuan then returned to Tientsin on the 21st, before going back once again to Peking that same day in response to the empress dowager's call for an audience at the Summer Palace. Sue Fawn Chung, "Tz'u-hsi and the Reform Movement."

19. Cited in Li Chien-nung, *The Political History of China*, p. 160. This version of the conversation originated in the tea houses of Peking, where it was told by anonymous palace eunuchs.

20. Kuang-hsu was kept a secluded prisoner until the Allies invaded Peking and the imperial family fled to Sian in August, 1900. Thereafter he was allowed to resume some of his ceremonial duties but never again held power. He supposedly died naturally in 1908, the day before Tz'u-hsi passed away, but he was more probably murdered because of her imminent death.

21. Hsiao Kung-ch'üan, "Weng T'ung-ho and the Reform Movements of 1898," *Tsing Hua Journal of Chinese Studies* (April, 1957) 116.

22. This quality of charismatic projection is described in the introduction to Peter Worsley, *The Trumpet Shall Sound: A Study of 'Cargo' Cults in Melanesia*, 2nd ed. (New York: Schocken Books, 1970).

23. From *fan-Ch'ing fu-Ming* (overthrow the Ch'ing and restore the Ming) to *fu-Ch'ing mieh-yang* (support the Ch'ing and exterminate the foreigners).

24. Five Chinese ministers were later executed by the government for remonstrating against this policy.

25. By the end of the siege, 66 foreigners had been killed.

26. This burden was passed on to the Chinese taxpayer. An additional 18.8 million taels per year were added to the provincial tax quotas, mainly in the form of increased land taxes. This supplementary tax increased popular disaffection from the government and played no small part in hastening the fall of the dynasty.

The End of the Mandate

THE OVERTHROW of the Ch'ing Dynasty initially appeared to be an instantaneous and voluntary act of violence. Reduced to momentary events, such as the Wuhan uprising of 1911, it was crystallized by the conspirator's rifle and sword. But a revolution is not merely a moment or a single discrete event. It must be seen as a continuing process which accompanies and surrounds the concrete act of political destruction. Divorced from that larger context, the single moment loses ultimate significance. Sometimes, in fact, the conspirator's act is betrayed by its involuntary effect, and we may even wonder if revolutionaries have the right to call a revolution their own.

The discrepancy between intention and result is not just an academic concern. A revolutionary regime has to plant new historical roots to legitimize itself, so that interpretations of the causes of a revolution are literally a matter of political survival. This was especially true in China, where the fall of the imperial government in 1911 not only entailed the destruction of an entire political order but also of the classical tradition that buttressed it. Successor governments consequently had to create a new past, a new history, to establish their claim to rule, and this necessitated the creation of a revolutionary legacy which could be bequeathed to future generations by some decisive leader like Sun Yat-sen, "father of his country" (*kuo-fu*).

Nationalist Version of the 1911 Revolution

The Chinese Nationalists (*Kuomintang*) have constructed their own version of the Revolution of 1911. According to their historiography, the Han people suffered two hundred and fifty years of alien Manchu rule before finding a national leader in the person of Sun Yat-sen. Born in Kwangtung, then educated in Hawaii and Hong Kong, Sun Yat-sen ostensibly practiced medicine, but his real goal in life was to overthrow the Manchus and restore China to the Chinese. Forming a revolutionary secret society in 1894 called the *Hsing-chung hui* (Society to Revive China), Sun organized branches in overseas Chinese communities throughout the world and then— through secret society contacts within China—launched the first of a series of revolts in 1895. Kidnapped in 1896 by Manchu secret agents in London, he narrowly escaped with his life and proceeded to immerse himself in the study of revolutionary theory. Gradually he developed a unique political philosophy of his own: the Three People's Principles (*San-min-chu-i*) of nationalism, populism, and socialism. At the same time he also formulated a plan for revolution in China, which called for the destruction of the ruling dynasty, to be followed by a period of political tutelage of the people by the victorious revolutionary party. These ideas, coupled with his revolutionary activities in a number of uprisings in south China, made him the natural leader of a Revolutionary Alliance (*T'ung-meng hui*) which was formed in 1905 by exiled Chinese radicals. During the next six years, the Revolutionary Alliance planned and perpetrated a number of revolts in Kwangtung, Yunnan, Hunan, and Chekiang, culminating in a coup in Canton in April, 1911, which cost the movement many devoted martyrs. Although each of these revolts failed, Sun's occupation of the vanguard of the movement continued to attract adherents to his cause.

Finally one of the revolts succeeded. On October 10, 1911, an uprising at Wuhan in central China incited a military mutiny against the regime, and revolution spread across the country. Sun Yat-sen quickly took charge of the situation from his headquarters in Shanghai, where he was elected president of a provisional republic, and by February 11, 1912, the dynasty had fallen. But north China remained under the control of the former viceroy of Chihli, Yuan Shih-k'ai. To achieve national unity, Sun Yat-sen therefore generously agreed to resign the presidency of the new republic and let Yuan take his place.

Unfortunately Yuan Shih-k'ai proved to be a reactionary and crushed the revolutionaries when they tried to overthrow his government in 1913. Once again Sun Yat-sen had to seek exile abroad. But within seven years he had organized a new Nationalist Party

(*Kuomintang*) which occupied Canton and began preparations for a northern expedition to reunify the country under progressive rule. By now Yuan Shih-k'ai was dead, but venal warlords continued to occupy the capital, fighting among themselves and sacrificing Chinese sovereignty in exchange for imperialist loans. Realizing that he needed allies to destroy the militarists, Sun therefore invited the Communists to form a united front and join his party. They accepted his invitation but ultimately betrayed Sun by continuing to work secretly for their own ends within the Nationalist Party. Sun Yat-sen realized this before his death in 1925, but he tried to hold the alliance together for the sake of the projected nothern expedition. The same policy was followed by his former military aide, Chiang Kai-shek, after Sun's death. Taking over the Kuomintang in order to realize Sun's dream of a united China, Chiang launched the northern expedition in 1926. Although the Communists turned on Chiang in 1927, the generalissimo managed by 1928 to unify the nation under Kuomintang rule, and so governed China from Nanking until the Second World War began.

Contradictions of Nationalist Historiography

This Nationalist version of the 1911 Revolution and its aftermath was designed to justify Chiang Kai-shek's assumption of power within the Kuomintang. Chiang is shown to deserve the chairmanship of the party because, by actually fulfilling Sun's plan to launch the northern expedition, he became the revolutionary founder's legitimate heir. That in turn required the exalting of Sun Yat-sen's stature within the revolutionary movement at the expense of other actors. The Revolution of 1911 is thus made to appear almost entirely Sun's handiwork and the republic his personal progeny.

Yet a closer look at the "father of the country" and the Revolution of 1911 makes multiple contradictions immediately evident. Sun Yat-sen not only had very poor relations with the secret societies, he personally participated in only one revolt. The Revolutionary Alliance of 1905 quickly fragmented, and by 1908 its Tokyo headquarters had completely lost touch with Sun Yat-sen who was then in Indochina. The crucial uprising at Wuhan on October 10, 1911, was a mutiny of subalterns and noncommissioned officers who had no contact whatsoever with Sun. In fact, when the revolution broke out, Sun Yat-sen was in Denver, Colorado. From there he went directly to Europe where he presented himself to the Western powers as the major leader of the revolution. Sun was elected president of the provisional republic in Shanghai as a compromise candidate because of an impasse between the New Army general, Li Yuan-hung, and the Hunanese revolutionary leader, Huang Hsing. The Revolutionary Alliance was able to seize power in only one of the eighteen provinces which revolted against the Ch'ing. This was in Sun's native province of Kwangtung where his revolutionary apparatus was the strongest. Yet even there the Revolutionary Alliance quickly lost out to merchants and reformist gentry who supported Sun's rival, Ch'en Chiung-ming.

Although Sun's paramountcy in the revolutionary movement of the 1920s is unquestioned,[1] it is a sharp distortion—as these contradictions suggest—to claim an equal prominence for him during the Revolution of 1911. There is even good reason to argue that the overthrow of the Ch'ing Dynasty was not a coherent, radically planned revolutionary coup at all. Rather, the Revolution of 1911 can be seen as a series of provincial secessions from the empire, led in every major province but one by officers of the New Army units or by gentry leaders of the new provincial assemblies. The fall of the old order was thus the culmination of processes which began during the 1850s in response to internal rebellion and external aggression: the development of regional armies, the rise of a rural managerial class, the political entrenchment of the gentry in provincial government, and so forth. Revolution was ideologically inspired by radical intellectuals, and revolutionary uprisings (however badly bungled) were important as demonstrations of profound social upheaval. But the extinction of the dynastic state was really the handiwork of the new elites that had emerged during the last half-century of Ch'ing rule. In fact, it was the dynasty's own military, political, economic, and educational reforms after 1901 that ironically hurried along this politically conscious process of elite formation, contributing considerably more to its own downfall than the activities of radicals like Sun Yat-sen.

Military Modernization and Its Consequences

The most salient example of the unexpected consequences of reform was the dynasty's military modernization program that continued the self-strengthening movement of the late nineteenth century. In 1896, after the Japanese victory, Sheng Hsuan-huai[2] had suggested replacing the 800,000 soldiers of the traditional Green Standard armies with a new army of 300,000 provincial troops recruited in the Prussian manner. The Kuang-hsu Emperor subsequently ordered that two new military units be formed: a "Self-Strengthening Army" (*Tzu-ch'iang chün*), consisting of 13 battalions commanded by Viceroy Chang Chih-tung at Nanking; and a "Newly Created Army" (*Hsin-chien lu-chün*) of 7,000 men, based in Chihli under the command of Yuan Shih-k'ai. Both were equipped with Western uniforms and weapons, especially Mauser rifles, and Chang's force was trained by 35 German officers.

The empress dowager, though in retirement, took immediate steps to counterbalance the Newly Created Army by getting Jung-lu appointed commander of all other imperial forces in Chihli. Jung-lu then quickly organized a German-trained vanguard under General Nieh Shih-ch'eng, who had earned an excellent reputation during the Sino-Japanese War. It was partly because of Jung-lu's overwhelming manpower that Yuan Shih-k'ai remained loyal to Tz'u-hsi during the 1898 coup and betrayed the reformers to her.

Tz'u-hsi's coup represented the reassertion of Manchu royal control over the government,[3] and this was quickly extended to the military sector. After her resumption of power, the empress dowager reorganized all of the northern Chinese armies, including Yuan Shih-k'ai's Newly Created Army, into a "Guards Army" (*Wu-wei chün*) of 60,000 men under the direct command of Jung-lu. Yuan retained control of his men, now known as the "Right Division" of the Guards Army, but the throne was assured of overall control of north China's military forces.

The allied attack on Peking in 1900 shattered the dynasty's military strength. As soon as hostilities broke out, the major viceroys of the South—Li Hung-chang, Liu K'un-i, Chang Chih-tung—privately arranged a truce with the foreign powers, promising to protect imperialist concessions and treaty-port interests. Yuan Shih-k'ai, then governor of Shantung, observed this agreement as well, and ignored Tz'u-hsi's orders to speed to the court's defense. It was consequently the forces of Jung-lu which bore the brunt of the first foreign onslaughts. General Nieh Shih-ch'eng was killed in battle south of Tientsin on July 9, 1900, and the imperial Guards Army emerged from the conflict severely diminished. Yuan Shih-k'ai's army, on the other hand, had been kept out of battle and survived intact.

Once the empress dowager decided on institutional reform in

1901, Yuan Shih-k'ai began to increase the size of his military forces, soon commanding 30,000 soldiers. Like Li Hung-chang before him, Yuan benefitted from the central government's determination to defend itself. It was mainly his officers who attended army colleges in Japan, and primarily his Northern (*Pei-yang*) Army which created military academies under imperial sponsorship. Moreover, a special Army Reorganization Bureau (*Lien-ping ch'u*) was created in December, 1903, and seconded to the Grand Council. This bureau, dominated by Yuan Shih-k'ai and the Manchu councillor T'ieh-liang, funneled provincial taxes into Yuan's military coffers, enabling him to double the size of his army in 1904—the year that Russia and Japan went to war over Manchuria and Korea. By then, with 60,000 well paid and disciplined soldiers under his command, Yuan was the leading military figure of north China.

Yuan Shih-k'ai's dominance of Chihli presented familiar problems to dynastic officials. His military position there seemed to be yet another example of the kind of regional administrative apparatus that Chinese viceroys like Tseng Kuo-fan, Li Hung-chang, and Chang Chih-tung had been erecting since Taiping times. The power of these officials seriously disturbed the original system of provincial checks and balances which the Shun-chih and K'ang-hsi emperors had devised in the late seventeenth century, relying on Manchu banner commanders to tip the scale in the dynasty's favor. Since then, however, the Manchu elite had lost much of its ethnic identity, and the banner troops had proven ineffective against both internal rebels and external aggressors. Yet even though the dynasty had lost an important weapon in the event of Chinese disaffection, it had— through its own sinification—won the cultural loyalty of its Confucian civil servants. In fact, the Manchu elite had become so identified with Chinese cultural conservatism that it had left specialization in Western military techniques to less defensive Han Chinese officials like Li Hung-chang or Yuan Shih-k'ai. By 1902, however, the empress dowager's reform measures had convinced the Manchu aristocracy of the necessity for its own adaptation to the times. Nobles were sent abroad to study and royal princes selected the Prussian aristocracy as a suitable model to follow. Within eight years, when the Manchus formed an Imperial Guard under Prince Yin-ch'ang (who married a German aristocrat), the dynasty had come to entertain hopes of recovering the ancient tribal vigor of the Collegium of Princes, and as Manchu Junkers dominate national military affairs.

T'ieh-liang, Yuan Shih-k'ai's former ally, began to carry out this policy of reasserting Manchu control over the so-called Peiyang Armies by 1906, when the Army Reorganization Bureau was replaced by a Ministry of the Army (*Lu-chün pu*) that absorbed four of Yuan's six divisions. Yuan was able to recover two of his lost divisions with the empress dowager's help, but as Tz'u-hsi's health failed, Yuan Shih-k'ai's own position at court weakened. His defeat was paradoxically signalled by his appointment to the Grand Council in 1907, which effectively removed him from field command of his remaining divisions. The empress dowager's death the following year deprived him of a valuable political ally, and the Manchu princes appeared to have won the top-level administrative struggle over military command in the North.

But their victory was illusory. First, Manchu junkerization simply increased Chinese racial fears and hatreds. By forsaking their Confucian robes for German epaulets, the princes had hoped to revive their identity as military aristocrats. But in the end this cost them their Chinese subjects' cultural loyalties and gave the dynasty an unfortunate ethnic taint. Second, T'ieh-liang and later Yin-ch'ang failed to recognize that Yuan Shih-k'ai's power was based on somewhat different foundations than that of Li Hung-chang or Chang Chih-tung. There were important similarities in that, like Li Hung-chang, Yuan Shih-k'ai could not operate independently of the central government, depending on personal allies in the bureaucracy to protect his regional military apparatus.[4] But, unlike the earlier viceroys, Yuan Shih-k'ai had led the way in training and nurturing a new and purely military elite. For years his Peiyang Army service academies had been producing hundreds of officers who owed their entire professional identity to him alone.

The armies of Tseng Kuo-fan and Li Hung-chang had been organized by literati along lines of super-subordinate loyalty, with each officer personally attached to the commander directly above him. Yuan's army, however, was staffed with cadres who had not been infused with particularistic Confucian norms of integrity to immediate friends and superiors, but instead were encouraged to devote their undivided loyalty to the supreme commander, Yuan Shih-k'ai.[5] As professional military men, they also possessed technical independence of the regular bureaucracy. Tseng Kuo-fan's *mu-yu*, on the other hand, had served in hopes of ultimate civil service status, and were as loyal to the existing system as they were to their patron. Although many of Yuan Shih-k'ai's officers later attained republican office,[6] they did not regard their military careers as stepping stones to civil rank. Conditioned by the formative experience of the military academy, they saw their own profession as an end in itself and placed duty to their calling over loyalty to a failing political system. This professional independence made Yuan's officers less reliable in the long run than morally committed Confucian followers, but in the years immediately following his transfer to the Grand Council, Yuan could continue to depend upon his former cadres. Placed in strategic military commands throughout the North, officers like Hsu Shih-ch'ang were quick to act at Yuan's command when revolution broke out in 1911.

Financial Difficulties

Yuan Shih-k'ai did not hold a national monopoly on military power. Other New Army units were trained and stationed elsewhere in China, while their civil commanders, the provincial governors of the early 1900s, took on more and more of the military and fiscal functions that had once belonged to the central government. Provincial fiscal autonomy especially hampered the throne's ability to pay for the ambitious reform effort which the Empress Dowager had initiated. Although the central government's expenses doubled between 1900 and 1910, revenue remained relatively inelastic.

The dynasty had four major sources of income: an annual land tax of 102 million taels, customs duties of 33 million, salt monopoly returns of 45 million, and inland transit duties (likin) on goods like opium of 21 million. Although the land tax represented only 35 percent of Peking's receipts, the government's collection system was so inefficient and lower gentry tax farming so ubiquitous, that the rate could not be raised. Major portions of other sources—customs duties and the salt monopoly—had already been pledged to pay off the enormous war reparations incurred during the previous two decades. The one possible internal source of income was provincial likin. But when the central government gave the Ministry of Finance powers in 1909 to audit and collect this revenue, it failed to provide the means to enforce its own decrees.[7] The only remaining source of funds lay outside China. The Ch'ing government could turn to the foreign powers for help, contracting loans which would be secured by pledging the meager sources of existing income as collateral for future repayment. There was no other way for the dynasty to finance long-needed military and economic projects. Yet to adopt such a policy meant exacerbating the tensions already separating the throne from the increasingly critical provincial gentry.

Between 1860 and 1900 the metropolitan gentry, composed of upper degree-holders, bureaucrats, and prominent literati, had become more and more deeply involved in their own provincial affairs. Just as they learned how to use the lower gentry as their rural managers, so also did they develop a complex administrative infrastructure of local water control boards, charity bureaus, and rental control agencies. During the 1890s many of these notables took their lead from the reformers' study societies and began to play an even more active role in the management of public works, the curriculum reform of local academies and schools, and commercial enterprises such as mining and textile manufacture. Becoming masters of their own estate, the gentry's provincial political consciousness widened in inverse proportion to the narrowing of their traditional bureaucratic interests at the imperial capital. It was becoming more and more common, in other words, for the higher gentry to feel that their provincial capitals were as appropriate an arena for political activities as the central administration in Peking. The dynasty's reform movement of 1901–1911 encouraged this political provincialization of the gentry both by drawing together the traditional gentry and an incipient bourgeoisie into modern economic enterprises, and by speeding the creation of new local educational systems.

New Educational Systems

One of the regime's first acts after Tz'u-hsi's reform announcement of 1901 was the establishment of a new educational system. In 1902 the government began to organize a nationwide pyramid of local schools, technical and prefectural middle schools, and provincial and national universities, all dedicated in part to studying Western mathematics, science, and geography. Two years later, following Yuan Shih-k'ai's advice, the court took an even more significant step by finally meeting reformist demands to abolish the traditional civil service examination system. For almost five hundred years mastery of the eight-legged essay had guaranteed the official

gentry its status. The examination system had been used by both
the Ming and Ch'ing dynasties to preserve classical orthodoxy, recruit civil servants, and keep local elites constantly aligned toward
the cultural and political capital of the Empire. Once the examinations were abolished, the gentry's ties with the monarchical state
attenuated. Other sources of status—Western learning, local political
prestige, wealth—now had a chance to compete with, and quickly
overcome, the prestige conferred by the old metropolitan degree.

Alliance of Gentry and Merchants

The devaluation of degree-holding status occurred just as the
bourgeoisie's standing was elevated. In 1902 the government finally
promulgated a commercial code to provide businessmen with legal
protection. At the same time the dynasty recognized formal chambers of commerce (shang-hui) in place of the old state-controlled
merchant guilds (hang and hui-kuan). For the first time in Chinese
history, merchants were granted the general right to organize public
associations. Given a voice in provincial affairs, the leaders of chambers of commerce soon became prominent spokesmen for business
interests in the major cities of China, and subsequently began to
ally with the newly flexible gentry on issues of common concern.

Merchants and gentry had long been informally connected, and
the division of urban society into mercantile and gentry spheres
was already a fiction by the eighteenth century. Prominent lineages
had members in both groups, and commercial pursuits were a surer
road to gentry rank than simple land-holding. But the connection
between the two was often formally denied, so that the relationship
among traditional merchants and scholar-officials was determined by
personal and private links rather than by public and collective
interests. In fact, the organization of monopoly capitalism under the
last two dynasties had been designed to prevent a coincidence of
interests between businessmen and scholar-officials. After 1902, however, the merchant-gentry alliance formally coalesced around such
mutual goals as the formation of new schools, mining investment,
and railway building, so that wealth soon became a legal criterion
for political involvement. The Revolution of 1911 was not, strictly
speaking, a bourgeois movement,[8] but the provincial elites' defense
of local enterprise against government appropriation, and of prop-

erty rights against radical attacks, reflected modern middle-class concerns.

The Constitutionalist Movement

The alliance between businessmen and urban gentry found one form of political expression in the constitutionalist movement. The intellectual inspiration for parliamentary assemblies can be traced to the proposals of Ho Kai,[9] and their first tangible predecessors were the voluntary associations of the 1898 reformers. Yet once again it was Tz'u-hsi's reform measures which provided the opportunity for implementation. Her impulse to encourage local assemblies, like her decision to support the Boxers in 1900, was based on the Chinese monarchical ideal of strengthening the bonds between the imperial throne and the minds (*hsin*) of the masses. Immediate examples of this phenomenon came from Japan, which had just heartened all Asians by defeating Imperial Russia. The Chinese attributed much of Japan's success in mobilizing its citizenry to institutions like the parliament (diet) which welded the Meiji Emperor and his subjects together, and seemingly coordinated a single body politic. In July, 1905, therefore, the empress dowager announced that a commission was to be formed to study foreign institutions as a model for Chinese political reforms. Thirteen months later the throne declared that it favored basic institutional changes, and, in August, 1907, it appointed a Constitutional Government Commission. Officials throughout the country responded by flooding Peking with memorials in favor of a parliamentary monarchy, and within a month the government had solemnly promised the nation that constitutional assemblies would eventually be formed. Finally, in August, 1908, a promulgation announced the immediate creation of local self-government bureaus (*ti-fang tzu-chih chü*), and scheduled provincial assembly (*tzu-i chü*) elections for 1909, national assembly (*tzu-cheng yuan*) elections for 1910, and an actual parliament for 1917.

To most contemporaries this declaration seemed proof that the Ch'ing government had recognized the popular demand for participatory government and was willing to transform the regime into a constitutional monarchy. Indeed, the dynasty garnered so much momentary support from the public that the radicals within the

Revolutionary Alliance found themselves losing previous gentry and merchant allies. Yet the surface concessions concealed a fundamental disagreement between the throne and the provincial gentry about the role that these new institutions were supposed to play. From the dynasty's point of view, the bureaus and assemblies were ultimately intended to build national unity without surrendering imperial sovereignty. To the provincial gentry, on the other hand, they seemed designed to facilitate the transfer of considerable local and national power into their own hands.

The local self-government bureaus, for instance, were assumed by most constitutionalists to be devices for asserting the gentry's local administrative responsibilities, while training the people in modern political practices. But the court envisaged a much more limited and traditional role for the bureaus. The Manchu princes certainly did not plan to let provincial notables turn these new institutions into political instruments of their own. Rather, they expected the gentry to use the bureaus to "enlighten" the peasantry by giving lectures on civic responsibility or by reading excerpts from vernacular newspapers. According to the regulations issued from Peking, the local self-government bureaus would merely "make up for the inefficiencies of official rule . . . under official control and not independent of it."[10]

A similar confusion characterized the provincial assemblies, whose members were elected in February, 1909. The elections themselves were highly elitist. Because of property and educational voting requirements, no more than .0004 percent of the population actually cast a ballot, and that was only to pick an electoral college which made the actual selection of provincial assemblymen. To stand for election to the assembly, one had either to be quite wealthy, earning more than 5,000 taels per year, or well educated, holding a provincial degree or having graduated from one of the new middle schools. Under these conditions the membership of the provincial assemblies was naturally dominated by the higher gentry. Nine out of every ten assemblymen held a degree from the old examination system, and an astonishingly high number—18 percent —had earned the highest metropolitan degree (*chin-shih*).

Yet even this elitist body was not trusted by Peking with provincial legislation. Instead, the provincial assembly was expected to live up to its name in Chinese (*tzu-i chü*), and function only as an "advisory bureau" to provide the central government with connections to the populace. From the throne's vantage point, the assemblies could also help curb the military governors' alarming tendency toward provincial autonomy. Providing an alternative means of contact with the empire's subjects, the assemblies were thus intended to provide the central government with an institutional route to bypass the governors and intermediate officials who continually blocked the throne's access to the provincial populace. Although this conception of the assemblies coincided to some extent with the statecraft conception of gentry home rule, it did not accord with the new theory of constitutional sovereignty that had initially inspired the demands for assemblies.

The National Assembly, standing at the apex of the system and composed of 5 percent of the provincial assemblymen, met in Peking in October, 1910. There the contradiction between the expectations of the constitutionalists and the restrictions of the government became glaringly evident. To the Grand Council this new *Tzu-cheng yuan* (literally, Court to Assist in Government) was merely a body of notables who served at the government's convenience to compile political treatises on reform for the councillors to ponder. Yet the national assemblymen, led by Liang Ch'i-ch'ao and Chang Chien's constitutionalist clique (*li-hsien p'ai*), thought that they had come to the capital to constitute a new government, not advise an old one. Their keen disappointment at discovering how slowly the regime was inching toward fundamental reform could do the dynasty nothing but harm—especially since these frustrations were linked with a growing protest movement in the provinces, directed against the railway building policies of the central government.

Railroad Construction

As early as the 1880s most self-strengtheners had felt that railroads were the foundation of rapid economic development. By 1905 Sheng Hsuan-huai, director of the Imperial Chinese Railway Administration, could say without much fear of public contradiction that "railways are the keys to national reform." He and his planners envisaged a vast network of railroads, stretching from Peking west to Ili, north to Aigun, and south to Canton, concretely drawing together the far corners of the empire. Sheng Hsuan-huai's enthusiasm for railroad construction was matched by foreign zeal—though by no means for the same reasons. Each of the Great Powers viewed participation in Chinese railway development as a splendid oppor-

tunity for its own bankers and as a major diplomatic victory over
rival countries. Every time that a foreign power signed a railway
construction agreement with the Chinese government, it at once
secured a new sphere of interest and tremendous profits for its
national investors. Once the agreement was signed, the foreign
power immediately extended a usurious loan[11] to the Chinese railway administration at almost no risk, since repayment was guaranteed by a lien on government revenues. Then the money so loaned
would be promptly returned to the foreigners' pockets as payment
for the construction costs charged by the foreign country's railroad
contractors. Once the railway was completed, the foreign power
also acquired jurisdictional rights on certain sections of the road,
jobs for its engineers and accountants, and the opportunity to exploit natural resources for ten miles on either side of the line. Thus
at every step of the way the country fortunate enough to secure such
an agreement reaped capital profits, extraterritorial legal rights, and
control of natural resources, all at the expense of the Chinese people.

Belgium was the first country to benefit from this arrangement
by winning a concession in 1898 to build the Peking-Hankow railway. Its success inspired furious competition from the other powers.
In fact, the competition was so intensely divisive that the powers
decided in 1909 to avoid potential conflict among themselves by
making international consortium loans to China. In the words of a
British foreign office spokesman at the time, "the old principle of
spheres of influence [will be replaced by] a new system [which] is
that of division among the various nations concerned."[12] Under
these circumstances, much as during the treaty-port cooperation era,
the Chinese government lost its leverage to play one nation's bankers against another country's investors, and by 1911 China owed
Great Britain, Germany, Belgium, France, and Japan a total of
£41,000,000 in railway loans.

The provincial gentry and merchants were quick to realize that
these loans were far from altruistic and instead represented concessions to the imperialist powers. They were also eager both to
patriotically protect national resources and to profit from this railroad construction themselves. Consequently, beginning in the early
1900s, gentry and merchants incorporated themselves under the
new commercial code and subscribed shares to repurchase railway
and mining rights from foreign investors. This railway recovery
movement had several successes, especially when the gentry of
Kiangsu and Chekiang managed to buy back the rights to a Shanghai-
Nanking line from the English-dominated Hong Kong and Shanghai

Bank. But foreign companies just as frequently refused to give up their concessions and countered adverse Chinese public opinion by having their governments put diplomatic pressure on the Peking regime, which preferred to keep railway building out of the provincial gentry's hands anyway. Provincial patriots, informed of these moves by modern newspapers, responded angrily to the central government's apparent willingness to give in to the imperialists and contract further expensive loans. Forty years earlier zealous gentrymen had accused specific local magistrates of "selling out the country." Now the dynasty itself received the blame, and anti-Manchu sentiments were voiced more and more openly.

Revolutionary Propaganda and Activities

The rationale for the belief that the Manchus were sacrificing China to save themselves came from radical intellectual circles abroad. In 1896 there were only nine Chinese students living in Japan. Ten years later fifteen thousand were studying there. Most of these Chinese students came to Tokyo or Yokohama to learn about Western subjects in a language more familiar to them than English, French, or German. The Ch'ing government thought Japan a safe place to study because the Meiji regime was regarded as a model form of enlightened monarchy. However, Japan also offered political refuge to the 1898 reformers-in-exile. The most prominent of these was Liang Ch'i-ch'ao.

Liang's widely read magazine, *The New Citizen* (*Hsin-min*), made an indelible impression upon these students, exposing them to a dizzying array of Western political and social theories. Between 1903 and 1906 *The New Citizen* introduced its readers to Copernican astronomy, Kantian liberalism, Platonic philosophy, Hegelian idealism, Rousseau's social contract, and European socialism. Japanese translations of Western works were also available to Chinese students, so that a young intellectual reading Montesquieu in 1903, as if the *Spirit of the Laws* were the latest treatise on modern government, might shortly be studying the works of Kropotkin, reading Kōtoku Shūsui's anarchist treatises, and following the editorials on socialism published in the Revolutionary Alliance's *Min-pao* (People's Paper). But Liang Ch'i-ch'ao's *The New Citizen* still remained the essential introduction to this world of new ideas.

Several themes were sounded again and again in Liang's editorials and articles. One was the importance of liberating Chinese youth from the social subjugation of Confucian values, freeing the individual's will to strengthen the nation. Praising English liberalism, Liang argued that countries like England were strong and powerful because their political systems gave each person the opportunity to develop his individual character free of arbitrary social fetters. China desperately needed to be liberated in the same fashion because, as the age of social Darwinism seemed to prove, only the fittest survive. Before 1906 Liang Ch'i-ch'ao also believed in the necessity for immediate revolution. The old order, with its strong cultural defenses, had to be destroyed before a new one could be constructed in its place. Later Liang backed away from this position on the grounds that the annihilation of the Manchu regime would strip China of its existing defenses against imperialism. By then, however, many of the students that he had influenced in the first place already had a solid commitment to carrying out a revolution against the Manchus, and so turned to other political leaders for guidance and inspiration.

The Hunanese were particularly activist, partly because of their intense disappointment at the failure of the 1898 reform in their province. Remembering the martyrdom of T'an Ssu-t'ung, the Hunanese in Tokyo, led by Huang Hsing, formed a revolutionary club, the *Hua-hsing hui* (China Revival Society), which led an unsuccessful uprising of secret societies in central China in 1900. The students from Chekiang were also involved in revolutionary activities, inspired by a brilliant scholar, Chang Ping-lin, who had been a member of K'ang Yu-wei's *Ch'iang-hsueh hui*, and who was now exiled in Japan, working as Liang Ch'i-ch'ao's editorial assistant. Chang's anti-Manchuism stemmed from classical roots, especially from the Ming loyalist writers of the seventeenth century who had emphasized the fundamental distinction between Chinese and barbarian cultures. In Chang Ping-lin's view, the Manchus had usurped the Chinese throne, stealing the country from its people, plunging China into stagnation and backwardness. Even now the Manchus continued to try to keep the Chinese people weak, betraying them to foreign aggressors in order to retain their stolen throne. Chang tried to propagate his theories by holding a student rally in 1902 in Tokyo to commemorate the fall of the Ming dynasty. The Japanese police prohibited the gathering, but Chang Ping-lin found other means of expressing his anti-Manchuism. One was by way of a young Hunanese friend named Tsou Jung, who wrote an inflammatory and impassioned tract called the *Revolutionary Army* (*Ko-ming chün*). Recalling the massacres of Ming loyalists and likening the Manchus to animals, the *Revolutionary Army* argued that the Han race had to purge itself of these barbarian parasites in order to recover the strength to expel the imperialists. When Chang Ping-lin returned to Shanghai and published Tsou Jung's broadside in 1903, it created a great furor. The Ch'ing authorities arrested both men, and Tsou Jung died in prison.

But the *Revolutionary Army* continued to be read, and some of its arguments seemed confirmed when the Ch'ing government failed to force the Russians to withdraw their garrisons from Manchuria in 1903. Chinese students in Tokyo were so aroused by this occupation that they formed a volunteer corps to fight the Russians. Then the Ch'ing ambassador to Japan persuaded the Meiji authorities to suppress the paramilitary force, giving the students all the proof they needed to believe that the Manchus were determined to betray Han patriots. This led many of the Chekiang students to return to China, pledged to destroy the dynasty. Joining Ts'ai Yuan-p'ei's Patriotic Academy (*Ai-kuo hsueh-she*) in Shanghai, they trained themselves in military tactics and tried to attract New Army soldiers in the lower Yangtze to their cause. The Chekiang revolutionary movement did engineer several uprisings in the next few years, but all failed.[13] In fact, these *coups de main* in Chekiang and Hunan— which usually involved secret society elements—may have done more to alarm potential allies among the provincial gentry than to further the revolutionaries' cause. Yet even if the radical intellectuals had decided to moderate their tactics in order to form a united front with the reformist gentry, it would have meant giving up any hope of arousing a mass popular uprising against the Manchus, and this was an ideal they were understandably loath to relinquish.

The young students exiled in Tokyo or hiding in Shanghai were —by virtue of their very distance from the Chinese peasantry— desperately conscious of their need to draw nearer the masses. In the act of becoming revolutionaries, this new generation of estranged intellectuals had cut itself off from traditional native roots. Consequently, there arose among them a deep longing to return to the masses and actually contact the peasantry which their populist rhetoric embraced. That was why anti-Manchuism had such a broad appeal for the students. It gave them a program, however limited, which they could share with the secret societies and, by projection, with the people.

Of course, there were other reasons as well for the prevalence of anti-Manchu racism in revolutionary circles. For instance, there was definite psychological comfort to be found in the belief that the Han Chinese had been humiliated by the imperialists because of Manchu cowardice and obscurantism. The Ch'ing Dynasty thus became a scapegoat for the military failures of the entire nation. Anti-Manchuism also provided a common denominator for the many different schools of revolutionary thought. Henry George socialists, admirers of English liberalism, Kropotkinites, and social revolutionary terrorists, could all agree upon their collective hatred for the Manchus, which was symbolized by cutting off the queue or pigtail imposed upon the Chinese in the seventeenth century. So uncomplicated a gesture also created a sense of martial involvement in the struggle. Remembering the great heroes of the past who had resisted barbarian invaders, the students fervently believed that the noble but bloody task of destroying the Manchus would restore racial pride and strength to the Chinese, who could then devote themselves to driving out the imperialists.

Sun Yat-sen

What the intellectuals most desired, then, was a means of translating their anti-Manchu fervor into direct popular action against the Ch'ing monarchy. That was why they turned to Sun Yat-sen in 1905. Sun's apparently extensive contacts with the underworld of the secret societies in south China and among *hua-ch'iao* (overseas Chinese) communities seemed to guarantee the exiles the means they sought. Historians now know that Sun Yat-sen's secret society connections were tenuous, but at the time intellectuals easily believed that this seasoned conspirator, equally at home in the tong halls of San Francisco as in the triad conclaves of Singapore, could put them in direct touch with popular allies. In fact, Chinese students would probably have turned to Sun sooner had he possessed better intellectual credentials. As a Western-trained doctor, he lacked the classical learning of a Chang Ping-lin or the theoretical subtlety of a Liang Ch'i-ch'ao. But, after being told by Chinese students in Brussels that he had little appeal for intellectuals other than as a man of action, Sun Yat-sen proceeded to throw together a potpourri of social theories[14] that eventually made up the Three People's Principles.

In the final analysis, however, Sun succeeded in uniting the exiles of Tokyo under his leadership because of his intense anti-Manchuism and his promise of secret society support. Brought together by Japanese sympathizers, Sun and the Hunanese leader, Huang Hsing, met in the Tokyo headquarters of the ultranationalist Black Dragon Society in the summer of 1905 to negotiate an alliance. Throughout the discussions Sun kept repeating that the revolution would not succeed unless the various provincial movements were combined into a single force. "If the secret societies can be put under a hard core of some hundred able men," he insisted, "then there can well be a successful uprising against the Manchus."[15] It was that confident guarantee, plus his personal magnetism, which brought the students cheering to their feet on August 20, 1905, when the Revolutionary Alliance (*T'ung-meng hui*) was finally inaugurated in public. For a moment their hearts were truly united, and in the flush of such enthusiasm the various provincial clubs and personal cliques laid aside their differences and pledged to work together against the Manchus.

As a functioning alliance, the *T'ung-meng hui* was relatively short-lived. Sun Yat-sen treated it as he had many of the groups, cells, and societies formed at his request in Chinese communities around the world. It was just one more organization designed to supply him with the money and arms to hire mercenaries for a series of abortive revolts along the Sino-Vietnamese frontier. According to Sun and his Cantonese allies, led by Hu Han-min, these revolts would eventually result in the revolutionaries seizing control of a province or two in the South where they could establish a republic, win diplomatic recognition, and build a base from which to conquer the North. Huang Hsing treated this "southern strategy" with contempt. In his view, the Ch'ing regime would hardly be affected if it lost control over a remote border province. He therefore insisted that the Revolutionary Alliance cease squandering precious funds on Sun's border bandits and devote itself wholeheartedly to striking at the heartland of China along the Yangtze. Sun Yat-sen tried to ignore such complaints, heightening animosities within the organization. Rumors even circulated about Sun's diversion of *T'ung-meng hui* funds into his own pocket, and a major rift developed between him and the head of the Tokyo office, Sung Chiao-jen. By 1908 the

Revolutionary Alliance was hardly more than a fiction, while each of the provincial groups went its own way.

Secret Societies

Despite their criticism of Sun's southern strategy, Huang Hsing and the Hunanese contingent did not find it easy to make significant advances in the central provinces. Major uprisings were staged in 1904 and 1906, but the revolutionaries were hard put to maintain a working alliance with the many secret societies of the Yangtze valley. Actually, the only belief they held in common with salt smugglers and highwaymen was anti-Manchuism. Thus relatively simple matters, such as deciding on the wording of a rebel pronunciamiento, posed embarrassing difficulties. The Revolutionary Alliance members wished to fight under the slogan of republican government, but the secret society chieftains usually bridled at such an unfamiliar and Western-sounding notion. Their followers instead preferred to announce the restoration of the Ming Dynasty or heaven's appointment of a new emperor. Although this was partly a question of political ignorance, it also reflected the secret societies' antiforeignism.

Popular xenophobia had continued to spread in central China after the anti-missionary riots of the 1860s and '70s. Secret societies played a prominent role in antiforeign movements during the last decades of the nineteenth century, and by the early 1900s treaty-port consuls were nervously collecting every shred of intelligence about the peasants' reactions to the occupation of Manchuria by the Russians. There was no doubt, in other words, that the largely illiterate Chinese masses were growing more and more conscious of imperialist threats to their country. Some of these fears took apocalyptic form, like the dark and irrational prophecies of the Boxers in north China. Yet there was a new tone and quality to these popular manifestations—not quite a fully awakened consciousness of Chinese national identity, such as the peasants experienced during the Japanese invasion of the 1940s, but at least a rational awareness that the individual's survival depended on the territorial perpetuation of the Chinese nation. At the same time the peasants' boundaries of identity began to enlarge. A farmer was not just a member of the Li lineage from San-men village; he belonged as well to Hunan province and felt himself a member of the Han people.

The growing nationalism coincided in part with the intellectuals' anti-imperialism. But what made it so difficult for secret society leaders to accept the revolutionaries' republicanism was the popular amalgamation of antiforeignism with antimodernism. The peasants and workers who joined secret societies were profoundly nativistic; they were revolutionists, not revolutionaries. Like the populace around them, they were puzzled and disturbed by the Ch'ing Dynasty's new reform efforts and by the provincial gentry's program of building new schools and constructing railroads. The peasants' resentment of these unfamiliar enterprises had economic origins. To fund their new armies and build their modern schools, the military governors and reformist gentry raised additional revenue by levying transit and commercial duties—a policy which struck especially hard at farmers who sold their produce in market towns. In highly commercialized areas like the Hsiang River valley in Hunan or the Pearl River delta in Kwangtung, it did not take long for the peasants to realize that they were footing the cost of provincial modernization. Already disposed to regard railroads and steamship companies as outlandish Western imports, the lower classes began to blame the reformist gentry and provincial authorities for their economic difficulties. At the same time old-fashioned rural gentrymen who felt squeezed out of the reformist gentry's urban enterprises began to encourage the peasants to strike out at foreign-seeming institutions (new schools, chambers of commerce, modern companies) in protest. When severe rice shortages exacerbated the peasants' struggle for a livelihood in 1909–1910, major riots broke out in central China. From the reformist gentry's standpoint, these were reactionary outbursts which divorced them from their former rural managers, the culturally conservative lower gentry, and which cut them off from popular support for their own programs. As we shall see, this rendered the reformist gentry all the more dependent on militarists during and after the Revolution of 1911.

The revolutionaries were also troubled by this popular antimodernism. They discovered that the secret societies were willing to run the risk of open rebellion primarily because their chieftains felt threatened by the improved communications and military forces of the authorities. In 1904, for instance, the Hunanese secret society leader, Ma Fu-i, agreed to join in a revolutionary uprising mainly because he feared that a new railway spur from the provincial capital would bring New Army units into his bailiwick and destroy his gambling empire. At the time, the China Revival Society simply welcomed this popular support and encouraged the secret society to revolt. The rebellion was quickly put down by the provincial authorities, however, and Ma Fu-i was killed. But when secret societies did win a momentary victory, the revolutionaries quickly discovered that the brigands were mainly interested in looting urban granaries, robbing the wealthy and adorning themselves with Ming titles.

Reacting against social change rather than hoping to carry it further, the secret societies lacked firm ideological commitments to the intellectuals' cause and proved to be fickle allies. Nevertheless, the republican revolutionaries had little choice but to continue working with the Triads and the Society of Elder Brothers (*Ko-lao hui*) up to and through 1911. Then, when revolution did break out in another quarter, the Revolutionary Alliance radicals found their former allies something of an embarrassment. In Hunan, for instance, where the China Revival Society hoped to ally with the reformists against the New Army officers, the activities of Chiao Ta-feng's secret society cohorts simply drove property-owners into the arms of the militarists. It would still be many years before a small core of intellectuals would learn how to direct peasant dissent into conscious social revolutionary action.

On the eve of the 1911 revolution, then, the Revolutionary Alliance was not only fragmented and strategically confused; it was also reeling from a series of failed uprisings and badly coordinated coups. In fact, some of its more impetuous members came to feel that concerted action was pointless and so, like Wang Ching-wei, turned to futile acts of terrorism. Although bomb attempts and assassins' bullets shook public confidence in the regime, the actions that decisively provoked revolution accompanied developments in other quarters: the agitation of the constitutionalists, the provincial railway movements, and the growing alienation of the military from the dynasty—all of which came to a head in the autumn of 1911.

Frustration of the Constitutional Movement

As we have seen, the national assemblymen had met in Peking the previous October to arrange for a parliament, and they soon discovered that the imperial government regarded them solely as advisors. Convinced that the dynasty had failed to realize that the public expected a parliament immediately, the delegates petitioned the throne to speed up the preparations for a constitution, even signing one of the appeals with their own blood. Prince Ch'un, the

Manchu regent, finally agreed to accept the petitions, but would only move up the date for a parliament from 1917 to 1913. Some of the delegates accepted this decision passively, but the more fervent constitutionalists were deeply dissatisfied with the dynasty's deliberate slowness. Led by Sun Hung-i, they formed a Society of Friends of the Constitution (*Hsien-yu hui*) in June, 1911, to coordinate protest against the delay. These men—most of them prestigious gentry leaders—then returned to their respective provincial assemblies shortly before the Wuhan mutiny erupted in October.

Railway Recovery Movement

In the meantime, the gentry railway recovery movement was also entering a more febrile phase. Three years earlier the gentry and merchants of Hunan, Hupeh, Szechwan, and Kwangtung had raised sufficient funds by selling railway bonds to plan to build two southern trunk lines, connecting Peking with Canton and Szechwan. Chang Chih-tung, who was in charge of the central government's southern trunk office in Peking, convinced the throne that this project would both strengthen provincial economic autonomy and slow down a genuine national railway network because each province's investors preferred to build their own branch lines first. The central government therefore gave Chang carte blanche to turn to foreign bankers. First Chang and then Sheng Hsuan-huai negotiated a large loan with a consortium of German, French, British, and American bankers. When news of this reached the provinces, and especially Hunan, the railway shareholders mobilized public opinion in their favor, and there was such agitation that the government refused to ratify the loan agreement. However, the consortium would not abide by this decision and had its diplomatic representatives send a series of threatening notes to the Ch'ing Ministry of Foreign Affairs. Peking soon backed down and agreed to accept the foreign loan, which was to be used by Sheng Hsuan-huai's railway administration to build the southern trunk lines for the central government. Consequently, on May 10, 1911, an order was issued from Peking, disbanding the provincial railway companies and promising to reimburse the shareholders for their bonds sometime in the future.[16]

The provincial investors exploded in angry protest. This time the Szechwanese were the most outraged. Their provincial newspapers spoke of the Ch'ing as "selling Szechwan to the foreigners" and vilified Sheng Hsuan-huai as a "traitor to China." Prominent assemblymen, spokesmen for the chambers of commerce, and patriotic students banded together to form a railway protection association which launched an intense public campaign. Students returned to their native districts to propagandize the peasants, and the Society of Elder Brothers became dangerously restive. As anti-Ch'ing feelings worsened, the provincial viceroy, Chao Erh-feng, feared rebellion on all fronts and on September 7, 1911, decided to nip the movement in the bud by arresting key leaders of the association and of the provincial assembly. Chao's action impelled the protestors into armed action. Within days gentry-led militia units had attacked the viceroy's yamen in Ch'eng-tu and had driven Chao from the province. Manchu troops were to impose order by the beginning of October, but Ch'ing control over this wealthy and populous province was never fully restored.

New Army Disaffection and the Wuhan Uprising

The central government could afford to defy the railway protection movement as long as the dynasty's armies remained loyal. But there were already serious signs of disaffection for the regime within the New Army garrisons stationed in central and southern China. The noncommissioned officers of these modern military units were quite unlike the squadron commanders of the old Green Standard forces. Trained in military schools and moderately literate, the New Army's sergeants had been a target of revolutionary propaganda since 1903. Tsou Jung's tract, newly discovered accounts of Manchu atrocities in the seventeenth century, and newspaper criticisms of the central government had all aroused anti-Manchuism in the rank and file, and widespread concern over China's national weakness led many subalterns and noncommissioned officers to organize revolutionary clubs which met to study republican political theory. Soldiers of the New Army garrison in the Wuhan area (Wuchang, Hanyang, and Hankow) were particularly active in forming study groups; their commanders had already broken up a number of these clubs, arresting their leaders and forbidding the dissemination of republican propaganda. But the clubs always managed to regroup, usually under a new name. The most revolutionary of these in the Wuhan sector was euphemistically known as the Literary Society (*Wen she*). During the summer of 1911, inspired by the agitation all around it, this club began to make plans for an uprising in the autumn of that same year.

The Revolutionary Alliance was informed of this plot but thought it premature. Consequently, there were no members of the *T'ung-meng hui* present on October 9, 1911, when the conspirators accidentally exploded a small bomb in their secret headquarters in Hankow.[17] But the police were nearby and seized the plotters' membership lists from the smoldering ruins of the room. The revolutionaries immediately realized that their organization and their lives were in jeopardy, and so decided to incite a military uprising that very night. But they failed to contact the rank and file in time. The next day, therefore, several leaders were arrested without warning by Governor-General Jui-ch'eng's military police, who rounded up suspects indiscriminately, even dragging some soldiers right off the drill grounds. As apprehensions increased, an altercation broke out that same evening—October 10, 1911—between a sergeant named Hsiung Ping-k'un and a suspicious officer in the Eighth Battalion of Engineers, detailed to guard the Wuhan ammunition dump. Even though Sergeant Hsiung was not one of the original conspirators, he shot the officers and persuaded his men to mutiny. Joined by other dissident units, the mutineers quickly seized the main Wuhan arsenal and forced a brigade commander, General Li Yuan-hung, to take charge of the uprising.

The Wuhan uprising succeeded for three reasons. First, the Manchu governor-general, Jui-ch'eng, panicked and fled, leaving the area in the rebels' hands. Second, the mutineers had at their disposal a complete arsenal, as well as the contents of the Wuhan treasury—arms and funds enough to hold out until the rest of the country was aroused to aid them. Third, their commander, Li Yuan-hung, proved to be an enthusiastic revolutionary leader once there was no turning back, and through his carefully cultivated contacts with provincial assembly leaders like the Hunanese T'an Yen-k'ai, was able to rally the constitutionalists to his side. Assured that this was not a terrorist adventure, gentrymen and New Army commanders elsewhere declared independence in their own provinces. The revolution was thus quickly taken over by an alliance of reformist gentry and militarists, who naturally looked to Yuan Shih-k'ai for support.

Yuan was then in nominal retirement in Chihli, protesting against the efforts of the regent, Prince Ch'un, to wrest control of the Peiyang Army from him. When news of the Wuhan uprising reached Peking, the mother of the young Hsuan-t'ung Emperor immediately decided that Yuan Shih-k'ai was the dynasty's only hope and wanted him back in the government to negotiate an armistice with the republicans. Prince Ch'un and the Manchu nobles, on the other hand, distrusted Yuan, opposed compromise, and urged an immediate attack against the enemy. However, in spite of Prince Ch'un's earlier attempt to create a military force under strict Manchu command, the nobles simply did not control the army. When they spoke against giving Yuan full powers, Peiyang Army generals loyal to Yuan Shih-k'ai threatened mutiny. The dynasty was thus forced to employ Yuan on his own terms.

In the meantime, the Revolutionary Alliance republicans had begun to dispute the reformists' leadership of the revolution. After the Wuhan garrison mutinied, Huang Hsing and other *T'ung-meng hui* leaders immediately returned to central China and tried to take advantage of the powerful wave of public support generated by the anti-Manchu uprising. As peasants enthusiastically cut off their queues and secret societies attacked Manchu outposts, the Revolutionary Alliance leaders attempted to organize their own mass movement. In most cases, they were defeated at the provincial level by the gentry-army alliance. At the national level, however, the *T'ung-meng hui* was recognized as a leading revolutionary group and thus sent delegates to join the provisional republican convention which met in Nanking on December 4. Although some of the moderates in the convention wished to elect Yuan Shih-k'ai president of the new republic if he would publicly change his allegiance, most of the delegates favored one of two other candidates: Li Yuan-hung, who was leader of the gentry-militarist group, and Huang Hsing, who was head of the more radical revolutionaries. Lacking agreement, both sides turned to Sun Yat-sen when he returned to Shanghai from exile on Christmas day, 1911, and on December 29 elected him president of the southern republic.

Sun Yat-sen had no illusions about his own strength compared to that of Yuan Shih-k'ai. He realized how many of the delegates had originally favored Yuan's candidacy and feared that the fragile alliance between Huang Hsing and Li Yuan-hung's respective groups could not long survive Yuan's blandishments. Yuan Shih-k'ai was also receiving strong support from the English and Japanese, who believed that his regime would be more friendly to their interests than Sun's revolutionary government. Fearing that a divided China encouraged imperialist ambitions, Sun Yat-sen made it clear from the moment he accepted the presidency that he would resign in Yuan's favor if the Manchus abdicated in favor of a united republic.

As negotiations continued between Yuan Shih-k'ai and the republicans, the Manchu nobles continued to oppose abdication. On January 27, however, several of Yuan's Peiyang generals declared themselves in favor of a republic. Playing on the empress dowager's fears of racial retaliation, Yuan Shih-k'ai persuaded her to secure Prince Ch'un's agreement to relinquish the throne. On February 12, 1912, the Hsuan-t'ung Emperor formally abdicated the monarchy that Dorgon had so proudly won 268 years earlier. The following day, abiding by his word, Sun Yat-sen turned the presidency over to Yuan Shih-k'ai, and the revolutionaries laid down their arms to prepare for the parliamentary politics of peacetime.

Sun personally showed no inclination to build a mass political coalition out of the old conspiratorial Revolutionary Alliance. Instead it was left to the former head of the Tokyo branch of the *T'ung-meng hui*, Sung Chiao-jen, to create a parliamentary party out of the welter of provincial factions and political cliques that each claimed the revolution for themselves. Now that the dynasty had been overthrown, many opportunists wished to climb aboard the victors' bandwagon. Sung Chiao-jen thus rapidly formed a loose alliance of former Revolutionary Alliance radicals and moderate provincial politicians into a *Kuomintang* (Nationalist Party),[18] which went on to sweep the elections for a constitutional convention to be held in the spring of 1913 in Peking. The coalition was a fragile one, but its electoral victory was so overwhelming that the southern republicans had considerable grounds for hoping to check Yuan Shih-k'ai's growing power in the North.

The "Second Revolution"

These hopes were dashed on March 20, 1913, when Sung Chiao-jen was mortally wounded by an assassin's bullet as he boarded a railway carriage in Shanghai to attend the Peking convention. Sung's death brought a quick end to the unity of the Nationalist Party, which had depended so heavily on his prestige and leadership. But just as Yuan Shih-k'ai was frightening some of the more timid Nationalist delegates into renouncing their membership, the public discovered that Sung Chiao-jen's assassin had been indirectly hired by the president himself. At that very same time, Yuan was also placing his Peiyang warlords in provincial governorships, thereby angering southern militarists who expressed interest in renewing their old alliance with the left against the North. With that strategy in mind, former Revolutionary Alliance leaders and Kuomintang activists declared a "second revolution" against Yuan Shih-k'ai in the summer of 1913.

The key to the success or failure of this second revolution was the attitude of the reformist gentry, who controlled the assemblies and legitimized the military governorships of provinces like Hunan, Hupei, and Kiangsi. If they rallied together and maintained a united front with the radicals, then Yuan Shih-k'ai might be defeated. Some leading assemblymen and militarists did come to the Nationalist Party's aid, but when the tide turned slightly in Yuan Shih-k'ai's favor, their support evaporated. By 1914 the old *T'ung-meng hui* revolutionaries were once again in exile and the Nationalist Party was outlawed. Sun Yat-sen's time would come again, but almost fifteen years were to pass before a new Kuomintang entered the gates of Peking.

The reformist gentry did not mourn the failure of the second revolution for very long. Some even welcomed Yuan Shih-k'ai's attack on the republican left wing because it removed provincial political competitors. Already deeply dependent on the new military governors, the reformist gentrymen who dominated the provincial assemblies, education associations, and chambers of commerce believed that they had won most of their victories anyway. The dynasty was destroyed, and for the moment they seemed in full command of their own civil affairs. Yuan Shih-k'ai was not the kind of president Sun Yat-sen had wanted, but that might also prove an advantage to the reformist gentry. If Yuan lacked popular support, he would be that much less able to build a strong, intrusive central government with a capacity to interfere in provincial home rule.

The Search for a New Mandate

Of course, Yuan Shih-k'ai himself realized that a presidency which had betrayed the electorate could not unite the country. He also discovered that he was beginning to lose control over the Peiyang generals, whose loyalty was proving to be shortlived. Searching for an unimpeachable source of unity and authority, he fell back on the old imperial model. After being advised by a doubtless well-meaning but politically presumptuous American professor that the Chinese were not ready for democracy, Yuan Shih-k'ai decided to cover himself with the one mantle he had respected most, and in

1915 covertly arranged for a "spontaneous" popular campaign to proclaim him emperor of a new dynasty.

This time the provincial gentry had no hesitation whatsoever. Yuan Shih-k'ai's restoration was paradoxically both comical and dangerous—comical because the monarchy had lost its Confucian significance for the elite, and dangerous because emperorship still had enough popular charisma to help Yuan unify the country on his own terms. Under such a dictatorship the provinces would lose their autonomy and the warlords their independence. In the winter of 1915–1916, therefore, the assembly leaders and provincial generals banded together against Yuan's imperial plans. The revolt began in the Southwest, led by Governor Ts'ai O and publicized by the constitutionalist, Liang Ch'i-ch'ao. As province after province proclaimed its opposition to a monarchy, Yuan was forced to abandon his plans and put away the imperial regalia he had so lovingly prepared for the coronation. Already struck by uremia, he became deeply despondent after this crushing defeat; in the spring of 1916 he died of nervous prostration.

The defeat of Yuan Shih-k'ai did not bring gentry democracy to the capital. Ideologues like Liang Ch'i-ch'ao, lacking either a mass party or a military machine of their own, tried to survive as advisors and grey eminences for the Peiyang warlord cliques that successively disputed the presidency. Their intellectual luster did serve occasionally as a political weapon—especially when it was withheld from particularly unpopular militarists. But it was a feeble weapon indeed against the muscular jostling of warlord politics. Intellectual powerbrokers no longer maintained the authority which Ming and Ch'ing literati had once wielded to decide whether a general deserved to become emperor. The military (*wu*) now dominated the civil (*wen*), and the gentry's traditional control over aspiration to the throne was lost with the throne itself.

Provincial gentrymen were also overpowered by local warlords. The reformists' maneuverings during the previous decade had already thrown them into the arms of the generals, but the provincial notables had always assumed that they were still indispensable social intermediaries for the militarists. The pre-revolutionary gentry had ensured their local dominance by connecting the state with rural society. Their lineages had stabilized the countryside and had given them an informal patriarchy over the peasantry. Under the Ming and early Ch'ing fiscal systems they had even eased the government's access to agricultural revenue.[19] But during the late nineteenth century the upper gentry—those who became assembly leaders later on—had turned their backs on rural China. Through a once forbidden alliance with the lower gentry, they had created a cadre of rural tax and rent managers whose efforts allowed them, the higher elite, to engage in the politics of their provincial capitals. There they discovered new roles as constitutionalists, railway investors, and sponsors of the modern schools that were rapidly educating Chinese youths away from the world of their ancestors. The new urban elite thus lost its strict former identity as classical gentrymen and began to look outward—to Shanghai, to Japan, and even beyond, to America and the universities that would train the next generation's engineers and lawyers. This cultural reorientation alienated them from the rural gentry-commoners who had once served them. And the latter, now landlords and usurers, consolidated themselves. Fifty years of rent collection and tax farming had left this class completely invulnerable to their former patrons and protectors. It was they, the managers, who now controlled the land registers, maintained the tax books, ran the local self-government bureaus, and turned rural militia (min-t'uan) into private police forces to bully tenants and punish debtors. This petty estate had no pretensions to squiredom; its members stood but a few rungs above the peasantry as unabashed parasites in a countryside sullen with class hostilities. When these lower-level landlords needed future protection from Communist organizers, they would turn directly to the warlords without any need of intermediaries.

Seen as a culmination, then, the Revolution of 1911 marked the final evolution, and extinction, of the Chinese gentry. But what did it signal as a beginning? When the monarchy fell, so did the center of a shared political universe, and the limited stability of late imperial China gave way to modern forms of struggle and class conflict. Yet the revolutionaries of 1911 assumed that unity would soon return, that the act of destroying the old would quickly be followed by the construction of the new. With that ultimate faith, they took their word for revolution, ko-ming, in its classical sense as a return of the mandate to the Han Chinese who were once again masters of themselves.

But if there was a mandate, to which of the Han did it belong? To the kuo-fu, Sun Yat-sen, whose claim was solipsistically established by his heir, Chiang Kai-shek? To Yuan Shih-k'ai and his warlords, who destroyed the republic? To the provincial gentry, whose short-term interests betrayed them in the long run? Or to the venal landlords, who abandoned this unfamiliar political world for their habitual realm of rent extortion and tax juggling?

There was really only one heir left intact from the old order, yet filled with promise for the new. The imperial mandate had once been heaven's to give, but—in the words of the *Book of Documents*—"heaven sees with the eyes of the people; heaven hears with the ears of the people." Vague and amorphous, a new tide was rolling toward Peking. As yet no one could name it: a proletariat, an armed peasantry perhaps. To define the people and determine how to mobilize its strength was a task for future revolutionaries. Until their time came, China would have no true unity and the revolution no enduring mandate to carry on.

Notes

1. That is why Sun Yat-sen's eminent position is also ensured in Communist historiography. Mao Tse-tung (who served Sun with enthusiasm during the united front period) insists that "China's anti-imperialist and anti-feudal bourgeois democratic revolution was, to put it correctly, begun by Mr. Sun Yat-sen." Mao Tse-tung, "Ch'ing-nien yun-tung te fang-hsiang" [The Direction of the Youth Movement], in *Mao Tse-tung hsuan-chi* [The Selected Works of Mao Tse-tung], 2:57.

2. Sheng Hsuan-huai, a protégé of Li Hung-chang, was soon appointed director of railways and telegraphs.

3. One of the major civil weapons used by Tz'u-hsi at the time of the coup was the Council of Princes and High Officials (*I-cheng ta-ch'en*), a body composed of Manchu princes and ministerial officials. Before imprisoning the emperor on September 23, 1898, the empress dowager consulted with the council and secured the backing of the Manchu nobility. It was this council, too, which was dominated by Prince Tuan during the Boxer War discussions.

4. For example, after Yuan was appointed to the Grand Council, his military interests were looked after by a protégé and friend, Feng Kuo-chang, who remained in command of the General Staff Council of the Ministry of the Army.

5. This was the same device employed by Chiang Kai-shek in 1924 when he directed the military education of Kuomintang cadets at the famous Whampoa military academy.

6. Of Yuan Shih-k'ai's Peiyang officers, five became presidents of the republic and one a premier. Many more were famous warlords.

7. The provincial governors had earlier forced the government to abolish the post of circuit intendant, depriving the ministry of a fiscal watchdog to report their transit tax collections.

8. A united bourgeoisie in the Marxian sense did not develop until the 1920s. The gentry were, after all, still a landowning class, and their economic interests did not always coincide with those of the merchants. Thus, before 1911, they cooperated most intimately on anti-imperialist issues, as well as joining together to protect local initiatives from the central government's interference. The latter point is strongly made in Mary Backus Rankin, "Provincial Initiative and Elite Politics: the Chekiang and Kiangsu Railway Controversies, 1906–1911," paper delivered at the Association for Asian Studies, April, 1974.

9. See p. 210.

10. Cited in Charles Hedtke, "The Revolution in Szechwan," paper presented at the Conference on the Chinese Revolution of 1911 (Laconia, 1965), p. 40. I have altered the translation slightly.

11. If the Chinese borrowed $1 million on paper, they paid a high interest on that amount, but actually only received $900,000.

12. E-tu Zen Sun, *Chinese Railways and British Interests, 1898–1911* (New York: Columbia University Press, 1954), p. 109.

13. The most famous was led by Ch'iu Chin at Hangchow in July, 1907. The uprising was defeated, however, and Ch'iu Chin was beheaded by the Ch'ing police.

14. Many of these ideas were inspired by the work of Maurice Williams, a Brooklyn dentist who popularized Henry George's single-tax socialism.

15. Sung Chiao-jen, *Wo chih li-shih* [My History], cited in Ta-ling Lee, *Foundations of the Chinese Revolution* (New York: St. John's University Press, 1970), pp. 28–29.

16. The government declared that it would pay 60 percent of the bonds' cash value and cover the remaining 40 percent with an interest-free note.

17. Lower echelon party affiliates (*t'ang-jen*) participated, but they were not really members of the *T'ung-meng hui*.

18. This was nominally the same, but actually different, from the *Kuomintang* which Sun Yat-sen established in 1919, and which became the ruling party of China from 1928 to 1940. The first KMT was a loose parliamentary coalition. The second KMT had stricter membership rules, abided by the Three Principles of the People, and demanded personal loyalty to Sun Yat-sen.

19. In the eighteenth century 75 percent of the state's revenue was agrarian. By 1900 only one-third came from land taxes. Commerce, the opium trade, and industry were now directly subject to the warlords' taxation.

Readings in Late Imperial
Chinese History

THE FOLLOWING ANNOTATED LIST, divided according to the chapters of the text, is not a bibliography. Rather it is a brief and idiosyncratic guide to books, and occasionally articles, in English about late imperial Chinese history.

Introduction

ALBERT FEUERWERKER, ed., *History in Communist China* (Cambridge: M.I.T. University Press, 1968).
An excellent collection of articles on Chinese Communist historiography.

JAMES P. HARRISON, *The Communists and Chinese Peasant Rebellions* (New York: Atheneum, 1969).
Professor Harrison traces the development of modern Chinese historical attitudes toward popular movements. Along the way, he provides much information about the rebellions as such.

Chapter I: Peasants

MARK ELVIN, *The Pattern of the Chinese Past* (London: Methuen, 1973).
A recently published survey of Chinese social history. Highly recommended.

FEI HSIAO-T'UNG, *Peasant Life in China: A Field Study of Country Life in the Yangtze Valley* (London: Kegan Paul, 1943).

A classic village study by one of contemporary China's leading anthropologists.

MAURICE FREEDMAN, *Lineage Organization in Southeastern China* (London: Athlone, 1958).

Although some of his conclusions are now contested, Freedman's work is the best ever done on lineage formation in south China.

HO PING-TI, *Studies on the Population of China, 1368–1953* (Cambridge: Harvard University Press, 1959).

A monumental work. Not a book to skim, but essential for understanding Chinese social history.

RAMON H. MYERS, *The Chinese Peasant Economy: Agricultural Development in Hopei and Shantung* (Cambridge: Harvard University Press, 1970).

This controversial study of the peasant economy of north China challenges Marxist generalities. The introductory chapter is particularly recommended for its survey of the historiography.

EVELYN SAKAKIDA RAWSKI, *Agricultural Change and the Peasant Economy of South China* (Cambridge: Harvard University Press, 1972).

The author forces other scholars to re-evaluate their assumptions about the peasant history of the Ming and Ch'ing periods.

JEAN CHESNEAUX, ed., *Popular Movements and Secret Societies in China, 1840–1950* (Stanford: Stanford University Press, 1972).

A recent collection of articles, which also includes an excellent bibliography.

IRWIN SCHEINER, "The Mindful Peasant: Sketches for a Study of Rebellion," *Journal of Asian Studies* (August, 1973).

Although focussed on Japanese sources, this is an important and suggestive essay for anyone interested in Chinese peasant movements.

Chapter II: Gentry

CHANG CHUNG-LI, *The Chinese Gentry: Studies on Their Role in Nineteenth Century Chinese Society* (Seattle: University of Washington Press, 1955); and *The Income of the Chinese Gentry* (Seattle: University of Washington Press, 1962).

Both of these books are essential to understanding what the gentry was and how it functioned. Chang's definition of the gentry is totally examination oriented, so it should be supplemented with the following two works.

WOLFRAM EBERHARD, *Social Mobility in Traditional China* (Leiden: E. H. Brill, 1963).

A study which uses clan genealogies to show the gentry lineage from within.

Ho PING-TI, *The Ladder of Success in Imperial China: Aspects of Social Mobility, 1368–1911* (New York: John Wiley and Sons, 1962).

Arguing for a high rate of social mobility in traditional China, Ho's work also contains fascinating capsule biographies of gentrymen.

CH'Ü T'UNG-TSU, *Local Government in China under the Ch'ing* (Cambridge: Harvard University Press, 1962).

A somewhat dry but authoritative study of district government. It should be supplemented by the following book.

HSIAO KUNG-CH'ÜAN, *Rural China: Imperial Control in the Nineteenth Century* (Seattle: University of Washington Press, 1960).

It is impossible to read this book at a single sitting, but it contains fascinating detail about the gentry's role in formal and informal local government.

JOHN WATT, *The District Magistrate in Late Imperial China* (New York: Columbia University Press, 1972).

Watt's thoughtful book contrasts the Confucian aspirations of the district magistracy with Legalist realities.

FREDERIC WAKEMAN and CAROLYN GRANT, eds., *Conflict and Control in Late Imperial China* (Berkeley: University of California Press, 1975).

A recent collection of essays which traces the evolution of the gentry and the development of popular movements from the late Ming to the twentieth century.

Chapter III: Merchants

W. E. WILLMOTT, *Economic Organization in Chinese Society* (Stanford: Stanford University Press, 1972).

An indispensable collection of authoritative articles on banking, salt production, silk and cotton manufacture, and so forth. The Elvin and Metzger essays are especially recommended.

Ho PING-TI, "The Salt Merchants of Yang-chou: A Study of Commercial Capitalism in Eighteenth Century China," *Harvard Journal of Asiatic Studies* (1954).

ARTHUR WALEY, *Yuan Mei, Eighteenth Century Chinese Poet* (New York: Grove Press, 1956).
Delightful.

Chapter IV: The Dynastic Cycle

ARTHUR WRIGHT, ed., *Studies in Chinese Thought* (Chicago: Chicago University Press); with David Nivison, *Confucianism in Action* (Stanford: Stanford University Press, 1959), and *The Confucian Persuasion* (Stanford: Stanford University Press, 1960); and with Denis Twitchett, *Confucian Personalities* (Stanford: Stanford University Press, 1962).

These famous volumes contain some of the best essays ever written in English on Chinese political thought and bureaucratic behavior.

C. K. YANG, *Religion and Chinese Society: A Study of Contemporary Social Functions of Religion and Some of Their Historical Factors* (Berkeley: University of California Press, 1961).

A structural functional study of religious sociology which shows how the higher and peasant cultures intertwined.

FREDERICK W. MOTE, *The Poet Kao Ch'i, 1336–1374* (Princeton: Princeton University Press, 1962).

A poet and his circle of friends during the years of turmoil when Chu Yuan-chang was founding the Ming dynasty.

CHARLES O. HUCKER, *The Censorial System of Ming China* (Stanford: Stanford University Press, 1966).

Detailed analysis of the Ming bureaucracy, emphasizing the issue of censorial criticism versus imperial despotism.

JAMES B. PARSONS, *The Peasant Rebellions of the Late Ming Dynasty* (Tucson: University of Arizona Press, 1970).

A study based upon Chinese chronicles of the late Ming rebellions.

Chapter V: The Rise of the Manchus

FRANZ MICHAEL, *The Origin of Manchu Rule in China: Frontier and Bureaucracy as Interacting Forces in the Chinese Empire* (Baltimore: Johns Hopkins University Press, 1942).

The basic work on frontier feudalism in the seventeenth century. Its conclusions have to be seriously modified in the light of Farquhar's work (see just below).

DAVID M. FARQUHAR, "Mongolian versus Chinese Elements in the Early Manchu State," *Ch'ing-shih wen-t'i* [Bulletin of the Society for Ch'ing Studies] (June, 1971).

Chapter VI: Early and High Ch'ing

ROBERT OXNAM, "The Politics of the Oboi Regency," *Journal of Asian Studies* (1973).

An important article, describing the harsh policies of the Manchu *beile* after Shun-chih's death.

JONATHAN SPENCE, *Ts'ao Yin and the K'ang-hsi Emperor, Bondservant and Master* (New Haven: Yale University Press, 1966).

A splendidly written, entertaining, and important work of scholarship.

SILAS WU, *Communication and Imperial Control in China: Evolution of the Palace Memorial System, 1693–1735* (Cambridge: Harvard University Press, 1970).

A technical study, based upon new Chinese sources, which shows exactly how the K'ang-hsi and Yung-cheng emperors further centralized the power of the throne by creating a private intelligence network.

CHANG TE-CH'ANG, "The Economic Role of the Imperial Household (*Nei-wu-fu*) in the Ch'ing Dynasty," *Journal of Asian Studies* (February, 1972).

Until Professor Chang published this article, few scholars besides Silas Wu knew much about the Imperial Household. This piece has opened up new vistas about the Ch'ing.

HAROLD L. KAHN, *Monarchy in the Emperor's Eyes: Image and Reality in the Ch'ien-lung Reign* (Cambridge: Harvard University Press, 1971).

The self-images of the Ch'ien-lung Emperor, masterfully analyzed with wit and erudition.

Chapter VII: The Western Intrusion

JOHN K. FAIRBANK, *The Chinese World Order: Traditional China's Foreign Relations* (Cambridge: Harvard University Press, 1968).

A symposium volume with an excellent introductory essay explaining the traditional diplomatic system of the Chinese.

TENG SSU-YÜ and JOHN K. FAIRBANK, eds., *China's Response to the West: A Documentary Survey, 1839–1923* (New York: Atheneum, 1965).

This carefully annotated collection of documents covers all of the nineteenth and early twentieth centuries, while the introductory chapter describes Sino-foreign relations before the Opium War.

WILLIAM C. HUNTER, *The 'Fan Kwae' at Canton before Treaty Days, 1825–1844* (Shanghai: Kelly and Walsh, 1911).

Local color by a firsthand observer. Recently reprinted.

LOUIS DERMIGNY, *La Chine et l'Occident. Le commerce à Canton au XVIIIe siècle, 1719–1833* (Paris: S.E.V.P.E.N., 1964), 3 Vols.

This is the only recommended work not written in English. It is mentioned simply because Dermigny's study is indispensable to anyone wishing to understand how the Canton trade worked.

MICHAEL GREENBERG, *British Trade and the Opening of China, 1800–1842* (Cambridge, Eng.: Cambridge University Press, 1951).

Using the archives of the country firms, Greenberg traces the involvement of the free traders in the Opium War.

Chapter VIII: Invasion and Rebellion

CHANG HSIN-PAO, *Commissioner Lin and the Opium War* (Cambridge: Harvard University Press, 1964).

Chang gives a balanced account of Lin Tse-hsu's activities during the Opium War.

FREDERIC WAKEMAN, JR., *Strangers at the Gate: Social Disorder in South China, 1839–1861* (Berkeley: University of California Press, 1966).

An attempt to assess the social effects of the Opium War upon Kwangtung province.

JOHN K. FAIRBANK, *Trade and Diplomacy on the China Coast: The Opening of the Treaty Ports, 1842–1854* (Cambridge: Harvard University Press, 1953).

A classic.

ARTHUR WALEY, *The Opium War through Chinese Eyes* (London: George Allen and Unwin, 1958).

Waley's famous translation of Chinese diaries (including Lin Tse-hsu's) which were written during the Opium War.

IMMANUEL HSU, *China's Entrance into the Family of Nations: The Diplomatic Phase, 1858–1880* (Cambridge: Harvard University Press, 1960).

The best diplomatic history of this period. It should be supplemented with the following work.

MASATAKA BANNO, *China and the West, 1858–1861: The Origins of the Tsungli Yamen* (Cambridge: Harvard University Press, 1964).
Especially good for understanding political factions in Peking.

FRANZ MICHAEL, *The Taiping Rebellion: History and Documents*, Vol. 1 (Seattle: University of Washington Press, 1965).
Excellent summary of the phases of Taiping development.

JEN YU-WEN, *The Taiping Rebellion* (New Haven: Yale University Press, 1973).
An encyclopedic study by one of the world's greatest experts on the Taiping movement.

VINCENT C. Y. SHIH, *The Taiping Ideology: Its Sources, Interpretations and Influences* (Seattle: University of Washington Press, 1967).
Exhaustive.

Chapter X: The Illusion of Restoration and Self-Strengthening

MARY C. WRIGHT, *The Last Stand of Chinese Conservatism: The T'ung-chih Restoration, 1862–1874* (Stanford: Stanford University Press, 1957).
One of the best books ever written on nineteenth-century Chinese history. Some of the late Professor Wright's assumptions are now debated, but the thoroughness and care of this monograph remain beyond question.

STANLEY SPECTOR, *Li Hung-chang and the Huai Army: A Study in Nineteenth-Century Chinese Regionalism* (Seattle: University of Washington Press, 1964).
Where Wright sees a restoration of imperial rule after the Taiping rebellion, Spector observes the development of regional political power.

PHILIP KUHN, *Rebellion and Its Enemies in Late Imperial China* (Cambridge: Harvard University Press, 1970).
Kuhn, on the other hand, distinguishes between regional and local militarization. This work has profoundly influenced historians' understanding of the late Ch'ing.

K. C. LIU, "Li Hung-chang in Chihli," in Albert Feuerwerker, ed., *Approaches to Modern Chinese History* (Berkeley: University of California Press, 1968).
Liu refutes Spector's argument that Li Hung-chang was a regionalist.

JOSEPH R. LEVENSON, *Confucian China and Its Modern Fate* (Berkeley: University of California Press, 1958–1965), 3 vols.

Perhaps the most profound study of modern Chinese intellectual history ever written; in a class all of its own.

ALBERT FEUERWERKER, *China's Early Industrialization: Sheng Hsuan-huai, 1844–1916, and Mandarin Enterprise* (Cambridge: Harvard University Press, 1958).

Why self-strengthening failed—an excellent study.

JOHN RAWLINSON, *China's Struggle for Naval Development, 1839–1895* (Cambridge, 1966).

How self-strengthening failed.

LLOYD EASTMAN, *Throne and Mandarins: China's Search for a Policy during the Sino-French Controversy, 1880–1885* (Cambridge: Harvard University Press, 1967).

The most interesting sections of this thoughtful book concern the "pure talk" clique.

Chapter IX: Dynastic Reform and Reaction

WILLIAM L. LANGER, *The Diplomacy of Imperialism, 1890–1902* (New York: Knopf, 1951), 2 Vols.

The scramble for concessions placed in a world perspective.

JOHN E. SCHRECKER, *Imperialism and Chinese Nationalism: Germany in Shantung* (Cambridge: Harvard University Press, 1971).

In addition to analyzing German policy, Schrecker shows how Ch'ing officials tried to preserve China's national sovereignty.

LLOYD EASTMAN, "Political Reformism in China before the Sino-Japanese War," *Journal of Asian Studies* (August, 1968).

A survey of the writings of Ho Kai, Cheng Kuan-ying, and other early reformists.

HSIAO KUNG-CH'ÜAN, "K'ang Yu-wei's Thought," *Chung Chi Journal* (1968).

Careful, work-by-work analysis of K'ang's thought, by a leading expert on traditional Chinese political theory.

JOSEPH R. LEVENSON, *Liang Ch'i-ch'ao and the Mind of Modern China* (Cambridge: Harvard University Press, 1953).

Liang here becomes a touchstone for China's modern identity crisis. Levenson's book has to be re-evaluated in light of the following work.

HAO CHANG, *Liang Ch'i-ch'ao and Intellectual Transition in China* (Cambridge: Harvard University Press, 1971).

Where Levenson's Liang is culturally tormented, Hao Chang's subject shows much more equanimity. Especially good for understanding the traditional sources of Liang's theories of sovereignty and social organization.

BENJAMIN SCHWARTZ, *In Search of Wealth and Power: Yen Fu and the West* (Cambridge: Harvard University Press, 1964).

Yen Fu translated Huxley, Spencer, Mill, and Montesquieu into Chinese at the end of the nineteenth century. His own ideas—which are placed in a universal context in this profound study—were extremely influential.

Victor Purcell, *The Boxer Uprising: A Background Study* (Cambridge, Eng.: Cambridge University Press, 1963).

Were the Boxers a spontaneous social uprising or an officially organized movement? In answering that controversial question, Purcell provides much insight into popular movements.

Chapter XI: The End of the Mandate

MERIBETH CAMERON, *The Reform Movement in China, 1898–1912* (Stanford: Stanford University Press, 1931).

Basic survey of the Manchu reforms.

JEROME CH'EN, *Yuan Shih-k'ai* (Stanford: Stanford University Press, 1972).

The second edition of an excellent political biography.

RALPH POWELL, *The Rise of Chinese Military Power, 1895–1912* (Princeton: Princeton University Press, 1955).

Stresses the struggle between Yuan Shih-k'ai and the throne for military supremacy. It should be read along with the following work.

STEPHEN R. MACKINNON, "The Peiyang Army, Yuan Shih-k'ai, and the Origins of Modern Chinese Warlordism," *Journal of Asian Studies* (May, 1973).

Mackinnon refutes Powell's thesis that the military reforms led to warlordism. His study is significant, but it does not settle the matter.

MICHAEL GASSTER, *Chinese Intellectuals and the Revolution of 1911* (Seattle: University of Washington Press, 1969).

The thought of Chang Ping-lin and other intellectual radicals, analyzed in detail.

HAROLD SCHIFFRIN, *Sun Yat-sen and the Origins of the Chinese Revolution* (Berkeley: University of California Press, 1970).

The first reliable account of Sun's revolutionary role.

MARY C. WRIGHT, ed., *China in Revolution: The First Phase, 1900–1913* (New Haven: Yale University Press, 1971).

This is a superb volume. Not only does it provide up-to-date scholarship on all aspects of the 1911 revolution; it also contains within its covers enough material for any reader to debate the issues with himself.

Index

Abahai, 78–80, 87, 91, 93
Aborigines, 12, 97, 101, 104, 117, 136, 147, 155
Africa, 113
Agriculture, 3, 5–17, 32, 42, 45, 72, 97, 100, 128, 136, 142, 153, 194, 212
Aigun, 237
  River, 72
  Treaty of, 138
Aisin Gioro, 75–76, 79
Albuquerque, Duke Alfonso de, 113, 117
Alcock, Rutherford, 179, 185
Alexeieff, Admiral, 220
Allied expeditionary force, 219–221, 229
Altan, 72
Amboyna Island, 118
Amherst, Lord, 106, 123
Amoy, 117, 119, 120, 121, 137, 155
Amur, 79
An Lu-shan, 7
An Te-hai, 180
Analects, 29, 56
Anarchism, 239, 242
Anglo-Chinese War (1856–1860), 156–159
Anhwei, 42, 44, 48, 124, 155, 172, 173, 175
Anking, 152, 173
Annam, 101, 111–113, 119, 189–190, 191, 243
Antiforeignism, 141, 183–186, 216–220, 221, 244–245
Anti-Manchuism. See Manchus
Antwerp, 118
Arabs, 112, 113
Aristocracy. See Nobility
Army, 7, 65, 66–69, 71–80, 89, 92, 104, 105, 142, 149–150, 152, 153, 154, 163–179, 212, 226, 227, 229–232, 243, 249
  Ministry of the, 231
  Reorganization Bureau of the, 230, 231
  See also Banners; Ever-Victorious Army; Green Standard; Military; New Army; Peiyang Army; Regionalism; Warlords
Art, 2, 23, 51, 52, 62, 101
Artisans, 5, 28, 39, 40–45, 72, 74, 77. See also Workers
Assemblies, 235–237. See also Provincial Government
Austria, 207

Bandits, 6, 62–64, 66–69, 141, 143, 145, 174, 216, 243, 244, 246. See also Rebels
Banking, 46–47, 176, 238, 239, 247

Banners, 8, 48, 76–78, 91, 92, 93–94, 95, 102, 103, 106, 137, 163, 214, 230
Barbarians, 7, 69, 71–82, 96, 111, 122, 127, 133, 144, 156, 159, 181, 205, 213, 216, 240, 241, 242
  management of, 139–142
  See also Diplomacy
Batavia, 117
Beile, 72, 74, 76–80, 88, 91, 94. See also Manchus
Belgium, 238, 242
Black Dragon Society, 243
Black Flags, 189
Board of Civil Appointments, 80, 91, 102, 188
Board of Justice, 91
Board of Revenue, 48, 50, 91, 94, 102, 178
Board of Rites, 91, 155, 214
Board of War, 91
Board of Works, 91
Bogue, 133, 134
  Supplementary Treaty of the, 137
Bondservants, 48, 87, 93, 94
Bonham, George, 141
Book of Changes, 59
Book of Documents, 56, 255
Book of Great Harmony, 205
Bourgeoisie, 50–52, 168, 233, 234–239
Bowring, Sir John, 141
Boxers, 207, 216–221, 235, 244
Bruce, Frederick, 157
Buddhism, 2, 6, 7, 34, 60–61, 86–87, 95, 100–101, 104–106, 143, 145, 212, 217
Bureau of Government Institutions, 211
Bureaucracy, 7, 19–24, 29, 43, 44, 46–50, 55–56, 58–59, 61–62, 65–66, 87, 88, 91–92, 93, 96–99, 102–106, 149, 150, 166, 167, 169, 179, 186, 187, 188, 193, 200, 210, 211, 212–214, 231
  salaries in, 26, 29, 31–32, 46
  See also Local Government
Burlingame, Anson, 179
Burma, 101, 104

Canton, 12, 40, 112, 113–116, 118, 119–126, 128–129, 131–137, 140–143, 155, 156, 171, 176, 190, 199, 203, 226, 227, 237, 243, 247
  customs office of, 94
Capitalism, 2, 43–44, 46–50, 194, 234, 247, 254
Catherine of Braganza, 119
Catholic. See Christian; Missionaries
Censors, 34, 88, 157, 211, 212